# Table of Contents

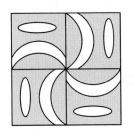

## Unit 19 • Past Tense of *Be*

## Unit 20 • Past Tense

## Unit 21 • Indirect Objects with *To*

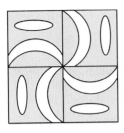

# Preface to *Grammar Dimensions: Form, Meaning, and Use*

## To the Teacher

### ABOUT THE SERIES

With the recent emphasis on communication, the teaching of grammar has often been downplayed, or even overlooked entirely. Although one would not want to argue the goal of having students be able to communicate successfully, it is important to recognize that a major means to this end is to teach students to use grammatical structures. Some grammatical structures may be acquired naturally without instruction, but it is assumed by the creators of this series that explicit focus on the troublesome aspects of English will facilitate and accelerate their acquisition. The teaching needs to be done, however, in such a way that the interdependence of grammar and communication is appreciated.

In this regard, it is crucial to recognize that the use of grammatical structures involves more than having students achieve formal accuracy. Students must be able to use the structures meaningfully and appropriately as well. This series, therefore, takes into account all three dimensions of language: syntax/morphology (form), semantics (meaning), and pragmatics (use). The relevant facts about the **form, meaning,** and **use** of English grammatical structures were compiled into a comprehensive scope and sequence and distributed across a four-book series. Where the grammatical system is complex (e.g., the verb-tense system) or the structure complicated (e.g., the passive voice), it is revisited in each book in the series. Nevertheless, each book is free-standing and may be used independently of the others in the series if the student or program needs warrant.

Another way in which the interdependence of grammar and communication is stressed is that students first encounter every structure in a meaningful context where their attention is not immediately drawn to its formal properties. Each treatment of a grammatical structure concludes with students being given the opportunity to use the structure in communicative activities. The point of the series is not to teach grammar as static knowledge, but to have students use it in the dynamic process of communication. In this way grammar might better be thought of as a skill, rather than as an area of knowledge.

It is my hope that this book will provide teachers with the means to create, along with their students, learning opportunities that are tailored to learners' needs, are enjoyable, and will maximize everyone's learning.

### ABOUT THE BOOK

This book deals with basic sentence and subsentence grammatical structures. It also introduces the grammatical forms associated with semantic notions such as time and place. The units have been sequenced in a way that allows students to add grammatical structures of increasing complexity to their repertoires. As the units have been designed to stand independently, however, it is possible for a syllabus to be constructed that follows a different order of structures than the one presented in the book. It is also not expected that there will be sufficient time to deal with all of the material that has been introduced here within a single course. Teachers are encouraged to see the book as a resource from which they can select units or parts of units that best meet students' needs.

# Unit Organization

## TASKS

One way in which to identify student needs is to use the **Tasks**, which open each unit as a pre-test. Learner engagement in the Tasks may show that students have already learned what they need to know about a certain structure, in which case the unit can be skipped entirely. Or it may be possible, from examining students' performance, to pinpoint precisely where the students need to work. For any given structure, the learning challenge presented by the three dimensions of language is not equal. Some structures present more of a form-based challenge to learners; for others, the long-term challenge is to learn what the structures mean or when to use them. The type and degree of challenge varies according to the inherent complexity of the structure itself and the particular language background and level of English proficiency of the students.

## FOCUS BOXES

Relevant facts about the form, meaning, and use of the structure are presented in **Focus Boxes** following the Task. Teachers can work their way systematically through a given unit or can pick and choose from among the Focus Boxes those points on which they feel students specifically need to concentrate.

## EXERCISES

From a pedagogical perspective, it is helpful to think of grammar as a skill to be developed. Thus, in this book, **Exercises** have been provided to accompany each Focus Box. Certain of the Exercises may be done individually, others with students working in pairs or in small groups. Some of the Exercises can be done in class, others assigned as homework. Students' learning styles and the learning challenge they are working on will help teachers determine the most effective way to have students use the Exercises. (The Instructor's Manual should be consulted also for helpful hints in this regard.)

## ACTIVITIES

At the end of each unit are a series of **Activities** that help students realize the communicative value of the grammar they are learning and that offer them further practice in using the grammar to convey meaning. Teachers or students may select the Activities from which they believe they would derive the most benefit and enjoyment. Student performance on these Activities can be used as a post-test as well. Teachers should not expect perfect performance at this point, however. Often there is a delayed effect in learning anything, and even some temporary backsliding in student performance as new material is introduced.

In all these ways, it is my hope that this book will provide teachers with the means to create, along with their students, learning opportunities that are tailored to learners' needs, are enjoyable, and will maximize everyone's learning.

## OTHER COMPONENTS

An **Instructor's Manual** is available for this book. The Manual contains answers to the Exercise questions and grammatical notes where pertinent. The Manual also further discusses the theory underlying the series and "walks a teacher through" a typical unit, suggesting ways in which the various components of the unit might be used and supplemented in the classroom.

A student **Workbook** also accompanies this book. It provides additional exercises to support the material presented in this text. Many of the workbook exercises are specially designed to help students prepare for the TOEFL (Test of English as a Foreign Language).

## To the Student

All grammar structures have a form, a meaning, and a use. We can show this with a pie chart:

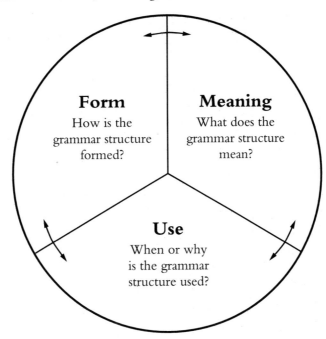

Often you will find that you know the answer to one or more of these questions, but not to all of them, for a particular grammar structure. This book has been written to help you learn answers to these questions for the major grammar structures of English. More importantly, it gives you practice with the answers so that you can develop your ability to use English grammar structures accurately, meaningfully, and appropriately.

At the beginning of each unit, you will be asked to work on a **Task.** The Task will introduce you to the grammar structures to be studied in the unit. However, it is not important at this point that you think about grammar. You should just do the Task as well as you can.

In the next section of the unit are **Focus Boxes** and **Exercises**. You will see that the boxes are labeled with **FORM, MEANING, USE,** or a combination of these, corresponding to the three parts of the pie chart. In each Focus Box is information that answers one or more of the questions in the pie. Along with the Focus Box are Exercises that should help you put into practice what you have studied.

The last section of each unit contains communicative **Activities.** Hopefully, you will enjoy doing these and at the same time receive further practice using the grammar structures in meaningful ways.

By working on the Task, studying the Focus Boxes, doing the Exercises, and engaging in the Activities, you will develop greater knowledge of English grammar and skill in using it. I also believe you will enjoy the learning experience along the way.

Diane Larsen-Freeman

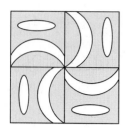

# Acknowledgments

## Series Director Acknowledgments

As with any project this ambitious, a number of people have made important contributions. I need to thank my students in the MAT Program at the School for International Training and audiences worldwide for listening to me talk about my ideas for reconciling the teaching of grammar with communicative language teaching. Their feedback and questions have been invaluable in the evolution of my thinking. One student, Anna Mussman, should be singled out for her helpful comments on the manuscript that she was able to provide based on her years of English teaching. A number of other anonymous teacher reviewers have also had a formative role in the development of the series. I hope they derive some satisfaction in seeing that their concerns were addressed wherever possible. In addition, Marianne Celce-Murcia not only helped with the original scope and sequence of the series, but also provided valuable guidance throughout its evolution.

I feel extremely grateful, as well, for the professionalism of the authors, who had to put into practice the ideas behind this series. Their commitment to the project, patience with its organic nature, and willingness to keep at it are all much appreciated. I insisted that the authors be practicing ESL teachers. I believe the series has benefited from this decision, but I am also cognizant of the demands it has put on the authors' lives these past few years.

Finally, I must acknowledge the support of the Heinle and Heinle "team." This project was "inherited" by Heinle and Heinle during its formative stage. To Dave Lee, Susan Mraz, Lisa McLaughlin, and especially Susan Maguire, who never stopped believing in this project, I am indeed thankful. And to Nancy Mann, who helped the belief become a reality, I am very grateful.

## Author Acknowledgments

We dedicate this book to our families and friends for their support throughout our writing process; to Joël, Melanie, and Michèle for their unwitting participation, extreme patience and cooperation; and finally to the power of enduring friendship. We would also like to thank Diane Larsen-Freeman for her guidance during the process of writing this book, and the reviewers of this book; Eva Bowman (University of North Texas), Mike Masyn (University of Colorado at Boulder), Pablo Buckelew (Santa Barbara City College), Judith Paiva (Northern Virginia Community College), Audrey Blackwell (University of Southern Mississippi), Steve Horowitz (University of Central Washington), and the field testers, Barbara Goddard (Hunter College), and Janet Miller and Maria Cantarero (Miami-Dade Community College) for their valuable suggestions. Special thanks to Sergio Aragones and to MAD Magazine for helping us track him down. Finally, we would like to express our gratitude to Nancy Mann and Shelley Clubb for their unceasing efforts and accommodating natures.

# 1

# The Verb *Be*
## Affirmative Statements;
## Subject Pronouns

## *Task*

Match each letter to a picture.

1.

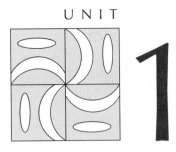

A. "Hi. My name is Fernando.
I'm Colombian.
I'm 30 years old.
I'm single."

2.

B. "Hello. I'm Young Soon.
I'm Korean.
I'm 20 years old.
I'm single."

3.

C. "My name's Chen.
I'm Chinese.
I'm from The People's Republic of China.
I'm 45 years old.
I'm married."

4.

D. "I'm Natalia.
I'm from Russia.
I'm 32.
I'm divorced."

Copy the information below onto an index card. Then fill out the information about yourself. Introduce yourself to the class.

| | |
|---|---|
| Name: | My name is_____ . |
| Country: | I am from_____ . |
| Nationality: | I'm_____ . |
| Age: | I'm_____ years old. |
| Married/Single/Divorced: | I'm_____ . |

# *Focus 1*

FORM

# Affirmative Statements with *Be*

FORM

- The normal word order in English is

  **Subject     Verb**

- The subject can be:
  - a noun phrase:     **(a) The student**   is from Korea.
  - a proper noun:     **(b) Young Soon**   is from Korea.
  - a subject pronoun: **(c) She**           is from Korea.
- The subject and the verb *be* must agree:

  | **Singular Subject** | **Singular Verb** | |
  |---|---|---|
  | (d) Young Soon | **is** | 25 years old. |
  | **Plural Subject** | **Plural Verb** | |
  | (e) Young Soon and Chen | **are** | Asian.* |

*Asian* is a term for people from countries in Asia, such as China, Japan, Thailand, Korea, India, Vietnam, etc.

*Hispanic* and *Latino* are terms for people who speak Spanish, such as people from Spain, South America, and Central America.

*Middle Eastern* is a term for people from countries in the Middle East, such as Israel, Lebanon, Iran, etc.

# *Exercise 1*

Use the information from the Task to fill in the blanks in the sentences below.

1. _____ is from Russia.

2. Young Soon _____ 20 years old.

3. _____ is Colombian.

4. Chen _____ married.

5. _____ are single.

6. Young Soon is from _____ .

7. Chen _____ Chinese.

8. _____ is in South America.

9. Moscow is in _____ .

10. Korea and The People's Republic of China _____ in Asia.

11. _____ is Hispanic.

12. _____ is divorced.

# Focus 2

FORM ● USE

## Subject Pronouns with *Be*

**FORM**
**USE**

- A subject pronoun takes the place of the noun phrase.

| | | |
|---|---|---|
| Fernando | = | He |
| Natalia | = | She |
| Colombia | = | It |
| Young Soon and Chen | = | They |

- Use subject pronouns in sentences only after the full noun phrase has been used.

**(a)** Fernando is Colombian. (He) is single.

| | **Subject Pronoun** | **Be** | |
|---|---|---|---|
| **Singular** | I | am | American. |
| | You | are | from the United States. |
| | He<br>She<br>It | is | 30 years old.<br>Russian.<br>in South America. |
| **Plural** | We<br>You<br>They | are | from Europe.<br>20 years old.<br>Asian. |

## Exercise 2

The subject pronouns in the following sentences are incorrect. Change the subject pronouns. Change the verb *be* when necessary. Say the correct sentences aloud. The first one has been done for you.

1. Miyuki and Seung are from Asia.

You are Asian. *They are Asian.*

2. Japan is an island.

He is in the Pacific Ocean.

3. George is 31 years old.

She is from Cyprus.

4. You and Mehmet are Turkish.

They are Turkish.

5. Young Soon is from Korea.

They are Korean.

6. Haiti is an island.

She is in the Caribbean.

7. Jean and I are from France.

They are French.

8. Marcio and you are from São Paulo.

They are Brazilian.

9. My name is Linda.

We are American.

## Exercise 3

Information Gap. Here are two lists of students in an ESL class. Look at List A. Make a statement about a student on your list. Your partner looks at List B, finds the person on his or her list, and makes a statement about the same student using a subject pronoun. Write the missing information in the blanks.

**EXAMPLES:** You say:               "Rodrigo is from Argentina."

Your partner says:       "He is Argentinian."

You say:               "Carla is Italian."

Your partner says:       "She is from Italy."

### List A:

| Name | Country | Nationality |
| --- | --- | --- |
| Rodrigo | Argentina | *Argentinian* |
| Carla | *Italy* | Italian |
| Miguel | _____ | Brazilian |
| Hiromi | Japan | _____ |
| Mohammed | _____ | Moroccan |
| Ivonne | Venezuela | _____ |
| Chin Hui | _____ | Taiwanese |
| Kyong Ho | _____ | Korean |
| Michele | France | _____ |
| Amir | Israel | _____ |
| Pany | _____ | Greek |
| Muhsin | _____ | Turkish |
| Bernice | The Dominican Republic | _____ |
| Stefanie | Germany | _____ |
| Ashi | _____ | Iranian |

5

**List B:**

| Name | Country | Nationality |
|------|---------|-------------|
| **Males:** | | |
| Muhsin | Turkey | _____ |
| Miguel | Brazil | _____ |
| Amir | _____ | Israeli |
| Pany | Greece | _____ |
| Rodrigo | _____ | Argentinian |
| Mohammed | Morocco | _____ |
| **Females:** | | |
| Ashi | Iran | _____ |
| Chin Hui | Taiwan | _____ |
| Michele | _____ | French |
| Hiromi | _____ | Japanese |
| Ivonne | _____ | Venezuelan |
| Bernice | _____ | Dominican |
| Stefanie | _____ | German |
| Carla | Italy | _____ |
| Kyong Ho | Korea | _____ |

# Exercise 4

Make seven summary statements about the students in the ESL class in Exercise 3. Write the number of students in the first blank. Write the correct form of the verb *be* in the second blank. Use *from* when necessary.

> **EXAMPLES:** _One_ student _is from_ France.
> _3_ students _are_ South American.

1. _____ student(s) _____ Iran.

2. _____ student(s) _____ Asian.

3. _____ student(s) _____ Europe.

4. _____ student(s) _____ South America.

5. _____ student(s) _____ Central American.

6. _____ student(s) _____ the Middle East.

7. _____ student(s) _____ French.

8. _____ student(s) _____ Hispanic.

# Focus 3

FORM

# Contractions with *Be*

FORM

- The subject pronoun combines with the verb *be* in speech and sometimes in writing. This is called a contraction. Contractions are short forms. An apostrophe (') is used above the line to make a contraction. Look at the placement of the apostrophe.

  **(a)** I'm American.

     NOT: I,m American.

| Subject Pronoun + *be* | *be* Contraction | |
|---|---|---|
| I am | I'm | Moroccan. |
| You are | You're | from Egypt. |
| He is | He's | 22 years old. |
| She is | She's | from Hong Kong. |
| It is | It's | in Asia. |
| We are | We're | in Level 1. |
| You are | You're | Japanese. |
| They are | They're | European. |

- Note: In spoken English, *is* and *are* are often contracted with nouns as well:

  **(b)** Victoria's American.

  **(c)** The woman's from Spain.

  **(d)** The students're from Korea. (in spoken English only)

## Exercise 5

Draw a line from the famous people on the left to the country they come from on the right. Next fill in their nationality in the column on the right. Then make two statements about each person. Use the name in the first sentence and the subject pronoun and the contraction in the second sentence.

**EXAMPLE:** Madonna ___*American*___ .

*Madonna is from the United States. She's American.*

| **Famous People** | **Country** | |
|---|---|---|
| 1. Madonna | France | 1. *American* |
| 2. Yoko Ono | South Africa | 2. _____ |
| 3. Sophia Loren | The United States | 3. _____ |
| 4. Arnold Schwarzenegger | Italy | 4. _____ |
| 5. Margaret Thatcher | Great Britain | 5. _____ |
| 6. The Rolling Stones | Japan | 6. _____ |
| 7. Luciano Pavarotti | Austria | 7. _____ |
| 8. Nelson Mandela | | 8. _____ |
| 9. Catherine Deneuve | | 9. _____ |
| 10. Robert Redford | | 10. _____ |

# Focus 4

# Introducing Yourself and Other People

USE

- To introduce yourself:

**(a)** Hello. My name's Mario Ortiz. I'm from the Philippines.

**(b)** Hi! I'm Lisa Jacobs. I'm from California. Nice to meet you!

- To introduce another person:
  - (c) Hello, Jay. This is Mario.
    He's from the Philippines.

- Here are some useful questions and responses to use when you first meet someone.

| Questions: | Responses: |
|---|---|
| (d) What's your name? | –My name is Frank.<br>–My name's Frank.<br>–Frank. |
| (e) Where are you from? | –I'm from Hong Kong.<br>–Hong Kong. |
| (f) How are you? | –Fine, thank you. How are you?<br>–Fine, thanks. And you? |

- Note: Use a title with someone's last name (family name).
  - (g) "Hello, I'm Dr. King."
  - (h) "Hello, I'm Ms. Smith."
- Do not use a title with a first name.
  - (i) "Hello, Susan."

    NOT: "Hello, Ms. Susan."

## Exercise 6

Choose five different people in your class. Ask each person the three questions in Focus 4.

## *Exercise 7*

Fill in the missing parts of the conversations.

1.   Frank:  Hello. I'm Frank.

Phillippe: ————————————————— ,   Frank.   —————————————————

Philippe.

2.   Lilik:  Hi! I'm Lilik. ————————————————— ?

Alvaro:  My name's Alvaro.

Lilik: ————————————————— , Alvaro?

Alvaro:  Venezuela. ————————————————— ?

Lilik:  I'm from Indonesia.

3. Michael:  Hi, Gregg. ————————————————— Jane.

Gregg:  Hi, Jane! ————————————————— ?

Jane:  Fine, thanks. ————————————————— ?

Gregg:  Great!

# Activities

### Activity 1

Make a list of all the students in your class. Make a list of the countries they come from and their nationalities.

| Names | Countries | Nationalities |
| --- | --- | --- |
| _____ | _____ | _____ |
| _____ | _____ | _____ |
| _____ | _____ | _____ |
| _____ | _____ | _____ |
| _____ | _____ | _____ |
| _____ | _____ | _____ |

### Activity 2

Write summary statements about the students in your class with the information you gathered above.

> **EXAMPLE:** Two students are Colombian.
> Six students are from Asia.

### Activity 3

On a separate piece of paper, write three sentences about yourself. Do not write your name on the paper. Then put your paper up on the board or wall with all your classmates' papers. On each of the other papers, under the sentences, write the name of the classmate you think the sentences are describing.

### Activity 4

Put all the index cards from Part 2 of the Task into a hat. Pick one card out and introduce that person to the class.

> **EXAMPLE:** "This is Maria. She's from Guatemala."

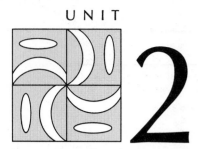

# 2

# The Verb *Be*

## Yes/No Questions;
## *Be* + Adjective;
## Negative Statements

## *Task*

Here are some advertisements from the classified section of the newspaper. Rewrite the questions on the lines in the correct ads.

CLASSIFIEDS

1. Are you single? Are you lonely?
   Is dating a problem for you?

2. Is English a problem for you?
   Are idioms difficult for you?
   Are you worried about your
   pronunciation?

3. Are you sad? Are you nervous?
   Is stress a problem for you?

4. Are you overweight?
   Are you out of shape?
   Are you tired?

**A.** Dr. Frend, Psychiatrist

_____

_____

_____

Call 222-HELP

**B.** 4-Ever Young Health Club

_____

_____

_____

Call now! 334-SLIM

**C.** The Lonelyhearts Dating Service

_____

_____

_____

Call 1-800-143-LOVE

**D.** The Cool School of English

_____

_____

_____

ENROLL NOW!
Call 777-4433

# Focus 1

## Yes/No Questions with *Be*; Short Answers

- To make a yes/no question with the verb *be*, put the correct form of the verb *be* in front of the subject. Put a question mark (?) at the end of the question.

| **Statement:** | **Yes/No Question:** |
|---|---|
| **(a)** Idioms are difficult. | Are idioms difficult? |
| **(b)** Stress is a problem. | Is stress a problem? |

- Short answers are used to answer yes/no questions.

| Questions | Affirmative | *Be* Contraction | Negative Contraction |
|---|---|---|---|
| Am I tense? | Yes, you are. | No, you're not. | No, you aren't. |
| Are you nervous? | Yes, I am. | No, I'm not. | * |
| Is he/she lonely? | Yes, he/she is. | No, he/she's not. | No, he/she isn't. |
| Is stress a problem? | Yes, it is. | No, it's not. | No, it isn't. |
| Are we overweight? | Yes, you are. | No, you're not. | No, you aren't. |
| Are you single? | Yes, we are. | No, we're not. | No, we aren't. |
| Are idioms difficult? | Yes, they are. | No, they're not. | No, they aren't. |

*There is no negative contraction with *am*. Use the *be* contraction with *not*.

- Note: After yes, do not use a contraction.

  **(c)** Yes, he is.
  NOT: Yes, he's.

## Exercise 1

Ask your partner the yes/no questions from the Task. Use short answers and contractions.

**EXAMPLE:** You:        "Are you single?"

Your partner:        "Yes, I am." (or)
                              "No, I'm not."

# Exercise 2

Write the missing parts of the correct form of the yes/no questions or the short answers in the blanks in the dialogues.

1. A: Hello, this is the 4–Ever Young Health Club.

   B: _____ you open today?

   A: Yes, ____ ____. We're open until 10:00 P.M.

2. Mitch: Hello, this is Mitch Brown. I got your telephone number from the Lonelyhearts Dating

   Service. _____ you Karen Smith?

   Karen: Yes, ____ ____.

   Mitch: ____ ____ free tonight?

   Karen: No, ____ ____. How about tomorrow?

   Mitch: Great!

3. A: Hello, is this Dr. Frend's office?

   B: Yes, ____ ____.

   A: _____ Dr. Frend busy? I need to speak to him.

   B: Hold on a minute, please.

4. (Hui Chen calls the "Cool School of English" for information.)

   Hui Chen: Hello, _____ this the "Cool School of English"?

   Secretary: Yes, ____ ____. May I help you?

   Hui Chen: I'd like some information about your program please.

   Secretary: Of course.

   Hui Chen: _____ the classes big?

   Secretary: No, ____ ____. We have only 10 people in a class.

   Hui Chen: _____ the teachers experienced?

   Secretary: Yes, ____ ____. They are excellent!

   Hui Chen: _____ the tuition expensive?

   Secretary: No, ____ ____. It's only $800 for ten weeks.

# Focus 2

## Be + Adjective

- After the verb *be*, you can use an adjective. An adjective *describes* a person, place, or thing.
  - **(a)** Dr. Frend is **busy**.
  - **(b)** The health club is **open**.
  - **(c)** Idioms are **difficult**.
- Do not put *s* on the adjective when the subject is plural.
  - **(d)** They are **excellent**.
    NOT: They are excellents.

## Exercise 3

Mark Stedman is 28 years old. He's single and he wants a girlfriend. He puts this advertisement in the newspaper. Write the correct form of the verb *be* in the statements and questions. Use contractions whenever possible.

---

I'm 28 years old.

I (1) _____ single.

I (2) _____ handsome and athletic.

I (3) _____ (negative) shy.

(4) _____ you under 30?

(5) _____ (6) _____ outgoing?

(7) _____ (8) _____ serious about a relationship?

Then call me!!! (222)593-6384

---

# Exercise 4

Write one of the adjectives below next to the correct picture. Then find the opposite of each adjective in the list at the bottom of the page. Write each opposite under the appropriate adjective. The first one has been done for you.

**Adjectives**

| | | | | | |
|---|---|---|---|---|---|
| sick | angry | funny | tall | poor | lazy |
| old✔ | overweight | strong | happy | beautiful | messy |

 1. _old_

_young_

 2. _____

_____

 3. _____

_____

 4. _____

_____

 5. _____

_____

 6. _____

_____

 7. _____

_____

 8. _____

_____

 9. _____

_____

 10. _____

_____

 11. _____

_____

 12. _____

_____

**Opposites**

| | | | | | |
|---|---|---|---|---|---|
| serious | healthy | energetic | sad | rich | calm |
| ugly | young✔ | weak | thin | short | neat |

16

# Exercise 5

Information Gap. Three women answered Mark's advertisement. You have Chart A with all the information about their physical characteristics and their personalities. Your partner doesn't have any information in Chart B. Your partner asks questions and puts a check in the correct space.

**EXAMPLE:** Your partner: "Is Cindy tall?"
You: "No, she isn't."
Your partner: "Is she short?"
You: "Yes, she is."

**Chart A**

| Name: | Cindy | Brigitte | Gloria |
|---|---|---|---|
| Age: | 22 | 27 | 30 |

**Physical Adjectives**

**A. Height**

| | Cindy | Brigitte | Gloria |
|---|---|---|---|
| 1. tall | | ✔ | |
| medium height | | | ✔ |
| short | ✔ | | |

**B. Weight**

| | Cindy | Brigitte | Gloria |
|---|---|---|---|
| 2. thin | ✔ | | |
| average weight | | | ✔ |
| overweight | | ✔ | |

**C. Personality**

| | Cindy | Brigitte | Gloria |
|---|---|---|---|
| 3. shy | | ✔ | |
| outgoing | ✔ | | ✔ |
| 4. quiet | | ✔ | |
| talkative | ✔ | | ✔ |
| 5. neat | | ✔ | ✔ |
| messy | ✔ | | |
| 6. funny | ✔ | | |
| serious | | ✔ | ✔ |
| 7. nervous | ✔ | | |
| calm | | ✔ | ✔ |

**Chart B**

| Name: | Cindy | Brigitte | Gloria |
|---|---|---|---|
| Age: | 22 | 27 | 30 |

**Physical Adjectives**

**A. Height**

1. tall _____

   medium height _____

   short _____

**B. Weight**

2. thin _____

   average weight _____

   overweight _____

**C. Personality**

3. shy _____

   outgoing _____

4. quiet _____

   talkative _____

5. neat _____

   messy _____

6. funny _____

   serious _____

7. nervous _____

   calm _____

## Exercise 6

Ask a classmate questions with the adjectives from Exercise 5. Use "Are you...?"

**EXAMPLE:** tall  You: "Are you tall?"
Your partner: "Yes, I am." or
"No, I'm not."

## Exercise 7

Write seven statements describing one of your classmates from the information you learned in Exercise 6.

**EXAMPLE:** *Juan is medium height. He's average weight.*

# Focus 3

FORM ● USE

## Negative Statements with *Be*;
## Negative Contractions

FORM
USE

- To form a negative statement with *be*, put *not* after the verb:

| Negative Statement (Full Form) | Be Contraction | Negative Contraction |
|---|---|---|
| I am not shy. | I'm not shy. | * |
| You are not short. | You're not short. | You aren't short. |
| He/She is not old.<br>It is not difficult. | He/She's not old.<br>It's not difficult. | He/She isn't old.<br>It isn't difficult. |
| We are not nervous.<br>They are not lonely. | We're not nervous.<br>They're not lonely. | We aren't nervous.<br>They aren't lonely. |

- Note: When the verb *be* is contracted and followed by *not* as a full word, it makes a stronger negative than a negative contraction. It is used to contradict or correct.

**Ping:** Wu's from the People's Republic of China.
**Chen:** Wu**'s not** from the People's Republic of China. He's from Taiwan.

## Exercise 8

Look at the hand-written student ID cards. Read the statements below the cards aloud. Are the statements correct? If the information is correct, say, "Yes, he/she/it is." or "That's right." If the information is not correct, make a negative statement with a *be* contraction + *not* and a correct affirmative statement.

**EXAMPLE:** 1. The last name is Yu-ho.

*The last name's not Yu-ho. It's Oh.*

| | |
|---|---|
| Last Name: | *Oh* |
| First Name: | *Yu-ho* |
| Country: | *Taiwan* |
| Nationality: | *Taiwanese* |
| Age: | *23* |
| Marital Status: | *single* |

1. The last name is Yu-ho.
2. He is Korean.
3. He's 25.
4. He's single.

| | |
|---|---|
| Last Name: | *Ryperman* |
| First Name: | *Aline* |
| Country: | *Holland* |
| Nationality: | *Dutch* |
| Age: | *32* |
| Marital Status: | *married* |

5. The first name is Alice.
6. She is Dutch.
7. She's from Germany.
8. She's 52.

| | |
|---|---|
| Last Name: | *Mafegna* |
| First Name: | *Abiy* |
| Country: | *Ethiopia* |
| Nationality: | *Ethiopian* |
| Age: | *30* |
| Marital Status: | *single* |

9. The first name is Mafegna.
10. He's Italian.
11. He's 30.
12. He's married.

| | |
|---|---|
| Last Name: | *Shram* |
| First Name: | *Jehad* |
| Country: | *Lebanon* |
| Nationality: | *Lebanese* |
| Age: | *27* |
| Marital Status: | *single* |

13. Jehad is Jordanian.
14. He is 29.
15. He's single.

# Activities

## Activity 1

Work with a partner. Ask each other questions to find out how you are *the same* and how you are *different*. Then write three sentences stating how you are similar and how you are different.

> **EXAMPLE:** "Are you energetic?"
>
> "Are you hard-working?"

### Similar

1. We are handsome.
2. We are intelligent.
3. We aren't modest!

### Different

1. My partner is hard-working. I am lazy!
2. He is 18. I'm 22.
3. He is nervous. I am calm.

## Activity 2

Based on your answers to Exercise 5, who is the best woman for Mark? Discuss your choice and explain why you picked her.

## Activity 3

Write your own personal ad for the newspaper or write one for a friend who is not married.

> **EXAMPLE:**
>
> My name is (1)_____.
> I'm (2)_____ (nationality).
> I'm (3)_____ years old.
> I'm (4)_____ (adjective).
> I'm (5)_____ (adjective).
> And I'm (6)_____ (adjective).
> Are you (7)_____ (adjective)?
> Are you (8)_____ (adjective)?
> **PLEASE CALL ME!**

## Activity 4

Describe someone in the class by writing five negative sentences. The other students guess the student you are describing.

> **EXAMPLE:** *This person is not tall.*
>
> *This person is not lazy.*
>
> *This person is not over 25 years old.*

# 3

# The Verb *Be*
## *Wh*-Questions

## *Task*

Test your knowledge. Try to answer the following questions. Discuss your answers with a partner.

**Answers**

1. What's the capital of Mexico? _____

2. Where is Katmandu? _____

3. Who is the head of the Catholic Church? _____

4. How is the weather in Argentina in June? _____

5. Where are the Himalayas? _____

6. When is Thanksgiving in the United States? _____

7. It's 9 A.M. in California. What time is it in New York? _____

8. What are the names of the seven continents? _____

_____

_____

9. How old are the Pyramids in Egypt? _____

10. Why is it cold at the North Pole? _____

# Focus 1

FORM ● MEANING

# *Wh*-Questions with *Be*

- To form *Wh*-questions with *be*, use a *Wh*-question word followed by the correct form of the verb *be*. Use *Wh*-questions to ask for specific information.

| *Wh*-Question Word + *Be* | Answer | Meaning |
|---|---|---|
| What is/'s the capital of Mexico? | It's Mexico City. <br> Mexico City. | THINGS |
| Where is/'s Katmandu? | It's in Nepal. <br> In Nepal. <br> Nepal. | PLACE |
| Who is/'s the head of the Catholic Church? | The Pope. | PEOPLE |
| How is/'s the weather in Argentina in June? | It's cold. | CONDITIONS |
| When is/'s Thanksgiving in the United States? | It's the last Thursday of November. | TIME |
| What time is/'s it in New York? | It's 12:00. <br> 12:00. | SPECIFIC TIME ON A CLOCK |
| How old are the Pyramids in Egypt? | About 4700 years old. | AGE |
| Why is/'s it cold at the North Pole? | It's cold because of the angle of the sun. <br> ...because of the angle of the sun. | REASON |

# Exercise 1

Using the answers to guide you, fill in the blanks with the correct *Wh*-question word.

| Questions | Answers |
|---|---|

1. _____ is the Great Wall of China?

    About 2200 years old.

2. _____ are the authors of Grammar Dimensions, Book 1?

    Victoria Badalamenti and Carolyn Henner-Stanchina.

3. _____ is Morocco?

    In North Africa

4. _____ are the summers in Washington, D.C.?

    Hot and humid.

5. _____ is the capital of Belgium?

    Brussels.

6. _____ is the first day of summer?

    June 21st.

7. It's 10 A.M. in Boston.

    _____ is it in Paris?

    4:00 P.M.

8. _____ is Independence Day in the United States?

    July 4.

9. _____ are you in this class?

    To learn English.

10. _____ are the names of the seven continents?

    North America, South America, Australia, Europe, Asia, Africa, and Antarctica.

# Exercise 2

Test your knowledge. Work with a partner. First, your partner chooses a category and an amount of money from the grid below. Then you ask a question about the information in the grid using *what* or *where*. If your partner answers correctly, he or she gets the amount of money chosen. Then you choose a category and an amount and your partner asks you a question. The person with the most "money" at the end wins.

**EXAMPLES:**
Your partner:  "*Monuments* for $30."
You:  "Where is the Colosseum?"
Your partner:  "It's in Rome, Italy."

Your partner:  "*Capitals* for $20."
You:  "What's the capital of Greece?"
Your partner:  "Athens."

| Amount $$$ | Categories | | | | |
|---|---|---|---|---|---|
| | Monuments | Capitals | Countries | Continents | Rivers, Mountains, Deserts |
| Questions | Where { is . . . / are . . . | What's the capital of . . . | Where's . . . | Where's . . . | Where { is . . . / are . . . |
| $10 | The Eiffel Tower | Afghanistan | Managua | Canada | The Sahara Desert |
| $20 | The Great Wall | Greece | Nagasaki | Chile | The Rocky Mountains |
| $30 | The Colosseum | Israel | Budapest | India | The Amazon River |
| $40 | The Pyramids | Peru | Capetown | Egypt | Mt. Everest |
| $50 | The Taj Mahal | Turkey | Zurich | Portugal | The Nile River |

## Exercise 3

Write the letter of the correct response in Column B next to the number in Column A.

**Column A**

_____ 1. What's your name?

_____ 2. Where are you from?

_____ 3. Where is Istanbul?

_____ 4. What's your nationality?

_____ 5. How old are you?

_____ 6. When's your birthday?

_____ 7. Why are you here?

_____ 8. How are you?

**Column B**

a. October 17.

b. I'm Turkish.

c. To study English.

d. Mehmet.

e. It's in Turkey.

f. 25.

g. Fine, thanks.

h. Istanbul.

## Exercise 4

Write five questions about other students in the class, using *who*. Then ask your partner the questions.

> **EXAMPLE:** *Who is from Asia?*
> *Who is 25 years old?*
> *Who is talkative?*

# Focus 2

USE

# Communication Strategy

USE

- When you need information about words in English, you can ask:
  **(a)** What is the meaning of *shy?*
  **(b)** What is the spelling of *shy?*
  **(c)** What is the pronunciation of *s-h-y?*

## Exercise 5

Read the following paragraph about Vancouver. Underline words if you don't know what they mean or how to pronounce them. Ask your teacher or a classmate questions. Use the two questions from Focus 2 to get the answers to your questions.

**EXAMPLE:** What is the meaning of *coast?*

Vancouver is a city in Canada. It's on the Pacific *coast*. The city is magnificent. It is clean and open. It isn't crowded. The hotels are modern and expensive. The people are polite. They are also warm and friendly. And, most importantly, the food is varied and delicious!

# Focus 3

USE

## Talking about the Weather

USE

- To talk about the weather, use *it* in the subject position followed by the verb *be*.

It's $\begin{cases} \text{sunny} \\ \text{humid} \\ \text{hot} \\ \text{muggy} \end{cases}$ in the summer.

It's $\begin{cases} \text{rainy} \\ \text{cloudy} \\ \text{mild} \end{cases}$ in the spring.

It's $\begin{cases} \text{cool} \\ \text{windy} \end{cases}$ in the fall.

It's $\begin{cases} \text{cold} \\ \text{chilly} \end{cases}$ in the winter.

- To ask questions about the weather, say:

How's the weather today?

How's the weather in Dallas?

What's the temperature today?

# Exercise 6

Information Gap. Here are two maps of the United States. You have some information about the weather in the different cities in Map A. Your partner has other information in Map B. Ask each other questions to find out the missing information.

**EXAMPLE:**  You:  "How's the weather in San Francisco today?"
Your Partner:  "It's sunny!"
You:  "What's the temperature?"
Your Partner:  "It's 65 degrees Fahrenheit."

**KEY**

| CLOUDY | SUNNY | PARTLY CLOUDY | RAINY | WINDY | SNOWY |

**MAP A**

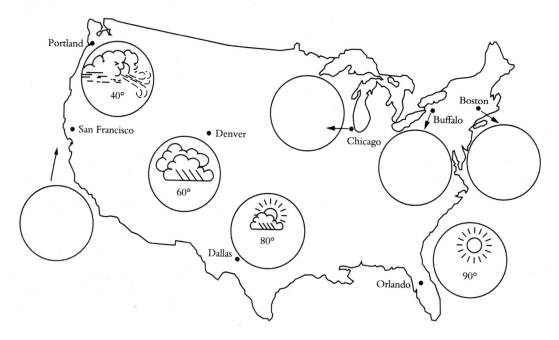

28

**MAP B**

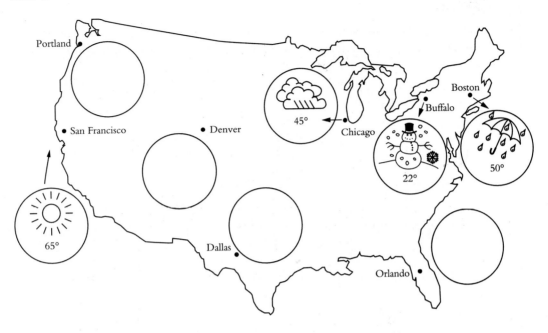

# *Focus 4*

## Talking about the Time

USE

- To talk about the time, also use *it* in the subject position followed by the verb *be*.
  - What time is it?  It's three o'clock.
    It's three P.M.
    It's 3:00.

**29**

## Exercise 7

Look at the map of the time zones in the United States. Ask and answer the following questions:

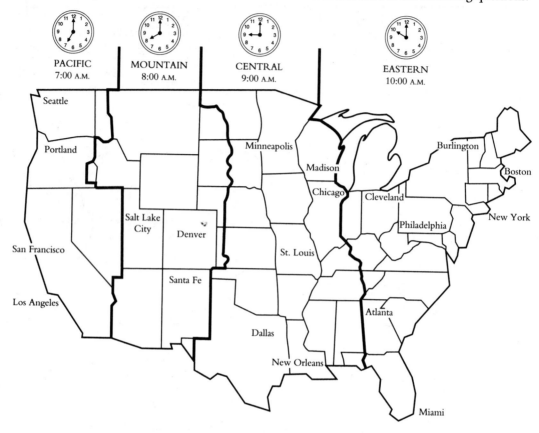

PACIFIC
7:00 A.M.

MOUNTAIN
8:00 A.M.

CENTRAL
9:00 A.M.

EASTERN
10:00 A.M.

1. It's 7:00 A.M. in San Francisco. What time is it in New York?_____

2. It's 10:00 P.M. in Miami. What time is it in Salt Lake City?_____

3. It's 6:00 P.M. in Minneapolis. What time is it in New Orleans?_____

4. It's 10:30 P.M. in Santa Fe. What time is it in Chicago?_____

5. It's 2:15 A.M. in Los Angeles. What time is it in Boston?_____

# Activities

**Activity 1**

Write the names of 20 big cities on pieces of paper and put them in a hat. The teacher will divide your class into two teams. Team 1 picks a piece of paper from the hat and asks Team 2 a question with *where*. Each team gets five points for a correct answer. The team with the most points at the end wins.

> **EXAMPLE:** Team 1 picks "Bogota" and asks: "Where is Bogota?"
>
> Team 2 answers: "It's in Colombia."

**Activity 2**

Use the time zone chart from Exercise 7 and make up other time questions for your partner to solve.

**Activity 3**

Using the adjectives below, interview a classmate about a city he or she knows. Ask yes/no and *wh*-questions.

> **EXAMPLE:** You: "Where are you from?"    Your Partner: "Acapulco."
>
> "Where's Acapulco?"    "It's in Mexico."
>
> "How is the weather?"    "It's hot in summer and mild in winter."
>
> "Are the people friendly?"    "Yes, they are."

| Weather | People | Other |
|---------|--------|-------|
| hot | happy | expensive |
| warm | friendly | cheap |
| mild | hard-working | small |
| cold | cold | big |
| sunny | religious | crowded |
| dry | outgoing | polluted |
| humid | quiet | safe |
| rainy | rich | dangerous |
| cloudy | poor | clean |

**Activity 4**

Write a short description of the city your partner described above.

> **EXAMPLE:** My classmate is from Mexico City. Mexico City is the capital of Mexico. Mexico City is big. It's crowded. It is hot in the summer. The people are friendly. The food is delicious.

# Noun Phrases
## Count and Non-Count Nouns

## *Task*

Match each word on the left with 2 words from the right. Write the words on the lines provided.

**CATEGORY**

1. Food  {  _____
         _____

2. Clothing (things to wear)  {  _____
                                _____

3. Electronic Equipment  {  _____
                           _____

4. Transportation  {  _____
                     _____

5. Entertainment (things to do)  {  _____
                                   _____

a. concerts

b. tv sets

c. sportswear

d. movies

e. trains

f. meat

g. shoes

h. radios

i. buses

j. vegetables

# *Focus 1*

## Two Kinds of Nouns

**MEANING**

- There are **two ways of seeing objects** in English.
  - Most often, objects are seen as separate things.
  - Sometimes, an object is seen as a whole, as one thing.
- There are **two kinds of nouns** in English:
  - **count nouns**—refer to objects seen as separate things. Some examples of count nouns are a telephone, a book, an apple.
  - **non-count nouns**—refer to objects seen as one thing. Some examples of non-count nouns are clothing, furniture, water.

## *Exercise 1*

Go back to the five categories in the Task. Divide the nouns in the Task into count and non-count nouns. Complete the list below.

| **Count Nouns** | **Non-Count Nouns** |
|---|---|
| 1. vegetables | 1. food |
| 2. things to wear | meat |
| _____ | 2. clothing |
| 3. _____ | _____ |
| _____ | 3. _____ |
| 4. _____ | 4. _____ |
| _____ | 5. _____ |
| 5. _____ | |
| _____ | |
| _____ | |

# Focus 2

## Indefinite Articles
## with Singular Count Nouns

- Count nouns can be **singular** or **plural**.
- Singular count nouns can be used with the indefinite articles *a / an*.

| *a* | *an* |
|---|---|
| a house<br>a movie<br>a uniform | an hour<br>an orange<br>an egg |
| *A* is used before a word beginning with a consonant sound. | *An* is used before a word beginning with a vowel sound. |

## Exercise 2

List all the words below in the correct categories. Then, read your lists aloud using *a / an*. Check to see if you have the same article as your classmates.

| | | | |
|---|---|---|---|
| earring | sofa | watch | emerald |
| dormitory | table | apple | house |
| orange | apartment | ring | desk |
| armchair | banana | pear | mobile home |

| Fruit | Furniture | Jewelry | Housing |
|---|---|---|---|
| *an apple* | | | |
| *a banana* | | | |
| | | | |
| | | | |

## Exercise 3

For each picture below, write a sentence identifying the person's occupation. Use *a/an*.

**EXAMPLES:**    She's an architect.    He's a police officer.

1. waiter _____

2. actor _____

3. athlete _____

4. secretary _____

5. dentist _____

6. flight attendant _____

**7.** nurse _____

**8.** engineer _____

**9.** cashier _____

**10.** doctor _____

**11.** hairdresser _____

**12.** construction worker _____

---

## *Exercise 4*

Write the occupations from Exercise 3 on small cards (one occupation per card). Choose a card. Use the information on the card to introduce one classmate to another classmate.

    **EXAMPLE:**    Gladys: Luis, this is Carmen. She's an architect.

                    Luis: Nice to meet you, Carmen.

            Carmen: Pleased to meet you too, Luis.

# Exercise 5

Test your knowledge. Read each question on the left aloud. Draw a line to the answer on the right. Fill in *a / an* when you read the answer aloud.

**EXAMPLE:** What's Poland?    It's _____*a*_____ country.

1. What's Poland?

2. What is Thanksgiving?

3. What's the Atlantic?

4. What is Puerto Rico?

5. What's the Sahara?

6. What is Africa?

7. What's New York?

8. What's the Concorde?

9. What's Big Ben?

10. What is the Louvre?

11. What is Harvard?

12. What's 60 minutes?

13. What's a Mercedes?

14. What's the Amazon?

a. It's _____ continent.

b. It's _____ car.

c. It's _____ museum.

d. It's _____ clock in London.

e. It's _____ river.

f. It's _____ city.

g. It's _____ holiday in the U.S. and Canada.

h. It's _____ hour.

i. It's _____ university.

j. It's _____ ocean.

k. It's _____ island.

l. It's _____ airplane.

m. It's _____ country.

n. It's _____ desert.

# *Focus 3*

## Spelling of Regular Plural Count Nouns

FORM

- Plural count nouns can be regular or irregular.
  - To form the plural of most regular count nouns, add *-s*. Do not use *a* or *an* before a plural noun.

|  | **Singular** | **Plural** |
|---|---|---|
|  | a car | two cars |
| (vowel + *y*) | a boy | three boys |
| (vowel + *o*) | a radio | four radios |

- Some regular plural count nouns require spelling changes.

| If the noun ends in: |  |  |  |
|---|---|---|---|
| consonant + *y* | change *y* to *i*, add *-es* | baby<br>city | babies<br>cities |
| *sh, ch, ss, x, z* | add *-es* | class<br>sandwich | classes<br>sandwiches |
| consonant + *o* | add *-es* | potato<br>tomato | potatoes<br>tomatoes |
| *fe* or *f* | change *f* to *v*, add *-es*\* | wife<br>life<br>thief | wives<br>lives<br>thieves |
| *\*Note: There are exceptions to the last rule:* |  | chief<br>chef | chiefs<br>chefs |

## *Exercise 6*

Write the plural forms of the words below.

1. party _____

2. shoe _____

3. box _____

4. banana _____

5. chair _____

6. glass _____

7. wife _____

8. watch _____

9. leaf _____

10. bed _____

11. month _____

12. key _____

## Exercise 7

Choose a noun from the list below. Make it plural. Complete the sentences.

city          story          holiday          university          state
mountain      country        continent        company              ocean

1. Thanksgiving and Christmas are _____.

2. The Atlantic and the Pacific are _____.

3. Africa and Asia are _____.

4. Harvard and Yale are _____.

5. IBM and Sony are _____.

6. "Cinderella" and "Beauty and the Beast" are _____.

7. The Alps are _____.

8. Colombia and Venezuela are _____ in South America.

9. Colorado and Vermont are _____ in the United States.

10. Paris and Rome are two _____ in Europe.

# Focus 4

FORM

# Pronunciation of Regular Plural Nouns

- /z/ **Group:** After **voiced** sounds (like l, m, b, y, g, n, r, v, z, and vowels), the *s* is pronounced z.

    schools          rooms          jobs          days

- /s/ **Group:** After **voiceless** sounds, (p, t, k, f) the *s* is pronounced s.

    books          maps          parents

- /ɪz/ **Group:** The final *s*/*es* is pronounced ɪz after the following:

| | |
|---|---|
| *s* sounds | classes, glasses, sentences, faces |
| *z* sounds | exercises, noises |
| *sh* sounds | dishes |
| *ch* sounds | sandwiches |
| *ge*/*dge* sounds | colleges, pages, lodges, oranges |

## Exercise 8

Look at the list of common measurements below. Make the measurement on the right plural and then read the statements aloud using the verb *equals*.

**EXAMPLE:** 98.6 degrees Fahrenheit = 37 degree____ Celsius
98.6 degrees Fahrenheit *equals* 37 degrees Celsius.

1. one foot = 12 inch____
2. one pound = 16 ounce____
3. one minute = 60 second____
4. one hour = 60 minute____
5. one day = 24 hour____

6. one year = 365 day____
7. one quart = 2 pint____
8. one gallon = 4 quart____
9. one inch = 2 1/2 centimeter____
10. one kilo = 2.2 pound____

# Focus 5

FORM

## Irregular Plural Nouns

FORM

- Some nouns do not take any form of *s* in the plural. They have irregular forms.
  - Some nouns change spelling in the plural.

    | child | – | children | person | – | people | tooth | – | teeth |
    | man | – | men | foot | – | feet | mouse | – | mice |
    | woman | – | women | | | | | | |

  - Some nouns do not change form in the plural.

    | a deer | – | two deer |
    | a sheep | – | three sheep |
    | a fish | – | four fish |

## Exercise 9

Use an irregular plural noun from Focus 5 to make each sentence true.

1. Big Bird is eight _____ tall.

2. Mickey and Minnie are famous _____.

3. Actresses are _____ and actors are _____.

4. "Bambi" is a movie about _____.

5. Famous _____ in Hollywood are rich.

6. Bugs Bunny has two big front _____.

7. "Sesame Street" is a television show for _____.

8. _____ of all ages like Disney movies.

# Focus 6

## Non-Count Nouns

| Count Nouns | Non-Count Nouns |
|---|---|
| • can be used with *a / an* in the singular<br>  **(a)** It's a watch.<br>  **(b)** It's an earring. | • cannot be used with *a / an* or *one*<br>  **(c)** Clothing is expensive in France.<br>  NOT: A clothing is expensive in France. |
| • can be plural<br>  **(d)** They have two computers. | • cannot be plural<br>  **(e)** He has homework.<br>  NOT: He has homeworks. |
| • can be used with singular or plural verbs<br>  **(f)** A house is expensive.<br>  **(g)** Houses are expensive in California. | • are always used with singular verbs<br>  **(h)** Housing is expensive in Japan.<br>  NOT: Housings are expensive in Japan. |

- **Some Common Non-Count Nouns in English**

| | | | |
|---|---|---|---|
| food | coffee | paper | information |
| bread | tea | medicine | news |
| rice | homework | hair | music |
| sugar | transportation | chalk | love |
| milk | electricity | luck | advice |
| fruit | furniture | money | clothing |
| water | mail | work | jewelry |

## Exercise 10

Use the cues to make questions. Add the names of the cities or countries represented by your classmates. Ask your classmates the questions, and then ask three questions of your own.

**EXAMPLE:** hamburgers / popular / in ... =

"Are hamburgers popular in....Russia?" "Yes, they are."

"No, they aren't."

1. American music / popular / in ...
2. bicycles / common / in ...
3. electricity / cheap / in ...
4. public transportation / good / in ...
5. families / big / in ...
6. taxes / high / in ...
7. fresh fruit / available / in ...
8. cars / big / in ...
9. sandwiches / popular / in ...
10. housing / expensive / in ...
11. accurate news about the world / available / in ...
12. ...
13. ...
14. ...

## Focus 7

USE

# Asking about Prices

USE

- Use the expressions *How much is* ... and *How much are* ... to ask about prices.

    **Singular:** How much is a television set in China?

    **Plural:** How much are newspapers in Russia?

    **Non-Count:** How much is gas in Italy?

## Exercise 11

Ask a classmate two questions for each cue. Add the name of the country. Write the answers in U.S. dollars.

> **EXAMPLE:** **1. a.** clothing / expensive (in ... Turkey)
> **b.** jeans
> **a.** "Is clothing expensive in Turkey?" "Yes, it is."
> **b.** "How much are jeans?" "Jeans are about $50."
> "Jeans cost about $50."

**Answers**

1. **a.** furniture / expensive in ...
   **b.** a sofa ... _____
2. **a.** public transportation / expensive in ...
   **b.** a bus ride ... _____
3. **a.** meat / expensive in ...
   **b.** steaks _____
4. **a.** housing / expensive in ...
   **b.** an apartment _____
5. **a.** fruit / expensive in ...
   **b.** an apple _____
6. **a.** entertainment / expensive in ...
   **b.** a movie _____
7. **a.** clothing / expensive in ...
   **b.** sneakers _____
8. **a.** electronic equipment / expensive in ...
   **b.** a VCR (a video cassette recorder) _____

# Activities

## Activity 1

This is a categorizing game. Your teacher will divide the class into three or four teams. Create category cards by writing one category on each card. For example, make the first category below into this category card:

> Things to eat that start
> with the letter *P*:
> *pizza (nc)*
> _____
> _____
> _____
> _____

**CATEGORIES:**

Things to Eat that Start with the Letter *P*:      Things that Give Light:

Things you Write or Draw with:      Parts of the Body that Come in Pairs:

Things at the Beach:      Things to Wear:

Then write each word from the list below on the correct category card. Next to each word, write **C** for Count Nouns and **NC** for Non-Count Nouns. Each correct answer is worth one point. The team with the most points wins.

## NOUNS FOR CATEGORY CARDS:

| | | | | |
|---|---|---|---|---|
| sand | shirts | pizza | people | eyes |
| matches | popcorn | towels | feet | glasses |
| peaches | candle | chalk | fire | lips |
| pencil | ink | socks | flashlight | pants |
| pen | pancakes | lamp | ears | pears |
| boats | shoes | markers | water | arms |

## Activity 2

Plan a surprise party for someone in the class. Make a list of all the things you need to buy for the party, including gifts.

## Activity 3

This is a guessing game about famous people. Think of a famous person. Make three or four statements about the person, and the class will then try to guess his or her name.

> **EXAMPLE:** "She's an actress.
> She's French.
> She is blonde.
> She's beautiful."
> Who is she? Catherine Deneuve.

## Activity 4

Tell your classmates what you have for:

Breakfast      Lunch      Dinner      Snack

UNIT

5

# The Verb *Have*

## Affirmative/Negative;
## Questions and Short Answers;
## *Some/Any*

## Task

Look at the photographs of two Inuit (Eskimo) women living in Northern Canada. Read each statement on the next page. Check **Mary** if the statement is true for Mary. Check **Nilaulaq** if the statement is true for Nilaulaq (Nila). Then, circle the correct name in each concluding statement.

**MARY**

**NILAULAQ**

45

|  | Mary | Nilaulaq |
|---|---|---|
| 1. She has a house. | _____ | _____ |
| 2. She has an Eskimo name. | _____ | _____ |
| 3. She has a tent. | _____ | _____ |
| 4. She has electricity. | _____ | _____ |
| 5. She has Eskimo clothing. | _____ | _____ |
| 6. She has dogs. | _____ | _____ |
| 7. She has furniture. | _____ | _____ |
| 8. She has canned food. | _____ | _____ |
| 9. She has fresh fish. | _____ | _____ |
| 10. She has a clock. | _____ | _____ |

Concluding statements:
Mary/Nilaulaq has a traditional Eskimo life-style.
Mary/Nilaulaq has a modern Eskimo life-style.

# Focus 1

FORM ● MEANING

## Affirmative Statements with *Have*

FORM
MEANING

- *Have* means to possess or own something.
- The verb *have* changes only when the subject is third person singular: he, she, it.

|  | Subject | Verb |  |
|---|---|---|---|
| Singular | I<br>You | **have** |  |
| Singular | He<br>Charlie<br>She<br>Mary<br>It<br>The house | **has** | a stove. |
| Plural | We<br>You<br>They | **have** |  |

## Exercise 1

Write the correct form of *have* to make statements about Nilaulaq and her family.

1. Nilaulaq _____ an Inuit name.

2. She _____ a husband named Charlie.

3. They _____ two children.

4. They _____ a traditional Eskimo life-style.

5. They _____ traditional Inuit clothing.

6. They _____ a tent.

7. They _____ dogs.

8. Charlie _____ a canoe.

9. He _____ a fishing net.

10. They _____ fresh fish.

## Exercise 2

Look back at the photograph of Mary. Mary has a more modern Inuit life-style. Complete the statements about what Mary has. Then complete the conclusions about what modern Eskimos have. Read the statements and conclusions aloud.

1. Mary (a) _____ wallpaper in her house. Mary (b) _____ a map. She

   (c) _____ pots. She (d) _____ canned food.

   Conclusion:

   Modern Eskimos live in towns. The towns (e) _____ stores. Modern

   Eskimos (f) _____ money. They (g) _____ jobs.

2. Mary (a) _____ a book of prayers.

   Conclusion:

   The town (b) _____ a school. It (c) _____ a church.

3. Mary (a) _____ photographs. She (b) _____ picture frames.

   Conclusion:

   Modern Eskimos (c) _____ cameras.

4. Modern houses (a) _____ lights.

   Conclusion:

   They (b) _____ electricity.

# Focus 2

## *Do* in Negative Statements with *Have*; Negative Contractions

**FORM**

- The verb *have* differs from the verb *be* in the negative.

| Be | Have |
|----|------|
| I **am** not Canadian.<br>She **is** not an Eskimo. | I **do** not **have** a tent.<br>She **does** not **have** dogs. |

- Add the auxiliary form *do + not* to make negative statements with *have*. Use the base form of the verb *have*. Use *does + not + have* if the subject is third person singular (he/she/it).

   **(a)** She **has** two children. — She **does** not **have** three children.
   
   NOT: She does not has three children.

|  | Subject | Auxiliary Form + Negative (Negative Contraction) | Base Form of the Verb |
|--|---------|-------------------------------------------------|----------------------|
| **Singular** | I<br>You | **do not**<br>**(don't)** | have three children. |
|  | He<br>She<br>It<br>(The tent) | **does not**<br>**(doesn't)** | have furniture. |
| **Plural** | We<br>You<br>They | **do not**<br>**(don't)** | have a car. |

## Exercise 3

Match the subjects with the noun phrases and make affirmative or negative statements aloud using the verb *have*. Make as many statements as you can.

**EXAMPLES:** *Traditional Eskimos don't have electricity.*
*Modern Eskimos have houses.*
*Mary has a radio.*

### Subjects

1. Nila
2. Nila and Charlie
3. Traditional Eskimos
4. Modern Eskimos
5. Traditional Eskimo women
6. Modern Eskimo women
7. Tents
8. A modern town
9. Mary

### Noun Phrases

a. sewing machine
b. jewelry
c. a school
d. a watch
e. a fishing net
f. a canoe
g. a high school diploma
h. a radio
i. a camera
j. electricity
k. a job
l. a stove
m. heat in the winter
n. canned food
o. stores
p. fresh milk
q. igloos
r. houses

## Focus 3

FORM

# *Do* in Yes/No Questions with *Have*

FORM

- Use the auxiliary form *do* to make questions with *have*. Use *does* if the subject is third person singular (he, she, it). Use the base form of the verb *have*.

   **(a)** They **have** children.—**Do** they **have** children?
   **(b)** He **has** a car.—**Does** he **have** a car?

      NOT: Does he has a car?
      NOT: Has he a car?

|  | Auxiliary Form | Subject | Base Form of the Verb |  |
|---|---|---|---|---|
| **Singular** | Do | I you | have | a child? |
|  | Does | he she it | have | furniture? |
| **Plural** | Do | we you they | have | books? |

- We commonly use negative contractions for short answers. Negative contractions with *not* as a full word are stronger negatives. We use them to correct or contradict.

| | Affirmative | Negative | Negative Contraction |
|---|---|---|---|
| **Singular** | Yes, { I / you } **do**. | No, { I / you } **do not**. | No, { I / you } **don't**. |
| | Yes, { he / she / it } **does**. | No, { he / she / it } **does not**. | No, { he / she / it } **doesn't**. |
| **Plural** | Yes, { we / you / they } **do**. | No, { we / you / they } **do not**. | No, { we / you / they } **don't**. |

# Exercise 4

Complete each question and give a short answer you think is correct. (The answers are not in the pictures.) If you are not sure of the answer, say "maybe." Discuss your answers in class. Then ask three questions of your own.

1. Q: _____ Mary _____ a television set?

   A: _____ .

2. Q: _____ a traditional Eskimo woman _____ a refrigerator?

   A: _____ .

3. Q: _____ modern Eskimos _____ igloos?

   A: _____ .

4. Q: _____ modern Eskimo houses _____ running water?

   A: _____ .

5. Q: _____ modern Eskimos _____ heat in the winter?

   A: _____ .

## *Exercise 5*

### Find Someone Who

Go around the classroom and ask your classmates if they have the following things. If the answer is "yes," write down your classmate's name. The first student who fills in names for all the things (or for the most things) wins.

**EXAMPLE:** "Do you have a cordless telephone?" . . . "Yes, I do."
"No, I don't."

| **Things** | **Students' Names** |
| --- | --- |
| 1. cordless telephone | _____ |
| 2. pet | _____ |
| 3. car | _____ |
| 4. children | _____ |
| 5. English-English dictionary | _____ |
| 6. jewelry | _____ |
| 7. job | _____ |
| 8. bicycle | _____ |
| 9. library card | _____ |
| 10. video cassette recorder (VCR) | _____ |

# *Focus 4*

## FORM ● MEANING

## *Some / Any*

- In general, use *some* in affirmative statements and *any* in negative statements and questions. Use *some/any* in front of plural count nouns and non-count nouns.

| Affirmative Statements (without *some*) | Affirmative Statements (with *some*) |
|---|---|
| Without *some,* the quantity is not important. <br> **Plural Count:** <br> **(a)** The children have **books**. <br> **(b)** The stores have **cigarettes**. <br> **Non-Count:** <br> **(c)** They have **money** in the bank. | With *some,* the quantity is important but is not specified. *Some* means *not all*. <br> **Plural Count:** <br> **(d)** The children have **some books**. <br> **(e)** The stores have **some cigarettes**. <br> **Non-Count:** <br> **(f)** They have **some money** in the bank. |

| Questions | Negative Statements |
|---|---|
| **Plural Count:** <br> **(g)** Do they **have any** children? <br> **(h)** No, they don't. <br> **Non-Count:** <br> **(i)** Do they **have any** money? <br> **(j)** No, they don't. | **Plural Count:** <br> **(k)** They **don't have any** children. <br> **Non-Count:** <br> **(l)** They **don't have any** money. |

- Note: When you want or expect the answer to be *yes,* you can ask a question using *some:*
  You are at a friend's house and you are thirsty. Say, "Do you have some water?"

## Exercise 6

Read the statements below. In each blank, write *some*, or *any*. In a group, decide if the statement represents something good or bad for Eskimos. Discuss your ideas with the whole class.

1. The town theater has _____ American movies.

2. Students don't have _____ Inuit teachers in school.

3. The stores have _____ magazines.

4. In school, classes are in English. Students don't have _____ classes in

   the Inuit language.

5. The stores have _____ cigarettes.

6. The Eskimos have _____ information about other people in the world.

7. Parents don't have _____ English classes.

8. Modern Eskimos have jobs. They have _____ money in the bank.

9. Children have _____ problems with their parents.

10. Schoolchildren don't have _____ traditional skills, like fishing, building

    an igloo, or hunting.

## Exercise 7

Read about the Amish people. Then use the cues on page 54 to write questions with *have*. Use *a* with singular count nouns. Use *any* with plural count or non-count nouns. Think carefully about the information in the text and answer the questions that you have written.

Imagine life without electricity, cars, or modern technology. The Amish are Americans with a traditional life-style. They do not have any of these things.

The Amish are farmers. They are called *Plain People*. They have simple, dark clothing. The women wear long dresses and bonnets. The men all have beards and wear hats.

Amish children have special one-room schoolhouses with Amish teachers. After school, they play with homemade toys.

The Amish are different. Today, we have about 85,000 Amish people in the United States.

1. Amish people / colorful clothing _____ ?

   _____

2. Amish women / jewelry _____ ?

   _____

3. Amish family / car _____ ?

   _____

4. Amish home / electricity _____ ?

   _____

5. Amish home / telephone _____ ?

   _____

6. Amish family / television set _____ ?

   _____

7. Amish child / computer _____ ?

   _____

8. Amish farmers / tractors _____ ?

   _____

9. Amish people / horses _____ ?

   _____

10. Amish children / special teachers _____ ?

   _____

# *Focus 5*

## Making Polite Requests

USE

- Use "Do you have ... ?" followed by a noun phrase to ask for something politely.
- To stop a person on the street, say, "Excuse me, do you have ...?"
- To answer a request:

  If the answer is **yes**, say: $\begin{cases} \text{"Yes, I do ..."} \\ \text{"Sure ..."} \end{cases}$ and give the object to the speaker.

  If the answer is **no**, say: $\begin{cases} \text{"No, I don't."} \\ \text{"Sorry, I don't."} \end{cases}$

- Note: To ask someone the time, say:

  "Excuse me, do you have the time?"

## *Exercise 8*

Look at the situations. Use the noun phrases below the pictures to make polite requests, and respond to them. Use *a/an/some/any.*

**1.** (match)

**2.** (milk)

**3.** (corkscrew)

55

**4.** (stamps)　　　　**5.** (change)　　　　**6.** (eraser)

# Focus 6

## Describing People

- The verb *have* is used to give physical descriptions of people.

He **has** black hair.

| HAIR COLOR | HAIR LENGTH | FEATURES | EYE COLOR |
|---|---|---|---|
| dark | long | a mustache | black |
| light | short | a beard | brown |
| black | medium–length | dimples | blue |
| brown | | freckles | green |
| red | **HAIR TYPE** | bangs | gray |
| blonde | straight | | hazel |
| gray | wavy | | |
| white | curly | | |

## Exercise 9

Refer to the photographs in the Task (Nilaulaq and Mary) and in Exercise 7 (The Amish). Complete the descriptions below using the verbs *be* or *have* and the correct noun phrases.

1. John Lapp is Amish.

   He _____ married.

   He _____ long _____.

   He _____ a long _____.

3. Daniel is young.

   He _____ long blonde hair.

   He _____ bangs.

2. Nilaulaq _____ an Inuit woman.

   She _____ long black _____.

   She _____ a nice smile.

4. Mary _____ a modern Eskimo.

   Mary _____ happy.

   She _____ dark hair.

## Exercise 10

Error Correction. Rewrite the following sentences correctly.

1. He have a car. _____ .

2. She have not a house. _____ .

3. He no have a TV set. _____ .

4. He doesn't is married. _____ .

5. She doesn't has children. _____ .

6. Does he has a canoe? _____ ?

7. Does she is an Eskimo? _____ ?

8. Excuse me, have you change? _____ .

# Activities

### Activity 1

Think of someone in your family—either of your parents, your brother, sister, a grandparent. What do you have that they do not have? Write three statements.

> **EXAMPLE:** *I have a car. My sister doesn't have a car.*
> *I have a college diploma. My parents don't have college diplomas.*

### Activity 2

Write a physical description of one of your classmates. Do not write the person's name on your paper. Read your description to the class. Your classmates will try to guess the student's name.

> **EXAMPLE:** "This student is tall. He has short hair. He has green eyes. He has a mustache."

### Activity 3

Go around the room. Make polite requests using *have*. Respond to your classmates' requests.

> **EXAMPLE:** "Excuse me, do you have a pencil sharpener?"

### Activity 4

Think of a person or people you know with traditional life-styles. Write about these people. Give a physical description of them. Tell how their lives are different; tell what they have and what they do not have. Then read your sentences to the class.

### Activity 5

Go to the library and take out a book about the Inuit or the Amish. Write down five new things that you learned about what they have and don't have.

### Activity 6

What American things do people in your country have today? Is it good or bad to have these things? Discuss this with a partner.

> **EXAMPLE:** "In Western Europe today, they have McDonald's restaurants. This is bad/good because . . ."

# Possessives

## Nouns, Adjectives, and Pronouns;
## Questions with *Whose;*
## *A/An* versus *The*

## Task

Each of the items on this page belongs to a person or people on the next page. Match the items to their owner(s) by writing the correct letter next to the item.

_____ 1.

_____ 2.

_____ 3.

_____ 4.

_____ 5.

_____ 6.

_____ 7.

_____ 8.

_____ 9.

_____ 10.

A. STAN

B. LEONA

C. CHRIS

D. BOB CAROL ALICE TED

E. JESSE GEORGE THOMAS

F. MONICA FRED

G. MRS. WOLF

H. SIMON

I. BERNIE

J. BONZO

# *Focus 1*

## MEANING

# Possessives

**MEANING**

- Use possessives to show that a person "has" something.
  - **(a)** Things:      Leona has a necklace.
                           Leona's necklace is expensive.
  - **(b)** Relationships:  Fred has a wife.
                           Monica is Fred's wife.
- There are different kinds of possessives. There are possessive nouns, adjectives, and pronouns.

# Focus 2

## Possessive Nouns

- Use possessive nouns in front of nouns to form noun phrases. Possessive nouns are formed with an apostrophe (') and *s*.

| Noun | Rule | Example | |
|------|------|---------|---|
| 1. Singular<br>–**boy**<br>–**Leona** | Add '*s*. | **(a)** The boy**'s** glasses are strong.<br>**(b)** Leona**'s** necklace is expensive. | '*s* |
| 2. Singular nouns and names ending in *s*<br>–**Thomas** | Add ' after the *s*.<br>OR Add '*s* after the *s*. | **(c)** Thomas**'** kite is broken.<br>**(d)** Thomas**'s** kite is broken. | '<br>'*s* |
| 3. Regular plural noun<br>–**boys** | Add ' after the *s*. | **(e)** The boys**'** kites are high up in the sky. | ' |
| 4. Irregular plural noun<br>–**people** | Add '*s*. | **(f)** The people**'s** dogs are lost. | '*s* |

- Note: When there are two or more subjects, make the last noun possessive:
    **Fred and Monica's** baby is six months old.

## Exercise 1

Go back to the Task. Point to the items and make statements using possessive nouns.

**EXAMPLES:** (point to the camera): "It's Bernie's camera."
(point to the two front teeth): "They're Chris' two front teeth."

## Exercise 2

Use possessive nouns in the following sentences.

1. _____ hobby is photography.

2. This is Ted. He's _____ husband.

3. _____ glasses are strong.

4. Where are the _____ dogs?

5. The old _____ cane is short.

6. _____ jewelry is expensive.

7. _____ hair is fake.

8. The _____ nose is funny.

9. _____ front teeth are gone.

10. The _____ kites are broken.

## Exercise 3

This is Carol's family tree. Read each statement and write each person's relationship to Carol under his or her name in the box. The first one has been done for you.

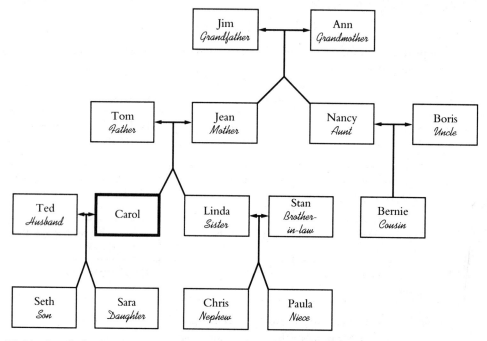

1. Ted is Carol's husband.
2. Seth is Ted and Carol's son.
3. Sara is Ted and Carol's daughter.
4. Linda is Carol's sister.
5. Stan is Carol's brother-in-law.
6. Chris is Carol's nephew.
7. Paula is Carol's niece.

8. Nancy is Carol's aunt.
9. Boris is Carol's uncle.
10. Bernie is Carol's cousin.
11. Jean is Carol's mother.
12. Tom is Carol's father.
13. Jim is Carol's grandfather.
14. Ann is Carol's grandmother.

## Exercise 4

Fill in the blanks with the correct possessive nouns and say each sentence aloud.

**EXAMPLES:** Carol is *Ted's* wife.

Carol is *Chris and Paula's* aunt.

1. Seth is _____ brother.

2. Boris is _____ father.

3. Paula is _____ sister.

4. Stan is _____ husband.

5. Jean is _____ mother.

6. Carol is _____ cousin.

7. Ted is _____ uncle.

8. Seth is _____ nephew.

9. Linda is _____ sister-in-law.

10. Jean is _____ mother-in-law.

# Focus 3

## Possessive Adjectives

- Possessive adjectives are used to show possession as well.

| Subject Pronoun | | Possessive Adjective | |
|---|---|---|---|
| **I** | have a dog. | **My** | dog is small. |
| **You** | have a dog. | **Your** | dog is big. |
| **He** | has a dog. | **His** | dog is friendly. |
| **She** | has a dog. | **Her** | dog is mean. |
| **The dog** | has a collar. | **Its** | collar is gold. |
| **We** | have a dog. | **Our** | dog is noisy. |
| **You** | have a dog. | **Your** | dog is quiet. |
| **They** | have a dog. | **Their** | dog is cute. |

- Use possessive adjectives only before nouns. Do not use the articles *a/an/the* with possessive adjectives:
  **(a)** My dog is cute.
     NOT: The my dog is cute.
- The form of the possessive adjective is determined by the person who has the thing or relationship.
  - *His* means a "male" has something.
  - *Her* means a "female" has something.
    **(b)** Ted has a son.　　　**His** son is ten.
    **(c)** Ted has a daughter.　**His** daughter is seven years old.
    　　　　　　　　　　　　　NOT: Her daughter is seven years old.
    **(d)** Carol has a daughter.　**Her** daughter is seven years old.
    **(e)** Carol has a son.　　　**Her** son is ten.
    　　　　　　　　　　　　　NOT: His son is ten.
  - NOTE: Do not confuse the possessive adjective (*its*) with the contraction of it is (*it's*).

# Exercise 5

Read the conversation between Mr. Wolf and an old neighbor he meets after four years. Circle the correct word in each sentence.

**Neighbor:** Hi, Mr. Wolf. How are you? How's (1) (you / your) wife?

**Mr. Wolf:** Well, (2) (I / my) am OK, but Mrs. Wolf has more and more aches and pains. Walking is difficult. (3) (She / Her) is 86 years old, you know!

**Neighbor:** Is she in a wheelchair now?

**Mr. Wolf:** No, she has a cane. (4) (She / Her) cane is a big help. (5) (It's / Its) important for her to go out and get some exercise.

**Neighbor:** Are you still in (6) (you / your) old apartment, Mr. Wolf?

**Mr. Wolf:** Yes, of course. (7) (We / Our) rent is cheap. (8) (It's / Its) only $350 a month.

**Neighbor:** And what about (9) (you / your) children?

**Mr. Wolf:** Well, (10) (I / my) son is married to a Chinese woman. (11) (He's / His) in business in California. (12) (He's / His) business is successful. (13) (He's / His) very happy. (14) (I / My) daughter is married to a Brazilian man. (15) (They're / Their) both professors at Stanford University. (16) (We / Our) also have three grandchildren now. (17) Unfortunately, (they're / their) all in California. (18) (We / Our) are very lonely here in New York.

# Exercise 6

Read the statements about the people in this unit. What conclusions can you draw? Match each statement on the left to a conclusion on the right. Then fill in the correct possessive adjectives. Read your answers aloud.

**EXAMPLE:** 1. Stan has a toupee. g. _His_ head is bald.

1. Stan has a toupee.

2. Leona doesn't have money problems.

3. Chris doesn't have any front teeth.

4. The people have leashes, but they don't have dogs.

5. Carol and Ted have three locks on their front door.

6. Simon has thick glasses.

7. Bernie has a camera.

8. Jean and Tom are grandparents.

9. This is the end of the exercise.

a. _____ neighborhood isn't very safe.

b. _____ camera is probably made in Japan.

c. _____ children have children.

d. _____ vision is poor.

e. _____ time is up!

f. _____ family is rich.

g. _____ head is bald.

h. The missing teeth are _____ baby teeth.

i. _____ dogs are lost.

## Exercise 7

Read the story about Sylkvester Mallone. Write the correct possessive adjectives in the blanks.

Sylkvester Mallone is a famous American actor. (1) _____ movies are very popular.

Sylkvester Mallone is a millionaire. He's married. He also has a girlfriend. (2) _____

wife, Dana, is angry. After one year of marriage, Sylkvester and (3) _____ wife are in

the middle of a divorce.

The story of (4) _____ divorce is in the newspapers every day. Dana isn't sad about

(5) _____ divorce. Dana and (6) _____ lawyer are after Sylkvester's money—$8

million of it!!!

"It's (7) _____ money," says Dana.

"Oh, no, it's not (8) _____ money; it's (9)_____ money," says Sylkvester.

Sylkvester is very worried about (10) _____ money now.

What about you? What is (11) _____ opinion about this story?

# Focus 4

USE

# Using Possessive Adjectives with Body Parts

USE

- Use possessive adjectives to talk about body parts. Look at these sentences below:

| | | |
|---|---|---|
| My hair is black. | His eyes are brown. | Their teeth are straight. |
| Your skin is dark. | Her legs are long. | Our hands are small. |

## Exercise 8

Describe a person in the class to your partner without saying his or her name. Have your partner guess who you are talking about.

**EXAMPLE:**  You say:  "Her hair is black. Her eyes are blue. Her skin is dark."
Your partner says: "Is it Luisa?"

# Focus 5

## Possessive Pronouns

- Possessive pronouns take the place of noun phrases.
    - **(a)** This is Leona's necklace.      The necklace is **hers**.
    - **(b)** This is Bernie's camera.      The camera is **his**.

| Possessive Adjectives | Possessive Pronouns |
|---|---|
| It is **my** apartment. | The apartment is **mine.** |
| It is **your** house. | The house is **yours.** |
| It's **his** dog. | The dog's **his.** |
| It's **her** jewelry. | The jewelry's **hers.** |
| They are **our** children. | The children are **ours.** |
| It's **their** money. | The money's **theirs.** |

- NOTE:
    1. *His* is the same whether it is a possessive adjective or a possessive pronoun.
    2. All possessive pronouns end in *s*, except *mine*.
    3. *Its* doesn't occur as a possessive pronoun.

## Exercise 9

Look at all the objects coming out of the bag. Identify each object. Then take turns reading each statement aloud. The class guesses who owns each object. Finally, make statements using the correct possessive pronoun.

**EXAMPLE:** Bernie is American. *The flowered shirt and shorts are his.*

## OBJECTS

| | | |
|---|---|---|
| flowered shirt and shorts | McDonald's hamburgers | saris |
| bowler hats and umbrellas | bottle of wine and cheese | can of coffee |
| pair of chopsticks | tulips | watches |
| salsa record | trophies | |

## STATEMENTS

1. Miyuki is Japanese.
2. Pierre and Mimi are French.
3. Arnaldo is Venezuelan.
4. We are American.
5. Philip and George are British.

6. Rene is Swiss.
7. Anjali and Namita are Indian.
8. Yolanda is Costa Rican.
9. Aline and Hans are Dutch.
10. You are good players.

# Focus 6

FORM ● MEANING

## Questions with *Whose*

FORM
MEANING

- The question word *whose* asks about possession.

| *Whose* + Noun Phrase | + Verb + | Subject? | Answers |
|---|---|---|---|
| Whose dog | is | it? | It's Carol's dog. It's her dog. It's hers. |
| Whose glasses | are | they? | They're Simon's glasses. They're his glasses. They're his. |

# Exercise 10

Use the vocabulary from the Task to make questions with *whose*. Then answer the questions aloud.

**EXAMPLE:** glasses

Whose glasses are they?    They're Simon's glasses.
                                                   They're his.

| | | | |
|---|---|---|---|
| 1. baby | 3. nose | 5. toupee | 7. teeth |
| 2. cane | 4. necklace | 6. camera | 8. kites |

# Exercise 11

The objects below belong to the people in Picture A, B, C or D. Using *whose*, ask questions to find out who the objects belong to. Make two statements, one with the possessive noun and one with the possessive pronoun.

**EXAMPLE:** Whose hammer is it?　　*It's Jackie's hammer.*
　　　　　　　　　　　　　　　　*It's hers.*

| A. John | B. Jackie | C. Jim | D. Pierre and Daniel |
|---|---|---|---|
| 1. Corkscrew | 2. Pencil Sharpener | 3. Lawn Mower | 4. Screwdriver |
| 5. Typewriter | 6. Flower Pot | 7. Hammer | 8. Shovel |
| 9. Sauce Pan | 10. Watering Can | 11. Envelope | 12. Can Opener |
| 13. Wrench | 14. Paintbrush | 15. Spatula | 16. Paper Clip |

# Focus 7

## MEANING
## A/An versus *The*

- Besides the indefinite articles *a/an*, which were introduced in Unit 4, there is another article in English. It is the definite article *the*.

| *A/An* (indefinite article) is | *The* (definite article) is |
|---|---|
| • used only with singular count nouns.<br>**(a)** Bernie has **a** camera. | • used with all nouns.<br>**(b)** **The** clown has a funny nose. (singular)<br>**(c)** **The** dogs are cute. (plural)<br>**(d)** **The** jewelry is hers. (non-count) |
| • followed by a non-specific noun. (The noun is one of many.)<br>**(e)** Mrs. Wolf has **a** cane. | • followed by a specific noun. (The noun is known to the listener or reader.)<br>**(f)** **The** sun is bright.<br>**(g)** **The** necklace is Leona's. |
| • used to introduce a noun phrase.<br>**(h)** Bernie has **a** new camera. | • used when the noun phrase has already been mentioned.<br>**(i)** Bernie has a new camera.<br>**The** camera is Japanese. |

## Exercise 12

Read the paragraph. Fill in *a/an* or *the*.

Exercise 7 is (1) __*a*__ story. (2) _____ story is about Sylkvester Mallone. Sylkvester

Mallone is (3) _____ rich movie star. He has (4) _____ problem. He is married, but he has (5)

_____ girlfriend. His wife wants (6) _____ divorce. Sylkvester has money, but his wife wants

(7) _____ money. He has (8) _____ incredibly beautiful house and she also wants (9) _____

house. His wife has (10) _____ good lawyer. (11) _____ lawyer's job is to get (12) _____

house and (13) _____ money for Sylkvester's wife.

## Exercise 13

Look at the pictures and read the mini-dialogues. Fill in *a/an* or *the*.

**1. Nurse:** "It's **(a)**_____ girl! Congratulations, Mr. Spade."

**2. Friend:** "Boy, it's hot. Do you have **(a)**_____ air conditioner in this car?"

**Driver:** "Yes, but **(b)**_____ air conditioner's broken. Sorry about that!"

**3. Husband:** "What's in **(a)**_____ box?"

**Wife:** "I have **(b)**_____ surprise for you."

**Husband:** "What's **(c)**_____ surprise?"

**Wife:** "Open it!"

**4. Man:** "Do you have **(a)**_____ room for tonight?"

**Clerk:** "Sorry, sir. **(b)**_____ motel is full tonight."

5. **Student:** "Hey! Are you **(a)**_____ new student?"

   **Teacher:** "No, I'm **(b)**_____ new teacher. Now please be quiet!"

6. **Husband:** "Do you have **(a)**_____ key or do I?"

   **Wife:** "I think **(b)**_____ key's in the car, honey."

7. **Receptionist:** "Take your feet off **(a)**_____ table, please, young man!"

8. **Woman:** "Who is it?"

   **Mailman:** "It's **(a)**_____ mailman, Mrs. Wallace. Here's your mail."

   **Woman:** "Thanks, Mr. Brown. Have a good day!"

## Exercise 14

Error Correction. Rewrite the following sentences correctly.

1. This magazine is my.
2. This is Paula bicycle.
3. Ted is married. Carol is her wife.
4. The my eyes are brown.
5. Here is a picture of my family. This is my sister and this is his husband.
6. Is Harry the boyfriend of Joan?
7. Who's class are you in?
8. Theirs children are Bolivian.
9. The Michael's car is expensive.
10. The necklace is her's.

# Activities

### Activity 1

As everyone in your class observes, the teacher will have each person put a personal object (watch, pen, book, key chain, etc.) into a bag. Each person will then take out one object. If the person doesn't remember the owner of the object, he or she will ask, "Whose is this?" After the owner says, "It's mine," the first student will make a sentence using the name of the object and a possessive noun, such as "This is Maria's pen."

### Activity 2

Fill in the information below about yourself. Then read the sentences aloud to a classmate. Next, interview your classmate to find out the same information about him or her. Use the questions to help you. Report this information to the class.

**INFORMATION ABOUT YOU:**

A. My name is (1) _____.

I'm (2) _____ years old.

My birthday is (3) _____.

I'm (4) _____ feet tall.

My eyes are (5) _____.

My hair is (6) _____.

**INTERVIEW QUESTIONS:**

What's your name?

How old are you?

When's your birthday?

How tall are you?

What color are your eyes?

What color is your hair?

**INFORMATION ABOUT YOUR CLASSMATE:**

B. My friend's name is (1) ————————————.

He or She is (2) ———————————— years old.

His or Her birthday is (3) ————————————.

He or She is (4) ———————————— feet tall.

His or Her eyes are (5) ————————————.

His or Her hair is (6) ————————————.

## Activity 3

Bring in a photograph of your family or friends or draw a simple picture. Then describe the photograph or picture to a classmate.

> **EXAMPLE:** "This is my family. This is my Uncle Sal and my Aunt Elena. Their son's name is Franco. Franco is my cousin. We have a house in a small town near Rome. Our house is beautiful."

## Activity 4

Create your own family tree. Then exchange your family tree with a partner. Write 5 sentences about your partner's family.

## Activity 5

Write 5 true statements and 5 false statements about your family tree. Show your tree to a partner and say the statements aloud. Your partner then says if the statement is true or false.

## Activity 6

Bring in objects from home that are special in your culture. Put all the objects into the center of the room. Then ask questions with *whose* to find the owners of the objects. Then try to explain why the objects are important.

> **EXAMPLE:** (You have a hand-painted fan.)
>
> Question:        Whose fan is this?
> Answer:          It's Wen-Chu's fan.
> The owner says:   It's my fan.
>                      It's mine.

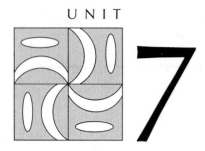

# Demonstratives
## Pronouns and Adjectives

## *Task*

Label each object in the picture of the room on the following page.

| | | |
|---|---|---|
| jacket | tennis racquet | sandwich |
| shirts | sneakers | gum |
| ties | sunglasses | beer can |
| sweatshirt | shoes | dirty clothes |
| pajamas | belt | address book |
| jeans | socks | shaving cream |

"Neat Ned" and "Messy Mike" are roommates in a college dormitory. Read their conversation. Then list Ned's things and Mike's things on the chart. In the drawing, who is "Neat Ned?" Who is "Messy Mike?"

**Ned:** Just look at this place, Mike. What a mess!

**Mike:** I know, Ned, I know. It's time to clean up.

**Ned:** O.K. This is my jacket. These are my shirts and ties. These shoes are mine.

**Mike:** Let's see. These are my sneakers and socks. That sweatshirt is mine. Are these jeans yours, Ned?

**Ned:** No, those are yours, Mike. They're not my size.

**Mike:** What about those pajamas? Are they yours?

**Ned:** No, they're yours, Mike. My pajamas don't have hearts on them. That belt is yours too.

**Mike:** Whose tennis racquet is that?

**Ned:** It's yours, Mike. I don't have a tennis racquet. That's your address book. And that shaving cream is yours too.

**Mike:** Are those your sunglasses?

**Ned:** No, Mike, they're yours. And what about the soda can? Is it yours?

**Mike:** It's not a soda can, Ned. It's a beer can.

**Ned:** Oh, what's the difference, Mike? This place is a wreck!
Whose dirty clothes are these?
Whose leftover sandwich is on the table?
And is this your gum?

**Mike:** Come on, Ned, give me a break!

| Ned's things | Mike's things |
|---|---|
| | |

# Focus 1

## Demonstrative Pronouns

- Use demonstrative pronouns in place of noun phrases.
- A demonstrative pronoun shows:

| Distance From Speaker | Number |
|---|---|
| whether the object is close to or far away from the speaker. | whether the object is singular, plural, or non-count. |

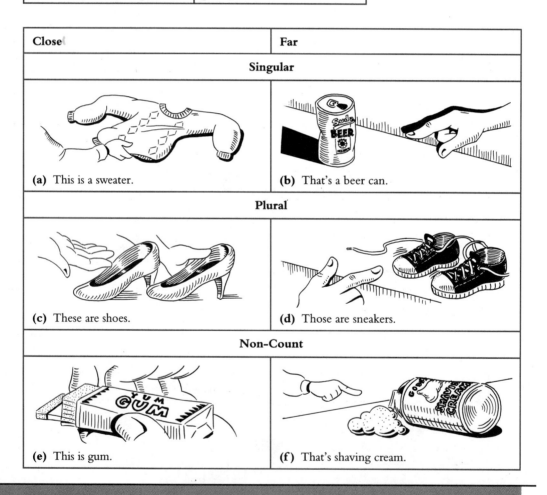

| Close | Far |
|---|---|
| **Singular** ||
| **(a)** This is a sweater. | **(b)** That's a beer can. |
| **Plural** ||
| **(c)** These are shoes. | **(d)** Those are sneakers. |
| **Non-Count** ||
| **(e)** This is gum. | **(f)** That's shaving cream. |

## Exercise 1

Go back to the dialogue in the Task. Find the sentences with demonstrative pronouns and write them below.

1. _____
2. _____
3. _____
4. _____
5. _____
6. _____
7. _____
8. _____
9. _____

## Exercise 2

Role-play the dialogue in the Task with a partner.

## Exercise 3

Underline the singular demonstrative pronouns in Exercise 1. Circle the plural demonstrative pronouns. Find one demonstrative pronoun that refers to a non-count noun.

## Exercise 4

Are the objects in the picture singular, plural, or non-count? Are the objects close to or far away from the speaker? Fill in the blanks with *this / that / these / those* and with the correct form of the verb *be*. The first one has been done for you.

1. _That_   _is_   a sweater.

2. _____ _____ high-heeled shoes.

3. _____ _____ a belt.

4. _____ _____ shorts.

5. _____ _____ a dress.

6. _____ _____ sunglasses.

7. _____ _____ jewelry.

8. _____ _____ a skirt.

9. _____ _____ blouses.

10. _____ _____ women's clothing.

# Focus 2

## Demonstrative Adjectives

FORM
MEANING

- Use demonstrative adjectives in front of nouns.
- Like demonstrative pronouns, demonstrative adjectives show:

| Distance From Speaker | Number |
|---|---|
| whether the object is close to or far away from the speaker. | whether the object is singular, plural, or non-count. Demonstrative adjectives agree in number with the nouns they precede. **This is the only case in English where an adjective agrees with a noun in number.** |

| Close | Far |
|---|---|
| **Singular** ||
| (a) This jacket is mine. | (b) That sweater is yours. |
| **Plural** ||
| (c) These sneakers are mine. | (d) Those sunglasses are yours. |
| **Non-Count** ||
| (e) This gum is yours. | (f) That shaving cream is mine. |

## Exercise 5

Go back to the Task. Find the sentences with demonstrative adjectives and write them below.

1. _____

2. _____

3. _____

4. _____

5. _____

6. _____

7. _____

8. _____

## Focus 3

FORM

# Yes/No Questions with Demonstratives

FORM

- To make a yes/no question with demonstratives, put the verb *be* in front of the subject.
- In short answers, use the subject pronouns *it* and *they*.

| Questions | | | Short Answers |
|---|---|---|---|
| Verb | Subject | | |
| Is | this | a doughnut? | Yes, it is. |
| Are | these | muffins? | No, they aren't. |
| Is | that doughnut | good? | Yes, it is. |
| Are | those muffins | fresh? | No, they aren't. |

# Exercise 6

Answer the question. If the answer is negative, make a negative short answer and give the correct response.

**EXAMPLE:**

 ← Is this soup hot?

a. <u>No, it isn't.</u>

b. <u>That soup's hot.</u>

 ← 1. Are these cupcakes fat-free?

a. _____

b. _____

 2. Is that coffee decaffeinated? ——→

a. _____

b. _____

3. Are those nuts mixed? ——————→

a. _____

b. _____

 ← 4. Are these popsicles sugar-free?

a. _____

b. _____

 ← 5. Is this yogurt fat-free?

a. _____

b. _____

6. Are those potato chips salt-free? ⟶

    a. _____

    b. _____

7. Is that skim milk? ⟶

    a. _____

    b. _____

⟵ 8. Is this soda caffeine-free?

    a. _____

    b. _____

# *Focus 4*

USE

## Using *What* Questions for Classification

USE

- Use questions with *what* + demonstratives to classify things or put things in groups.

| QUESTION | ANSWER |
|---|---|
| **(a)** What's **this**? | SINGULAR COUNT NOUNS<br>**It** is **a** sandwich.<br>**It**'s **an** egg. |
| **(b)** What are **these**?<br>**(c)** What are **those things**? | PLURAL COUNT NOUNS<br>**They** are French fries.<br>**They**'re muffins. |
| **(d)** What's **that** dish? | NON-COUNT NOUNS<br>**It**'s soup. |

## Exercise 7

Fill in the correct subject pronoun, verb, and article. Then match each sentence to the correct picture.

**Letter of the Picture**

1. What's this?  _____It's a_____ hamburger.  _____D_____

2. What's that?  _____ hot dog.  _____

3. What are those? _____ French fries.  _____

4. What's this?  _____ ketchup.  _____

5. What's that?  _____ pizza.  _____

6. What's this?  _____ sandwich.  _____

7. What are these? _____ doughnuts.  _____

8. What are those? _____ cookies.  _____

9. What's this?  _____ muffin.  _____

10. What's that?  _____ ice cream.  _____

## Exercise 8

Look at the answers and the pictures. Are the objects singular, plural, or non-count? Are the objects close to or far away from the speaker? Make questions using *what* and demonstrative pronouns. The first one has been done for you.

1. Q: *What are those*____?

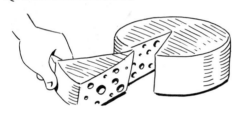

A: They're strawberries.

2. Q: _____?

A: It's cheese.

3. Q: _____?

A: It's an apple.

4. Q: _____?

A: It's spaghetti.

5. Q: _____?

A: They're peanuts.

6. Q: _____?

A: It's yogurt.

7. Q: _____?

A: It's an egg.

8. Q: _____?

A: It's a pie.

## Exercise 9

Now look around the room. Can you name the things around you? Write five questions of your own about those things.

**EXAMPLES:** What is this? It's a blackboard. What are these? They're tape recorders.
What's that? It's chalk. What are those? They're electrical outlets.

# Activities

### Activity 1

The Blindfold Game

Take out the personal objects you have with you in class. (Name all these objects before playing the game.) The teacher will blindfold half of the students. The non-blindfolded students will give an object to the blindfolded students and ask, "What's this?" or "What are these?" Blindfolded students guess—"It's not a _____, it's a _____." or "They're not _____, they're _____," etc.

### Activity 2

Make up menus of typical foods, drinks, and desserts from your countries. Then work in pairs, asking each other for information about the foods and drinks.

**EXAMPLE:** The menu says, "egg rolls."
You ask: "What are these?"

### Activity 3

Using an authentic American menu, ask your teacher questions about the food items on the menu. Make a list of the new food items you learn about.

### Activity 4

Bring in objects from your country that you think will be interesting to your classmates. For example, you can bring in objects with cultural meaning, clothing, eating utensils, photos, etc. Ask each other questions about these objects. Then write about one of them.

**EXAMPLE:** (object—silver ankle bracelets from India)
You write: These are silver ankle bracelets from India.
An Indian woman usually has two of them.

### Activity 5

Look through supermarket flyers and cut out different items. Then set up a supermarket scene in class with the different items. Role-play a scene where one person is the clerk and another is the customer. The customer asks questions about the different items.

**EXAMPLE:** Customer: Is this regular yogurt?
Clerk:    No, it isn't. It's low fat.

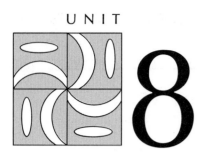
# Be + Prepositional Phrase; *Where* Questions

## *Task*

Read the dialogue and look at the picture. Find all the items George cannot find. Circle those items in the picture.

Judy Harris is sick today. It is 7:30 in the morning. Her husband George is getting the children ready for school. He's having problems.

**George:** Honey, where's the peanut butter?

**Judy:** It's in the cupboard above the stove.

**George:** Oh, and where are the kids' lunch boxes?

**Judy:** In the cabinet, under the sink.

**George:** Now, where is the plastic wrap?

**Judy:** On the counter, next to the toaster.

**George:** What's next? Oh, the cheese! I know that's in the refrigerator. Now what about some fruit?

**Tommy:** No, we want cookies!

**George:** Judy—where are the cookies?

**Judy:** They're in the cabinet against the wall.

**George:** OK kids, we're all ready to go. Where are your jackets?

**Tommy:** They're in the closet, Dad.

**George:** Cindy, do you have your books?

**Cindy:** Yes, Dad. They're in my backpack.

**George:** What else? Oh, the keys! Judy, where are the car keys?

**Judy:** They're on the wall, behind the bird cage.

**George:** Oh, of course! Now, one more thing. Where are my glasses?

**Tommy &
Cindy:** They're right on your head, Dad!

# *Focus 1*

FORM ● MEANING

## Prepositional Phrases about Place

FORM
MEANING

- To talk about place, use *be* and a prepositional phrase.
- To form a prepositional phrase, use a preposition and a noun phrase.

|  |  |  | Prepositional Phrase |  |
|---|---|---|---|---|
| Subject | + | *Be* + | Preposition + | Noun Phrase |
| **(a)** The cheese | | is | in | the refrigerator. |
| **(b)** The keys | | are | behind | the bird cage. |

## *Exercise 1*

Go back to the dialogue in the Task and put parentheses ( ) around the prepositional phrases. Then circle all the prepositions.

**EXAMPLE:** It's ((in) the cupboard) ((above) the stove).

# Exercise 2

Role-play the dialogue in the Task with students in the class.

# Exercise 3

Match each prepositional phrase to a diagram by writing the number on the line next to the letter.

1. in the box
2. above the box
3. under the box
4. next to the box
5. on the box
6. behind the box

_____ A.

_____ B.

_____ C.

_____ D.

_____ E.

_____ F.

# Exercise 4

Think of an object in the classroom. Then make sentences with prepositional phrases so that your classmates can guess what the object is.

**EXAMPLE:** This object is in front of the room. It's behind the teacher's desk. It's on the little shelf under the blackboard. (It's a piece of chalk.)

## Exercise 5

Here is a photograph of George, Judy, and their children on vacation in Paris, France. Match the underlined prepositions to the diagrams that represent them on the next page. Write the correct number on the line next to the letter.

1. Here we are <u>in front of</u> the Eiffel Tower in Paris, France.
2. Can you see Cindy? She's <u>in back of</u> me. She's camera-shy!
3. Oh, and that's our French friend, Henri, <u>between</u> Judy and me.
4. Our hotel is <u>near</u> the Eiffel Tower.
5. The souvenir shop is <u>opposite</u> our hotel.

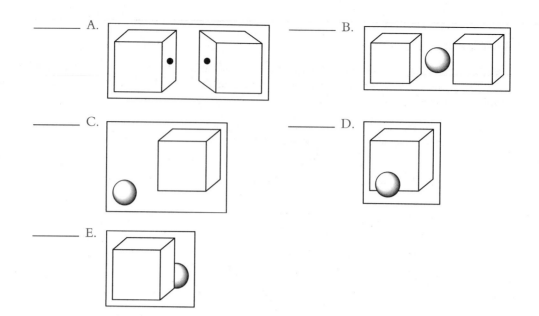

_____ A.

_____ B.

_____ C.

_____ D.

_____ E.

## Focus 2

### *Where* Questions to Ask about Place

FORM
MEANING

- Use *where* to ask about place. The answers to *where* questions can be complete sentences, phrases, or single words.

  Where are my glasses?    They're on your head.
  On your head.
  Here.

# Exercise 6

Pretend you cannot find items 1–6 in Picture A. Ask your partner where they are. Your partner cannot find items 7–12 in picture B. Your partner asks you where they are. Draw the missing objects in the correct places in your pictures.

**EXAMPLE:** Student A asks: Where is my volleyball?

Student B says: It's on the sofa.

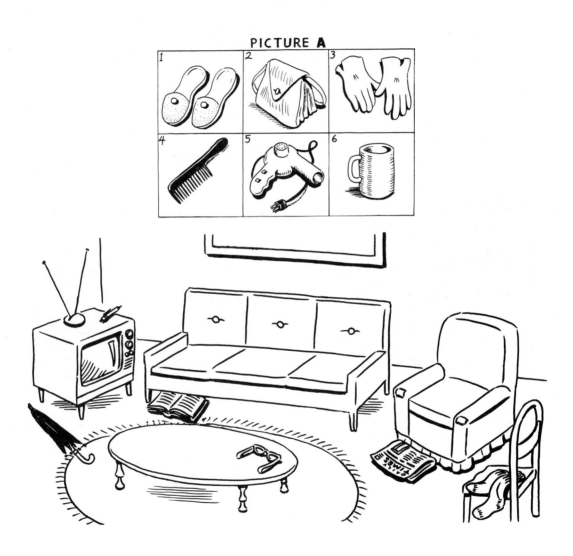

## Exercise 7

This is a map of your new neighborhood. The names of the places are missing. Your neighbor has given you all the locations of these places. Read the information below and fill in the names on the map.

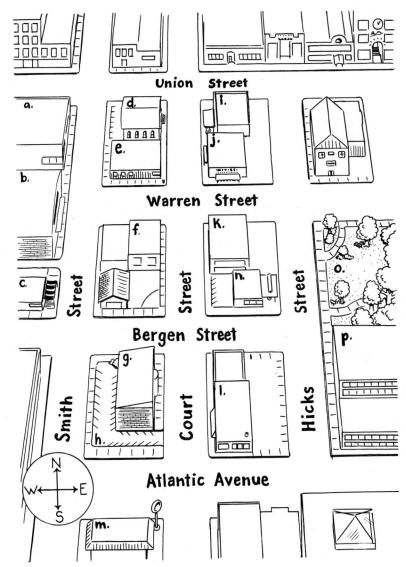

1. The hospital is on the corner of Hicks Street and Atlantic Avenue.
2. The park is next to the hospital.
3. The bank is on the southwest corner of Court Street and Union.
4. The drugstore is next to the bank.
5. The liquor store is across the street from the bank.
6. The video store is near the liquor store.

7. The movie theater is on the west side of Court Street between Bergen and Atlantic.
8. The parking lot is behind the movie theater.
9. The bakery is across the street from the movie theater.
10. The gas station is on the corner of Hicks and Bergen.
11. The hardware store is on the southeast corner of Court Street and Warren.
12. The bookstore is opposite the hardware store.
13. The supermarket is between the pet store and the newsstand on Smith Street.
14. The newsstand is on the corner of Bergen and Smith Streets.
15. The diner is on Atlantic Avenue.

# Activities

### Activity 1

Hide a pen somewhere in the classroom. Write the location on a piece of paper and don't tell the other students in the group. The other students ask questions to find out where the pen is. If the person is very far away, you can say, "You're cold." When the person gets closer, say, "You're warm." When the person is very close, say "You're hot."

| | | |
|---|---|---|
| **EXAMPLE:** | Question: | Is the object near the window? |
| | Answer: | You're cold. |
| | Question: | Is it in front of the room? |
| | Answer: | Now you're warm! |

### Activity 2

Draw a map of your hometown or the place where you live now. Describe your map to your partner. Then write down the description, using prepositions.

**EXAMPLE:** This is my house. It's on Main Street. The drugstore is on the corner of Main and 1st Avenue. The supermarket is opposite the drugstore.

### Activity 3

Using items from the list below, draw a plan of your own bedroom. Then work with a partner. Ask your partner *where* questions about the items in his or her bedroom. Draw a plan for that room. Then check whether your plan matches your partner's original plan. Finally, have your partner ask you *where* questions and follow the same procedure.

| | | | | |
|---|---|---|---|---|
| lamp | chair | dresser | bed | desk |
| night table | poster | rug | bookcase | mirror |
| stereo | computer | plant | TV | telephone |

# Intensifiers

*Be* + Adjective + Noun

## *Task*

Rate the following items in terms of how necessary and how useful they are to you. A rating of 5 means that the item is very necessary and very useful to you. Circle the appropriate number.

| Television | | | | | | |
|---|---|---|---|---|---|---|
| A television set is unnecessary. | 1 | 2 | 3 | 4 | 5 | A television set is very necessary. |
| A television set is not useful. | 1 | 2 | 3 | 4 | 5 | A television set is very useful. |
| **Microwave Oven** | | | | | | |
| A microwave oven is unnecessary. | 1 | 2 | 3 | 4 | 5 | A microwave oven is very necessary. |
| A microwave oven is not useful. | 1 | 2 | 3 | 4 | 5 | A microwave oven is very useful. |
| **Walkman** | | | | | | |
| A walkman is unnecessary. | 1 | 2 | 3 | 4 | 5 | A walkman is very necessary. |
| A walkman is not useful. | 1 | 2 | 3 | 4 | 5 | A walkman is very useful. |
| **Computer** | | | | | | |
| A computer is unnecessary. | 1 | 2 | 3 | 4 | 5 | A computer is very necessary. |
| A computer is not useful. | 1 | 2 | 3 | 4 | 5 | A computer is very useful. |

## *Focus 1*

MEANING

# Intensifiers

MEANING

- Intensifiers are adverbs that affect the strength of adjectives.

| | | |
|---|---|---|
| **(a)** A car is | **very** | expensive. |
| **(b)** A television is | **quite/rather/pretty\*** | expensive. |
| **(c)** A microwave oven is | **fairly** | expensive. |
| **(d)** A walkman is | **somewhat** | expensive. |

  *\*Pretty* is an intensifier with the same meaning as *quite* or *rather*, but is very informal.

- Note: Negative sentences can only occur with *very*:

  **(e)** A compact car isn't very expensive.

       NOT: A compact car isn't somewhat expensive.

           A compact car isn't fairly expensive.

           A compact car isn't pretty expensive.

## Exercise 1

Go back to the Task and use intensifiers to make sentences about the items in terms of how useful and necessary you feel they are.

**EXAMPLES:** *A television set is very necessary.*

*A television set isn't very necessary.*

*A television set is pretty necessary.*

## Exercise 2

Fill in the blanks below with the affirmative or negative of the verb *be* and an intensifier. Compare your answers with your partner's answers.

**EXAMPLES:** A portable telephone *is pretty* convenient.

1. A portable telephone _____ _____ convenient.

2. Sneakers _____ _____ comfortable.

3. French restaurants _____ _____ expensive.

4. A gold necklace _____ _____ cheap.

5. A vacuum cleaner _____ _____ useful.

6. A dishwasher _____ _____ practical.

7. An encyclopedia _____ _____ informative.

8. A word processor _____ _____ efficient.

9. A big car _____ _____ economical.

10. American movies _____ _____ popular in my country.

## Exercise 3

Guess the object by using the clues below.

1. This is fairly long and thin.
   People eat it.
   It is very popular in Italy.

   What is it?_____

2. This is a liquid.
   People drink it.
   It is yellow on the bottom and white on the top.
   It is very cold.
   It's not very expensive.

   What is it?_____

3. This is an electrical appliance.
   It is silver in color.
   Sometimes it is very hot.
   You put bread into it.
   It's fairly common in people's homes.

   What is it?_____

4. This is a vehicle.
   It is somewhat expensive.
   It is very practical in cities.
   It has two wheels.
   Children love to ride it too.

   What is it?_____

5. This is very cold.
   It's also pretty hard.
   People put it in drinks.
   It's somewhat slippery.

   What is it?_____

## Exercise 4

Make sentences using the affirmative or negative form of the verb *be,* the adjectives in parentheses, and intensifiers.

1. My father _____ . (serious, quiet, confident)

2. My best friend _____ . (understanding, dependable, funny)

3. My boss _____ . (generous, kind, hardworking)

4. My teacher _____ . (patient, creative, interesting)

5. My sister/brother _____ . (shy, helpful, sociable)

# Focus 2

USE

## Asking for Information

USE

- To find out about a person, place, or the weather, ask questions like these:
  **(a)** What's the capital city like?       It's very big and crowded.
  **(b)** What's your boyfriend like?         He's pretty athletic and rather intelligent too.
- You can also ask more specific questions with *how* + *adjective*:
  **(c) How big**        is your city?         It's very big. The population is over 8 million!
  **(d) How humid**      is it?                It's very humid in the summer.

## Exercise 5

Match the questions from Column A with the appropriate responses from Column B.

**COLUMN A**

1. What's your apartment like?
2. What's your neighborhood like?
3. What's your girlfriend like?
4. What's the weather like in your hometown?
5. What's your job like?
6. What's your English class like?
7. What's your city like?

**COLUMN B**

a. It's not very hot in the summer, and somewhat cold in winter.
b. It's very crowded, and it's rather polluted.
c. It's quite large. I have four rooms.
d. It's very busy and noisy, and fairly safe.
e. She's very smart, friendly, and kind.
f. It's pretty interesting. The students are from all over the world.
g. It's somewhat difficult. My boss is pretty demanding, and the salary is not very good!

## Focus 3

FORM

# Be + Adjective + Noun

FORM

- Adjectives can come after the verb *be*:

| Subject | *Be* | Adjective |
|---|---|---|
| (a) New York City | is | big. |
| (b) The people | are | interesting. |

- Or they can come before the noun:

| Subject | *Be* | Article | Adjective | Noun |
|---|---|---|---|---|
| (c) New York City | is | a | big | city. |
| (d) They | are | | interesting | people. |

- In sentences where the adjective comes before the noun, place the intensifier before the adjective:
  **(e)** Quebec is a **very exciting** city.

# Exercise 6

Unscramble the words in parentheses to complete the dialogue.

**Carol:** What's the Dominican Republic like?

**Bernice:** (a / country / it / very / beautiful / is) (1) _____.

_____ . It has miles and miles of beaches.

**Carol:** What's the capital of the Dominican Republic?

**Bernice:** Santo Domingo.

**Carol:** (like / the / what / capital / is) (2) _____?

**Bernice:** Well, (very / is / city / it / big / a) (3) _____.

It's very crowded, but (clean / it / quite / is) (4) _____.

**Carol:** And (the / how / is / inflation / high) (5) _____?

**Bernice:** (fairly / it / high / is) (6) _____.

**Carol:** And the people? (they / like / are / what) (7) _____?

**Bernice:** (people / are / Dominicans / friendly / pretty) (8) _____

_____. They're always ready to help you.

**Carol:** Of course they are, if they're like you! Well, really, is it a good place for me to go on my

vacation?

**Bernice:** You'll love it there. (place / is / very / a / it / interesting) (9) _____

_____.

You're adventurous. Take a chance. Go there and see!

# Exercise 7

Write one sentence using the form **be + adjective + noun** and an intensifier for each of the cues below. Choose an adjective from the list below. You can use an adjective more than once.

**EXAMPLE:** French _____ language.

French *is a somewhat difficult* language.

| | | | | |
|---|---|---|---|---|
| exciting | violent | tall | expensive | dangerous |
| crowded | popular | talented | nutritious | satisfying |

1. The Twin Towers _____ buildings in New York.

2. Disneyworld _____ place.

3. Pavarotti _____ singer.

4. "Rambo" _____ movie.

5. A Mercedes _____ car.

6. A bowl of granola _____ meal.

7. Baseball _____ sport in Japan.

8. Tokyo _____ city.

9. Scuba diving _____ sport.

10. Teaching _____ profession.

# Activities

## Activity 1

This game is called 20 Questions—first put an object in a bag, but don't show it to the rest of the class. Then the other students can ask you up to 20 yes/no questions to guess what is in the bag. When your classmates guess the correct object, show the object to them.

**EXAMPLE:** Object: (chalk)

Questions: "Is it big?" No, it isn't.
"Is it heavy?" No, it isn't.
"Is it white?" Yes, it is.
"Is it chalk?" Yes, it is.

## Activity 2

Using the following categories, ask three different people about a city or country they know. Write the information on the chart. After you get all the information, report to the class on one of the countries you learned about. Here are some useful adjectives.

Weather       (hot, cold, wet, dry, humid, tropical, mild)
Food          (spicy, hot, sweet, tasty, bland, expensive)
People        (friendly, helpful, polite, generous, cold, warm, hospitable)
Capital city  (big, crowded, polluted, small, quiet, safe, dangerous)
Land          (mountainous, flat, hilly, dry)
Nightlife     (exciting, interesting, boring, expensive)
Inflation     (high, low, average)

Ask questions like these:

**EXAMPLE:** "How's the weather in your hometown?" or "What's the weather like?"
"Is it very humid?"
"How humid is it?"

|  | _____ (name) _____ (place) | _____ (name) _____ (place) | _____ (name) _____ (place) |
|---|---|---|---|
| Weather |  |  |  |
| Food |  |  |  |
| People |  |  |  |
| Capital city |  |  |  |
| Land |  |  |  |
| Nightlife |  |  |  |
| Inflation |  |  |  |

## Activity 3

Check all the adjectives that describe you and write an appropriate intensifier in Column A. Then ask your partner questions to find out which adjectives describe him or her and check the box. Then ask a second question with *how* and write the intensifier in Column B. Finally, your partner asks you questions.

**EXAMPLE:** You ask:              "Are you shy?"
Your partner answers:   "Yes, I am."

You ask:              "How shy are you?"
Your partner answers:   "I'm very shy."

| Adjective | Column A | | Column B | |
|---|---|---|---|---|
| | You | Intensifier | Your Partner | Intensifer |
| shy | | | ✔ | very |
| lazy | | | | |
| quiet | | | | |
| romantic | ✔ | pretty | | |
| sociable | | | | |
| optimistic | | | | |
| pessimistic | | | | |
| old-fashioned | | | | |
| organized | | | | |
| jealous | | | | |
| talkative | | | | |
| athletic | | | | |
| healthy | | | | |

## Activity 4

Use the information you collected from Activity 3 to make five sentences about your partner using intensifiers.

**EXAMPLE:** My partner is a *very romantic* person. He is *pretty old-fashioned*, and he is *very jealous*.

## Activity 5

You are a salesperson. Your partner is a customer. Convince your partner to buy the following items. The adjectives in the list will help you. Use intensifiers too.

**EXAMPLE:**   **Salesperson:** Buy this new skin cream. It is very soft and fragrant.
                **Customer:** Oh, no, thanks. I don't need it. I don't want it.
                **Salesperson:** But it's very healthy for your skin. And very cheap!
                **Customer:** Well, all right. I'll try it.

**POSSIBLE ADJECTIVES:**

| | | | | |
|---|---|---|---|---|
| cheap | practical | necessary | small | powerful |
| light | comfortable | delicious | nutritious | convenient |
| useful | effective | attractive | expensive | healthy |

**PRODUCTS:**

1. Stay Young 4-ever Skin Cream
2. A portable car phone
3. An electric towel warmer
4. No-Fat, No-Cholesterol, No-Calorie Yogurt
5. A vacuum cleaner

## Activity 6

Read each of the following statements. Think about the students in your class. Try to match each statement to one of your classmates, and then write the name of the student in the column marked "Guesses." After you do this, check your guesses by asking the students questions to find out if your guess was right or wrong. Put a check in the "Facts" column if your guess is correct.

|  | **Guesses** | **Facts** |
|---|---|---|
| 1. This person is a good dancer. | _____ | _____ |
| 2. This person is a diligent student. | _____ | _____ |
| 3. This person is a fantastic singer. | _____ | _____ |
| 4. This person is a wonderful cook. | _____ | _____ |
| 5. This person is a creative artist. | _____ | _____ |
| 6. This person is a patient friend. | _____ | _____ |
| 7. This person is an unusual dresser. | _____ | _____ |
| 8. This person is a late sleeper. | _____ | _____ |
| 9. This person is a fast worker. | _____ | _____ |
| 10. This person is a neat housekeeper. | _____ | _____ |

# There + Be

## Task

Look at the picture. Whose apartment is this? Make guesses about the person who lives here. Circle your guesses and then explain them by circling the clues in the picture.

| | | |
|---|---|---|
| 1. | The person is | a man / a woman |
| 2. | The person | has a baby / doesn't have a baby |
| 3. | The person | has a pet / doesn't have a pet |
| 4. | The person is | athletic / not athletic |
| 5. | The person is | a coffee drinker / not a coffee drinker |
| 6. | The person is | well-educated / not well-educated |
| 7. | The person is | a smoker / not a smoker |
| 8. | The person is | middle class / poor |
| 9. | The person is | a music lover / not a music lover |
| 10. | The person is | on a diet / not on a diet |

# Focus 1

## Showing Existence or Location

**MEANING**
**USE**

- Use *there* for describing.
- Use *there* to show the **existence** or **location** of something that is **new information**. (With new information, use the indefinite articles *a/an*.)
- In English, this new information comes after the verb *be*.

From the Task, we know that the woman in this apartment has a cat.

Which sentence best shows the existence or location of the new information (a cat) in the picture ?

**A. A cat is under the bed.**

This sentence doesn't have the new information (a cat) after the verb *be*. This sentence is grammatically correct, but native English speakers do not use this sentence to show the existence or location of the new information (a cat).

**B. There's a cat under the bed.**

This sentence has the new information (a cat) after the verb *be*.
The indefinite article *a* is used.
*There* is used in the subject position.
Native English speakers use this sentence to show the existence or location of the new information (a cat).

## Exercise 1

Circle the sentence in each pair that best describes this picture.

**EXAMPLE:** a. Two men are in this picture.

b. There are two men in this picture.

1. **a.** There's a bowl of soup on the table.
   **b.** A bowl of soup is on the table.
2. **a.** An angry man is at the table.
   **b.** There's an angry man at the table.
3. The angry man says:
   **a.** "Waiter, a fly is in my soup."
   **b.** "Waiter, there's a fly in my soup."

# Focus 2

## Affirmative Statements with *There + Be*

FORM

- *There* is usually at the beginning of the sentence, in the subject position.
  - **(a) There** is a cat under the bed.
    NOT: Is a cat under the bed.
- *There* is usually followed by a form of the verb *be*.
  - **(b) There is** a cat under the bed.
    NOT: There have a cat under the bed.
- The verb *be* agrees with the noun phrase that follows it, even if there is more than one noun phrase. The noun is usually non-specific. The indefinite articles (*a/an*) are used.
  - **(c)** There **is a** cat under the bed.
  - **(d)** There **is a** bathroom, a kitchen, and 2 bedrooms in my apartment.
  - **(e)** There **are two** cats under the bed.
  - **(f)** There**'s soup** in his dish.
- Note : *There is* is often contracted to *There's*.

## Exercise 2

Go back to the Task. Write sentences to describe the clues you circled in the picture.

   **EXAMPLE:** a cat under the bed = *There's a cat under the bed.*

1. one bed in the apartment =

   _____ .

2. women's clothing in the closet =

   _____ .

3. high-heeled shoes in the closet =

   _____ .

4. women's jewelry in the box on the dresser =

   _____ .

**107**

5. a tennis racquet in the closet =

_____ .

6. sneakers in the closet =

_____ .

7. an exercise bicycle in the apartment =

_____ .

8. a coffee pot on the stove =

_____ .

9. books on the shelf =

_____ .

10. a computer on the desk =

_____ .

11. an expensive rug on the floor =

_____ .

12. a fur coat in the closet =

_____ .

13. records on the shelf =

_____ .

14. stereo equipment on the shelf =

_____ .

15. a big cake on the counter =

_____ .

## Exercise 3

Divide into groups and choose one student in each group to read the following sentences. Listen to the description and draw a picture of what's described. Then compare your drawings.

1. There's an apartment building in the center of the picture.
2. There is graffiti on the walls of the building.
3. There are bars on each window.
4. There's a fire hydrant to the right of the building.
5. There are parking meters in front of the building.
6. There are five parked cars in front of the building.
7. There's a bus stop to the left of the building.
8. There's a young woman, an old man, and two children at the bus stop.

## Focus 3

FORM

# Negative Statements with *There + Be*

FORM

|  | *There + Be* / *There + Be Contraction* } *+ No* | *There* + **Negative Contraction** |
|---|---|---|
| Singular Count Nouns | **There is** / **There's** } no ashtray on the table. | **There isn't** any ashtray on the table. |
| Plural Count Nouns | **There are** no women in the restaurant. | **There aren't** any women in the restaurant. |
| Non-count Nouns | **There is** / **There's** } no silverware on the table. | **There isn't** any silverware on the table. |

## Exercise 4

Think back to the picture in the Task. Make an affirmative statement if the apartment has the item. Make a negative statement if the apartment does not have the item.

**EXAMPLE:** (baby carriage) *There's no baby carriage in the apartment.*

1. television set
2. rug
3. men's clothing
4. computer
5. ashtrays
6. cigarettes
7. books
8. toys
9. exercise bicycle
10. crib
11. coffee pot
12. ties

## Exercise 5

Look at the chart below about the city named Utopia. Write affirmative and negative statements about the city of Utopia. Compare your ideas. Then make five statements of your own using new noun phrases.

**EXAMPLE:** *In Utopia, there aren't any guns.*
*In Utopia, there are no guns.*

|  | YES | NO |  | YES | NO |
|---|:---:|:---:|---|:---:|:---:|
| **1.** guns |  | X | **6.** universities | X |  |
| **2.** public transportation | X |  | **7.** noise |  | X |
| **3.** crime |  | X | **8.** jobs | X |  |
| **4.** museums | X |  | **9.** parks | X |  |
| **5.** traffic |  | X | **10.** poor people |  | X |

## Exercise 6

Read the politician's speech about the city of Utopia. Fill in the blanks with the appropriate affirmative or negative forms.

Good evening, Ladies and Gentlemen. I am the Mayor of Utopia. I am here tonight to talk about our wonderful city.

Today, (1) _____ 50,000 people in our city. We are all happy. (2) _____ problems in our city.

(3) _____ jobs for all our people. (4) _____ good schools for the children. (5) _____ nice houses for all our families. The houses are comfortable. They aren't expensive.

(6) _____ homeless people on our streets. Our streets are safe.

(7) _____ crime here. (8) _____ drugs. Our streets are clean.

(9) _____ garbage on the streets. (10) _____ pollution.

(11) _____ many museums, theaters, and parks in our city. (12) _____ entertainment for everyone. (13) _____ good public transportation for your convenience.

(14) _____ many reasons why Utopia is a great city! (15) _____ a good life waiting for you too here in Utopia. Please come and live in our wonderful city!

Thank you, and good night!

# Focus 4

FORM

## Yes/No Questions with *There + Be*

FORM

- In affirmative statements, put the verb *be* in front of *there.*
  **(a) Is there a cat** under the bed?

| Yes/No Questions | | Short Answers *Be* Contractions |
|---|---|---|
| **Singular Count Nouns** | | |
| **Is there a cat** | under the bed? | Yes, there is. No, there is not. No, there isn't. |
| **Plural Count Nouns** | | |
| **Are there any books** | on the shelves? | Yes, there are. No, there are not. No, there aren't. |
| **Non-Count Nouns** | | |
| **Is there any jewelry** | in the box? | Yes, there is. No, there is not. No, there isn't. |

## Exercise 7

Complete the questions corresponding to each picture.

**1.** _____
messages for me?

**2.** _____
doctor in the house?

**3.** _____
anything in here to eat, Mom?

**4.** _____
post office near here?

**5.** _____
tickets available for the 10:00 show?

**6.** _____
room for me?

**7.** _____
instructions in the box?

**8.** _____
mail for me?

**9.** _____
small sizes?

**10.** _____
witnesses?

## Exercise 8

Test your knowledge. Make questions using the cues below. Then work with a partner, asking your questions and answering your partner's questions.

> **EXAMPLE:** eggs in an eggplant = *Are there any eggs in an eggplant? / No, there aren't.*

1. rain in a desert
2. 12 planets in our solar system
3. 2 billion people in China
4. 52 states in the United States
5. earthquakes in California
6. billions of stars in the universe
7. cure for the common cold
8. life on other planets

## Exercise 9

Error Correction. Rewrite the following sentences correctly.

1. It's a picture on the wall.
2. There are a bathroom, a kitchen and a living room in my house.
3. There have three bedrooms and two bathrooms in the apartment.
4. Is a good restaurant in my neighborhood.
5. There aren't milk in the refrigerator.
6. In my picture, have one woman and two men.
7. No have women in the restaurant.
8. Are homeless people in your city?

# Activities

### Activity 1

Picture Differences. Work with a partner. You look at Picture A while your partner looks at Picture B. Describe your pictures using *there is / there are* or ask each other yes/no questions with *there*. When you have determined the differences, write a description of your partner's scene.

### Activity 1 (Picture A)

113

**Activity 1 (Picture B)**

**Activity 2**

Work in pairs. Ask each other questions about cities you know. Share your information with the class.

> **EXAMPLE:** zoo / Is there a zoo in Beijing?
>
> skyscraper / Are there any skyscrapers in Santo Domingo?

**Activity 3**

Use the categories below (or categories of your own) to find out about the people in your class. Then write statements about the make-up of your class.

**Categories**

| | |
|---|---|
| Nationality or Ethnic Group | Mexican, Cambodian, Asian, African |
| Sex | Male, Female |
| Level of Education | High School graduate, college graduate... |
| Occupation | secretary, teacher, doctor... |
| Personal Characteristics | shy, outgoing, sad, happy... |

> **EXAMPLE:** There are ten Asians, three South Americans, and two Europeans in our class.

**Activity 4**

Think of a place that is important to you—a room, a city, etc. Describe this place to a partner, using *there is* and *there are*. Have your partner draw a picture of the place you are describing. Your partner can ask questions to get more information from you.

> **EXAMPLE:** "This place is an island near Sicily. There are two sides of the island. On one side, there's a hotel. On the other side, there are houses. There are two restaurants on the island."

**Activity 5**

Think about the problems in your city or your neighborhood. Write as many statements as you can about these problems. Discuss these problems with the class.

> **EXAMPLE:** There's crime in the neighborhood.

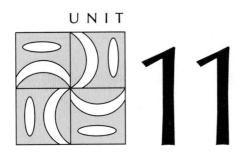

# 11

# Simple Present Tense

## Affirmative and Negative Statements; Time Expressions; *In/On/At; Make* and *Do*

## *Task*

Read about the life-styles of the Lowes and the Ticks.

**THE LOWES**

The Lowes live a quiet life in a small town. Mel Lowe is a mailman. Jane Lowe works in the local elementary school. They both love their jobs. The Lowes wake up at 7:00 every morning. They have breakfast together. They leave for work at 8:00. Mel drives to work. Jane walks. Mel and Jane both go home for lunch every day. She gets home from work at 3:15. She prepares her lessons and waits for Mel. Mel gets home at 5:30. They cook dinner together. After dinner, they take a walk, play tennis, or visit friends. They go to bed at 10:30 every night.

**THE TICKS**

The Ticks lead a busy life in the big city. Fran Tick is a banker, and her husband Fred is a lawyer. Every day they get up at 6:30. They skip breakfast. They leave home at 7:00. Fred rushes to the subway station. Fran takes a cab to the bank. Fred sees his clients all day. At 12:00, he has a business lunch with a client. They have a cocktail, eat a big lunch, and smoke cigars. He finishes work at 8:00. Fran discusses money problems every day. She leaves work at 8:00 too. She feels hungry and tired. She meets Fred every evening at 8:30. They order in food from the neighborhood restaurant. After dinner, they work in their office at home. They go to sleep at 1:00 A.M. every night.

Which life-style do you think is healthy? Discuss your reasons with your classmates.

# *Focus 1*

FORM

# Affirmative Statements
# in the Simple Present

**FORM**

- A sentence in the simple present tense has a subject and one verb.

| **Subject** | **Verb** |
|---|---|
| He | works. |
| NOT: He | is work. |

- With the simple present, there is only one verb change—for third person singular subjects. With the subjects *he, she,* and *it,* add *s* to the verb. With all other subjects, use the base form of the verb.

  - Use the base form of the verb with:

    I
    You
    We
    They
    } work.

  - Add *s* to the base form of the verb with:

    He
    She
    It
    } works.

# *Exercise 1*

Go back to the Task. Underline all the simple present tense verbs. Connect each verb to its subject with an arrow.

**EXAMPLE:** The Lowes <u>live</u> a quiet life in a small town.

# *Exercise 2*

Circle the correct form of the verb.

1. Mel Lowe is a mailman. He (deliver/delivers) mail.
2. Jane Lowe is a teacher. She (work/works) in an elementary school.
3. Mel and Jane (love/loves) their jobs.
4. Mel (take/takes) his car to work.
5. Jane (walk/walks) to work.
6. Mel and Jane (prepare/prepares) dinner together every night.
7. Fred Tick is a lawyer. He (talk/talks) to clients every day.
8. Fran Tick is a banker. She (manage/manages) people's money.
9. Fred and Fran (stay/stays) at work late every night.
10. Fred and Fran (eat/eats) fast food for dinner.

# Focus 2

## USE

# Talking about Habits and Routines

USE

- Use the simple present to talk about habits and routines.
  - **(a)** Fred and Fran Tick wake up early every morning.
  - **(b)** Mel Lowe drives to work every day.

## Exercise 3

Read the statements below. Check the statement that is generally true for you. Then exchange papers with a classmate. See how you are the same or different. Make statements aloud.

**EXAMPLES:** I live a busy life. My partner lives a quiet life.

My partner and I both wake up early.

1. I live a quiet life. _____

   I live a busy life. _____

2. I wake up early. _____

   I wake up late. _____

3. I eat breakfast every morning. _____

   I skip breakfast every morning. _____

4. I walk to school. _____

   I drive to school. _____

   I take the bus to school. _____

   I take the train to school. _____

5. I eat a big lunch. _____

   I eat a small lunch. _____

6. I work after school. _____

   I stay home after school. _____

   I exercise after school. _____

   I take a nap after school. _____

7. I cook dinner. _____

   My mother/father cooks dinner. _____

   My husband/wife cooks dinner. _____

   My roommate cooks dinner. _____

8. After dinner, I exercise. _____

   After dinner, I watch TV. _____

   After dinner, I visit friends. _____

   After dinner, I do homework. _____

9. I go to bed early. _____

   I go to bed late. _____

10. I feel tired every day. _____

    I feel good every day. _____

# Focus 3

## Time Expressions

FORM
MEANING

- Use time expressions with the simple present to talk about habits. Time expressions specify how often we do these habitual activities:

  | | |
  |---|---|
  | every day | once a week |
  | every summer | twice a month |
  | every year | three times a year |
  | all the time | |

- Time expressions usually come at the end of a sentence:

  **(a)** They cook dinner together every night.

- Time expressions can sometimes occur at the beginning of a sentence. Use a comma after the time expression when it is placed at the beginning of a sentence:

  **(b)** Once a week, they go out to eat.

- Time expressions cannot occur between the subject and the verb:

  **(c)** NOT: He every day eats a small lunch.

- When you have two time expressions, more specific time often goes before more general time.

  **(d)** She plays tennis **at 3:00 on Saturday.**

## Exercise 4

Make true statements about yourself by adding a time expression. Skip the statements that are not true for you.

1. I eat fruit *twice a day*.

2. I take a vacation _____.

3. I take a nap _____.

4. I exercise _____.

5. I sleep late _____.

6. I go to the doctor _____.

7. I eat chocolate _____.

8. I write letters _____.

9. I read a book _____.

10. I drink coffee _____.

11. I take a shower _____.

12. I brush my teeth _____.

13. I eat fast food _____.

14. I go to the movies _____.

# Focus 4

## Spelling and Pronunciation: Third Person Singular

**FORM**

| Base Form of the Verb | Spelling | Pronunciation |
|---|---|---|
| **1.** The final sound of the verb is "voiceless."* (e.g., p/t/f/k)<br><br>**sleep** | Add *s*.<br><br>He **sleeps** 8 hours a night. | /s/ |
| **2.** The final sound of the verb is "voiced."** (e.g., b/d/v/g/l/m/n/r or a vowel)<br><br>**drive** | Add *s*.<br><br><br>Mel **drives** to work. | /z/ |
| **3.** The verb ends in *sh, ch, x, z,* or *ss*.<br>**rush** | Add *es*.<br>Fran **rushes** to work every day. | /ɪz/ |
| **4.** The verb ends in a consonant + *y*.<br>**hurry** | Change *y* to *i* and add *es*.<br>He **hurries** to class every morning. | /z/ |
| **5.** The verb ends in a vowel + *y*.<br>**play** | Add *s*.<br>She **plays** tennis every afternoon. | /z/ |
| **6.** Irregular Forms:<br>    **have**<br>    **go**<br>    **do** | Jane **has** a quiet life.<br>She **goes** jogging after work.<br>She **does** her exercises every day. | /z/ |

*To know if a sound is voiceless, put your hand on your throat and say the sound. If you do not feel a vibration, then it is voiceless.

**To know if a sound is voiced, put your hand on your throat and say the sound. If you feel a vibration, then it is voiced.

## Exercise 5

Look at the pictures about Lazy Louie and his wife Horrible Hannah. The pictures are not in the correct order. Number them to show the correct order. Then write the number of each picture next to the corresponding caption.

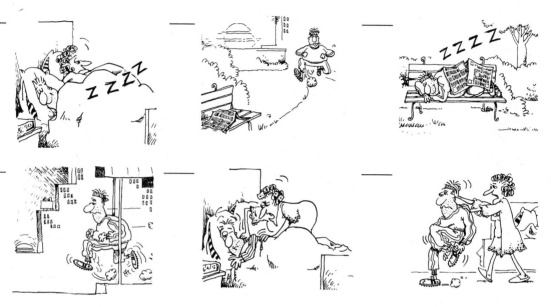

### Captions

_____ A. Poor, miserable Lazy Louie leaves the house and goes jogging. He doesn't look very happy.

_____ B. He lies down on the bench. He covers himself with the newspapers. Then Lazy Louie goes to sleep. Finally, he feels free!

_____ C. Lazy Louie hates exercise. He wants to sleep, but he gets up. He gets dressed in a hurry. He puts on his sneakers. Hannah pushes him out of the house.

_____ D. Lazy Louie loves to sleep. He is happy and he smiles in his sleep. But he snores all the time and his wife, Horrible Hannah, can't sleep.

_____ E. He jogs about three blocks. He runs into the park. He finds his favorite park bench.

_____ F. Hannah has a plan. Every morning at 6:45, she wakes Louie. He is lazy. She shakes him. She screams in his ear, "Come on, honey! Time to get up! You need your exercise, dear!"

## Exercise 6

Go back to the story about Lazy Louie and make a list of all the third person singular verbs. (Do not include the verbs *be* and *have*.) Make a chart like the one below and check the correct column to show the sound you hear at the end of the verb. Then read the verbs aloud.

| Verb | /s/ | /z/ | /ɪz/ |
|------|-----|-----|------|
| 1. loves |  | ✔ |  |
| 2. wakes | ✔ |  |  |
| 3. pushes |  |  | ✔ |

## Focus 5

USE

# In/On/At

USE

- Prepositions of time can be used to talk about habits and routines. Notice how these prepositions are organized from general to specific.

**general**  **in**  October, 1964, the spring, the morning, the afternoon, the evening*

**on**  Monday, Tuesdays, the Fourth of July, January 1, weekends

**specific**  **at**  6:15, noon, midnight

*Note: We say "at night."

WOW

## Exercise 7

Look at Wendy's weekly schedule below. Then fill in the blanks below the chart with the correct simple present tense or time expression.

| | Monday | Tuesday | Wednesday | Thursday | Friday |
|---|---|---|---|---|---|
| 7:00 | wake up | | | | |
| 7:30 | eat breakfast at home | | | | go out for breakfast |
| 9:30 | teach French | go skydiving | teach French | do aerobics | teach French |
| 12:00 | eat lunch at school | eat lunch at home | eat lunch at school | eat lunch at home | attend meetings |
| 3:00 | play tennis | prepare lessons | play tennis | go food shopping | clean apartment |
| 6:00 | meet a friend for dinner | go to cooking class | go to the movies | take dancing lessons | go out with friends |
| 8:00 | do the laundry | talk on the phone | read novels | prepare lessons | |
| 10:30 | go to bed | | | | |
| 12:00 | | | | | go to bed |

1. Wendy _____ every day at 7:00.

2. She eats breakfast at home _____.

3. Once a week on Fridays, she _____.

4. She _____ three times a week.

5. She does aerobics on Thursday _____.

6. She eats lunch at school _____.

7. She skips lunch _____.

8. Twice a week she _____.

9. She goes to cooking class _____.

10. She reads novels _____.

11. On Friday nights, she _____.

12. She goes to bed early _____.

13. She _____ at midnight on Friday.

14. She does the laundry _____.

15. She _____ at 8:00 on Thursday night.

## Exercise 8

Complete the sentences with *in, on,* or *at.*

1. Wendy wakes up every morning _____ 7:00.

2. She goes skydiving _____ Tuesdays.

3. I play tennis _____ the summer.

4. Wendy sees her boyfriend _____ weekends.

5. She has lunch _____ noon.

6. She watches a video _____ the evening.

7. She teaches French _____ Monday, Wednesday, and Friday.

8. My friends and I drink champagne _____ New Year's Eve.

9. Fran and Fred go to sleep _____ 1:00 A.M. every night.

10. I celebrate my birthday _____ April 10.

## Exercise 9

Make true statements about yourself by completing the time expressions below.

1. Every weekend . . .
2. Twice a week . . .
3. Once a year . . .
4. On Friday night . . .
5. In the morning . . .

6. On December 31 . . .
7. In the summer . . .
8. In August . . .
9. Every Wednesday . . .
10. At 6:00 . . .

# Focus 6

## Do in Negative Statements in the Simple Present

**FORM**

- Form the negative in the simple present the same way you form the negative for the verb *have*. Use the auxiliary *do/does* + *not* + the base form of the verb to make negative statements.

Base form = *have*          Base form = *smoke*
**(a)** He **doesn't have** a cigarette.     **(b)** He **doesn't smoke**.

| Subject | Do/Does + Not (Contraction) | Base Form of the Verb |
|---|---|---|
| I<br>You<br>We<br>They | do not<br>don't | smoke. |
| He<br>She<br>It | does not<br>doesn't | work. |

## Exercise 10

Read the statements about habits and daily routines below. Check the answers that are true for you. Then compare your answers with a classmate's. Write five affirmative or negative statements about your partner.

**EXAMPLES:** My partner doesn't smoke cigarettes.
He jogs.
He doesn't drink alcohol.

|  | YES | NO |  | YES | NO |
|---|---|---|---|---|---|
| 1. I smoke. | ___ | ___ | 7. I take vitamins. | ___ | ___ |
| 2. I exercise. | ___ | ___ | 8. I put sugar in my coffee. | ___ | ___ |
| 3. I drink alcohol. | ___ | ___ |  |  |  |
| 4. I eat meat. | ___ | ___ | 9. I like fast food. | ___ | ___ |
| 5. I play soccer. | ___ | ___ | 10. I eat fruits and vegetables. | ___ | ___ |
| 6. I drink coffee. | ___ | ___ |  |  |  |

# Focus 7

## Making Generalizations

USE

- Use the simple present to make statements about things that happen or that are true in general. These statements can be both affirmative and negative.

   **(a)** The sun rises in the East and sets in the West.

   **(b)** A healthy person exercises every day.

   **(c)** A healthy person doesn't use drugs.

## Exercise 11

Read the list of activities below. Decide if a healthy person does these things or not and check the correct column. Then make affirmative or negative statements. Discuss your statements with a partner.

|  | YES | NO |
|---|---|---|
| 1. eat hamburgers every day | ___ | ✔ |
| *A healthy person doesn't eat hamburgers every day.* |  |  |
| 2. watch his diet | ___ | ___ |
| 3. smoke | ___ | ___ |
| 4. eat fruit and vegetables | ___ | ___ |
| 5. worry all the time | ___ | ___ |
| 6. find time to relax | ___ | ___ |
| 7. use drugs | ___ | ___ |
| 8. enjoy life | ___ | ___ |
| 9. sleep only five hours a night | ___ | ___ |
| 10. overeat | ___ | ___ |
| 11. exercise | ___ | ___ |

# *Focus 8*

## Using Common Expressions with *Go*

USE

• You can use the verb *go* with many expressions.

| **Go to the** | **Go to** | **Go** | **Go + Base Verb + *-ing*** |
|---|---|---|---|
| Go to the store | Go to bed | Go home | Go shopping |
| Go to the supermarket | Go to sleep | Go downtown | Go fishing |
| Go to the post office | Go to school | Go uptown | Go swimming |
| Go to the park | Go to high school | Go out | Go skiing |
| Go to the bank | Go to college | Go away | Go dancing |
| Go to the doctor | Go to class | | Go jogging |
| Go to the dentist | Go to jail | | Go hiking |
| Go to the movies | Go to work | | Go biking |
| Go to the beach | Go to lunch | | |
| | Go to church | | |

## Exercise 12

Circle the correct form:

**EXAMPLE:** She goes to ((the park)/park) every Sunday.

1. My father goes to (the doctor/doctor) once a year.
2. Her parents go to (the bed/bed) late every night.
3. I go to (the bank/bank) twice a week.
4. Wendy doesn't go to (the work/work) every day.
5. Wendy goes to (the college/college).
6. My mother goes to (the supermarket/supermarket) every Monday morning.
7. Jane doesn't go to (the lunch/lunch) at 2:00 every day.
8. My family and I go to (the church/church) every Sunday.
9. Criminals go to (the jail/jail).
10. The students go (to home, home, to the home) at 3:00.

## Exercise 13

Change the base verb in parentheses to the structure *go* + base form of the verb + *-ing* and say your sentences aloud.

Wendy and her boyfriend are very active.

1. Every summer, Wendy _____ (swim) in a big lake.

2. Her boyfriend, Tod, _____ (fish) in the lake.

3. In the fall, they _____ (hike) in the mountains.

4. They _____ (bike) on mountain trails.

5. In the winter, Wendy _____ (ice skate).

6. Tod _____ (ski).

7. They both _____ (jog) every week.

8. And every Friday night they _____ (dance).

# Focus 9

USE

## Choosing *Make* or *Do*

USE

- In English, the verbs *make* and *do* are used in different expressions.

| *Make* | *Do* |
|---|---|
| –the bed | –the dishes |
| –breakfast/lunch/dinner | –the laundry |
| –a cake/pie | –the cooking |
| –a reservation | –the shopping |
| –an excuse | –exercise/aerobics |
| –a request | –an assignment |
| –plans | –your homework |
| –a decision | |
| –a dress | |
| –a telephone call | |

## Exercise 14

Think about your present living situation or your living situation back home. Fill in the blanks with appropriate subjects and circle either *do* or *make*. Then make a statement aloud and compare your statement with a partner's statement.

**EXAMPLE:** *In my family, my father does the dishes.*

**In my family,**

1. _____ do/make the dishes.

2. _____ do/make the bed.

3. _____ do/make breakfast.

4. _____ do/make lunch.

5. _____ do/make dinner.

6. _____ do/make the decisions.

7. _____ do/make vacation plans.

8. _____ do/make my homework.

9. _____ do/make the laundry.

10. _____ do/make the shopping.

## Exercise 15

Error Correction. Rewrite the sentences below correctly.

1. She is smile every day.
2. He every day takes a walk.
3. He finish his dinner every night.
4. He don't is cook dinner on Sundays.
5. We are study in the library on Saturdays.
6. She don't work on Tuesdays.
7. We go to shopping every week.
8. She doesn't goes to school on Thursdays.
9. She isn't goes jogging on Mondays.

# Activities

## Activity 1

On a separate sheet of paper, make a grid like the one in Exercise 7. Fill out your own daily schedule on the grid, using only the base form of the verb. Then exchange schedules with a partner. Compare your daily routines. Write as many affirmative and negative sentences as you can about your partner's habits and routines.

## Activity 2

For each category, write short sentences about things you do every day, every month, every year, etc. Compare your information to a partner's. Find the special things that only you do. Make a list of the special things that each person in the class does.

| Every Day | Once a Week | Once a Year |
|---|---|---|
| Every Night | Once a Month | Every Sunday |

## Activity 3

Write ten statements about the habits of people in your country. Share this information with your classmates.

**EXAMPLES:** *In Greece, people drink wine with their meals.*
*In France, stores close between 12:00 and 2:00.*

## Activity 4

Write one thing you do and one thing you don't do for the following categories. Exchange papers with a partner. Each student then tells the class about his/her partner.

**EXAMPLE:** Entertainment: Mario watches TV. He doesn't go to the movies.

| Entertainment | Hobbies | Music | Family | Food | Sports | Languages |
|---|---|---|---|---|---|---|
|  |  |  |  |  |  |  |

## Activity 5

Think of a person you admire and write five sentences telling why you admire the person. Think of a person you are worried about and write five sentences telling why you are worried about that person.

**EXAMPLES:** I admire my mother. She loves our family. She enjoys her work. She cooks good food. She doesn't get angry.

I am worried about my friend. He doesn't eat good food. He doesn't exercise. He doesn't sleep. He sits in front of the TV all the time.

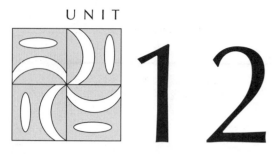

# 12

# Simple Present Tense

## Questions;
## Adverbs of Frequency

## Task

You are all "language learners" in this class. But are you **good** language learners? What is a **good language learner**? What do good language learners do?

Read the text below. Then check Yes/No to answer the questions.

Good language learners think about how to learn. They don't try to avoid the new language. They practice the new language every day. They read, write, and listen to the new language. They find people to speak to. When they don't understand, they don't get nervous. They try to guess the meanings of new words and expressions. They always ask questions about the language. They find ways to remember new words. They try to use new words and expressions in sentences. They listen to correct pronunciation. They repeat words out loud. They sometimes talk to themselves in the new language. They also think about grammar. They try to understand how the new language works.

Good language learners know that learning a new language is not easy. They don't feel bad when they make mistakes. They try to understand their problems in the new language. They review every day.

### WHAT DO GOOD LANGUAGE LEARNERS DO?

|  | Yes | No |
|---|---|---|
| 1. Do they think about how to learn? |  |  |
| 2. Do they try to avoid the new language? |  |  |
| 3. Do they get nervous when they don't understand? |  |  |
| 4. Do they ask questions about the new language? |  |  |
| 5. Do they guess the meanings of new words? |  |  |
| 6. Do they find ways to remember new words? |  |  |
| 7. Do they listen to pronunciation? |  |  |
| 8. Do they think about grammar? |  |  |
| 9. Do they feel bad when they make mistakes? |  |  |
| 10. Do they think language learning is easy? |  |  |

# *Focus 1*

## FORM

# *Do* in Yes/No Questions in the Simple Present

FORM

- Yes/no questions in the simple present tense are like yes/no questions with the verb *have*. Use the auxiliary verb *do/does* in front of the subject. Use the base form of the main verb after the subject. For short answers, use the auxiliary *do/does*.

| Auxiliary | Subject | Base Verb | | Short Answers |
|---|---|---|---|---|
| Do | I / you | spcak | English? | Yes, you do. <br> Yes, I do. |
| Does | he <br> she <br> it | work? | | Yes, he does. <br> No, she does not. <br> No, it doesn't. |
| Do | we <br> you <br> they | remember | new words? | Yes, we do. <br> No, we do not. <br> No, they don't. |

## *Exercise 1*

Find Someone Who . . .

What good learning strategies do your classmates use? Go around your classroom and ask your classmates questions using the cues below. Write down the names of the students who answer yes. Discuss the results with the class.

**EXAMPLE:** You:      Do you speak English outside of class?
Your partner:   Yes, I do.

1. speak English outside of class     _____

2. find different ways to say things when people don't understand you     _____

3. practice pronunciation     _____

4. ask people to correct your English     _____

5. ask people questions about English     _____

6. watch TV in English     _____

**131**

7. guess the meanings of new words _____

8. make lists of new words _____

9. read something in English every day _____

10. write something in English every day _____

11. try to understand how English works _____

12. avoid English _____

# Exercise 2

Sophia and Mohammed are two different types of language learners. Find out how they are different. Working with a partner, ask and answer questions in order to complete each learner's chart.

**EXAMPLES:** A. Does Mohammed like English? Does he like English? / No, he doesn't.

B. Does Sophia like English? Does she like English? / Yes, she does.

**Student A:**

| | Sophia | | Mohammed | |
|---|---|---|---|---|
| | yes | no | yes | no |
| 1. like English | x | | | |
| 2. need English | | | x | |
| 3. think English is difficult | | | x | |
| 4. study with other students | x | | | |
| 5. think grammar is important | | | x | |
| 6. learn more by speaking and listening to English | x | | | |
| 7. learn more by reading and writing English | | | x | |
| 8. feel good using English | x | | | |
| 9. have any American friends | x | | | |
| 10. feel bad about making mistakes in English | | | x | |

**Student B:**

| | Sophia | | Mohammed | |
|---|---|---|---|---|
| | yes | no | yes | no |
| **1.** like English | | | | x |
| **2.** need English | x | | | |
| **3.** think English is difficult | | x | | |
| **4.** study with other students | | | | x |
| **5.** think grammar is important | x | | | |
| **6.** learn more by speaking and listening to English | | | | x |
| **7.** learn more by reading and writing English | | x | | |
| **8.** feel good using English | | | | x |
| **9.** have any American friends | | | | x |
| **10.** feel bad about making mistakes in English | | x | | |

# Exercise 3

What are some of your personal habits? Ask a partner yes/no questions using the cues below. Then have your partner ask you the questions.

**EXAMPLE:** You:        Do you smoke?
             Your Partner: No, I don't.

**Partner's Answers
(Yes/No)**

1. smoke        _____

2. drink alcohol        _____

3. listen to loud music        _____

4. cook        _____

5. have parties on weekends        _____

6. make friends easily        _____

7. go to bed late        _____

8. talk on the telephone all the time        _____

9. study hard        _____

10. clean your apartment every week        _____

# Exercise 4

What do students do in other countries? Make questions using the cues below. Find a partner from a different country and ask him or her the questions. Then write sentences about school in your partner's country.

**EXAMPLE:** *Do children go to nursery school?*
*Yes, they do./No, they don't.*

**Answers**

1. a child / start school at age five          _____

2. students / wear uniforms to school          _____

3. boys and girls / go to separate schools          _____

4. children / go to school on Saturdays          _____

5. students / study religion in school          _____

6. a student / take difficult exams after high school          _____

7. college / cost a lot of money          _____

8. the government / pay for higher education          _____

9. parents / pay for their children's education          _____

10. students / work after school          _____

1. _____

2. _____

3. _____

4. _____

5. _____

6. _____

7. _____

8. _____

9. _____

10. _____

# *Focus 2*

## Adverbs of Frequency

FORM
MEANING
USE

- Use simple present questions to ask about things that are true in general, or things you do as habits or routines.
- Simple present questions can be

  - yes/no questions

    **(a)** Do you watch TV?

    Yes, I do.

    No, I don't.

  - yes/no questions of frequency

    **(b)** Do you **ever** watch TV?

    Yes, I **always** watch TV.

    No, I **never** watch TV.

- Adverbs of frequency tell how many times a habit is repeated; they tell, in a general way, what percent of the time this habit occurs.

|  | **Adverbs of Frequency** | **Percent of the Time** |
|---|---|---|
| **Positive Meaning** | always<br>almost always<br>usually }<br>generally }<br>often }<br>frequently }<br>sometimes | 100% of the time<br>90–99% of the time |
| **Negative Meaning** | seldom }<br>rarely }<br>never | 0–10% of the time<br><br>0% of the time |

## Exercise 5

The chart below shows learning habits and adverbs of frequency. Check the box that is true for you.

| Learning Habits | Adverbs of Frequency | | | | | | |
|---|---|---|---|---|---|---|---|
| | Always | Almost Always | Usually; Generally | Often; Frequently | Sometimes | Seldom; Rarely | Never |
| 1. use a dictionary | | | | | | | |
| 2. make a telephone call in English | | | | | | | |
| 3. speak to native speakers | | | | | | | |
| 4. discuss learning problems with classmates | | | | | | | |
| 5. practice the sounds of English | | | | | | | |
| 6. record your voice on tape | | | | | | | |
| 7. read books or stories in English | | | | | | | |
| 8. ask questions about English | | | | | | | |
| 9. think in English | | | | | | | |
| 10. think about how to learn English | | | | | | | |

## Exercise 6

Read the questions and answers. Circle the appropriate adverb of frequency.

1. **Q:** Do you ever use your hands when you speak English?

   **A:** I (never/always) use my hands. My hands help me explain things.

2. **Q:** Do you ever guess the meanings of new words?

   **A:** I (never/always) guess the meanings of new words. I use my dictionary all the time.

3. **Q:** Do you ever think in English?

   **A:** I (never/usually) think in my native language first. Then I translate my words into English.

4. **Q:** Do you ever sing songs in English?

   **A:** I (often/seldom) sing songs in English. I don't like to sing.

5. **Q:** Do you ever write letters in English?

   **A:** I have an American friend in Boston. I miss him. I (rarely/sometimes) write letters to him in English.

6. **Q:** Do you ever make telephone calls in English?

   **A:** I live with my aunt. My aunt speaks English. She makes the phone calls. I (never/always) make phone calls in English.

7. **Q:** Do you ever talk to yourself in English?

   **A:** English is fun. I (usually/rarely) talk to myself in English.

8. **Q:** Do you ever think about how English works?

   **A:** Grammar is interesting. I (never/always) try to understand how English works.

# Focus 3

FORM ● USE

## Position of Adverbs of Frequency

FORM
USE

- In general, place adverbs of frequency between the subject and the verb.

    **(a)** They **always** come to class.

    **(b)** He **sometimes** asks questions in class.

    **(c)** He **never** asks questions.

- You can also place *sometimes/often/frequently* (and adverbs that express the same frequency) at the beginning or the end of the sentence for emphasis.

    **(d)** That's not true. He asks questions **often**.

    **(e)** **Sometimes** I ask questions in class.

- Note : In general, with the verb *be*, place the adverb of frequency *after* the verb. (If the adverb is stressed, you can place it before *be*.)

    They **are always** in class.

## Exercise 7

Go back to the chart in Exercise 5. Write statements about your personal learning habits using adverbs of frequency.

> **EXAMPLES:** *I always use a dictionary.*
> *I seldom think in English.*

## Focus 4

FORM ● MEANING

### *Wh*-Questions in the Simple Present

FORM
MEANING

- *Wh*-questions ask for **specific information** about habits. Place the *Wh*-question word before the auxiliary *do/does*.

| Information Wanted | Question Word | Auxiliary | Subject | Main Verb | |
|---|---|---|---|---|---|
| **Things/ Activities** | What | do | they | do | in class? |
| **Time** | When | does | the class | begin? | |
| | What time | does | the class | begin? | |
| **Place** | Where | do | you | study | English? |
| **Reason** | Why | does | he | need | English? |
| **Means/Ways** | How | do | we | learn | English? |
| **Frequency*** | How often | does | she | speak | English? |

* Note: Adverbs of frequency in answer to *how often* questions can be unclear and impolite. The answer to a *how often* question is usually a specific time expression.

How often do you go to the movies?   I go to the movies every weekend.
                                     NOT: I go to the movies often.

# Exercise 8

Match each question to its answer by writing the letter of the appropriate answer next to each question.

_____ 1. Why does he need English?

_____ 2. When does the semester begin?

_____ 3. What do they do in class?

_____ 4. What time does your class start?

_____ 5. Where does he study English?

_____ 6. How often does he speak English?

_____ 7. How do students learn to speak English?

(a) every day

(b) at the City University of New York

(c) They practice all the time

(d) They speak, read, write, and listen to English

(e) because he wants to go to school in the United States (He needs English because he wants to go to school in the United States.)

(f) at 8:30

(g) on September 10

# Exercise 9

Read the following case history of a student named Carla and then look at the cues. Choose the correct *Wh*-word to write questions. When you are done, read the text again and answer the questions aloud.

Carla is a Haitian student in New York. She speaks three languages—Creole, French, and English. She wants to be a bilingual teacher. Her English is very good, but she speaks with an accent. Sometimes people don't understand her when she speaks. Carla feels embarrassed. She seldom speaks English. She feels angry because she says Americans only speak English. Americans don't understand the problems people have learning a new language.

**EXAMPLE:** (Carla/live) *Where does Carla live?*

1. (Carla/come from )_____ ?

2. (Carla/feel when she speaks English)_____ ?

3. (Carla/feel this way)_____ ?

4. (Carla/want to be)_____ ?

5. (Carla/speak English)_____ ?

6. (Carla/feel angry)_____ ?

Now ask two questions of your own about this story.

# Focus 5

## Answering *How* Questions with *By* + Noun Phrase

USE

- *How* questions can also be used to ask about transportation. The answer to a *how* question about transportation can be *by* + noun phrase.
  - How do you get to school?

    by bus (I go by bus.)
    by train
    by car
    on foot
  - Note: Other possible answers to *how* questions are

    I take the bus.
    I take the train.
    I drive.
    I walk.

## Exercise 10

Complete each question with the name of a country. Then ask a classmate the question. He or she should choose an answer from the expressions below.

| | | | |
|---|---|---|---|
| by bus | by airplane | by subway | by helicopter |
| by train | by boat | by car | by limousine |
| by taxi | by bicycle | by truck | |

1. How do students get to school in _____?

2. How do rich people go to work in _____?

3. How does the President get to work in _____?

4. How do average people get to work in _____?

5. How do people go shopping in _____?

6. How do people get to airports in _____?

7. How do people travel to different cities in _____?

8. How does fresh food get to markets around the country in _____?

# Focus 6

## FORM ● MEANING
## Wh-Questions with *Who/Whom*

**FORM**
**MEANING**

- Use *who* and *whom* to ask questions about people.

| *Who* questions | Answers |
|---|---|
| **(a)** Who practices English every day? | Mei-Lin practices every day. Mei-Lin. |
| **(b)** Who learns English fast? | Takeiko and Tiziana learn English fast. Takeiko and Tiziana. |

- In questions **(a)** and **(b)**, *who* is the **subject** of the question.
- Do not use the auxiliary verb *do/does* in the question.

| *Whom* questions | Answers |
|---|---|
| **(c)** Who(m) do you meet after class? | I meet Henri after class. Henri. |
| **(d)** With whom do you study? | I study with Sam and Mary. . . . with Sam and Mary. |

- In question **(c)**, *who(m)* is the **object** of the verb. Use the auxiliary *do/does* in the question.
- In question **(d)**, *whom* is the **object** of the preposition *with*. Use *whom* with verbs followed by the prepositions *to, for,* and *with*. When *whom* is the object of a preposition, place the preposition at the beginning of the question.
- Note: *What* can also be used as the subject of a question. When *what* is the subject, do not use the auxiliary *do/does*.

  **Riddle:** What goes up but never comes down?

  Answer: Your age !!!

---

# Exercise 11

Using *who*, ask your classmates questions about their family life. Then have your classmates ask you the questions.

**EXAMPLE:** cook / Who cooks in your family?
My mother usually cooks. Sometimes, my father cooks.

1. earn money . . .
2. make important decisions . . .
3. take out the garbage . . .
4. take care of the children . . .

5. clean the house . . .
6. go shopping . . .
7. be the boss . . .
8. pay the bills . . .

# *Focus 7*

## Choosing *Who/Whom* in *Wh*-Questions

USE

- *Who* is often used instead of *whom* in questions in **informal** spoken English.
- Use *whom* in questions in **formal** English. The use of a Preposition + *whom*—**With whom do you study?**—is the most formal way to ask a question.

## *Exercise 12*

Use *who* or *whom* in the questions below. (Remember *who* = subject and *who(m)* = object.) Some questions have two possible forms. Ask and answer the questions aloud.

1. _____ likes English?

2. _____ avoids English?

3. _____ bites his nails before a test?

4. _____ do you meet after class?

5. To _____ do you write letters in English?

6. _____ makes mistakes in English?

7. With _____ do you come to school?

8. _____ understands the difference between *who* and *whom?*

# Focus 8

# Communication Strategy

USE

- In a new language, you do not always know the words to express what you want to say. When you have a problem, ask for help.

| When you want to know: | Use the expressions below to ask questions or get information about English |
|---|---|
| the **meaning** of a word, say: | What does the word *decision* mean? What does *strategy* mean? |
| the **spelling** of a word, say: | How do you spell *remember*? |
| the **pronunciation** of a word, say: | How do you pronounce *communicate*? |
| **When you don't know the word for something, explain your meaning and say:** | How do you say *a machine to clean floors*? How do you say *the opposite of happy*? |

# Exercise 13

Ask the appropriate *Wh*-question.

1. Q: _____ ?

   A: You pronounce it: læŋwɪdʒ _____ .

2. Q: _____ ?

   A: The word *guess* means you don't know the answer, but you think and try to find the answer

   in your head.

3. Q: _____ ?

   A: You say *thin*.

4. Q: _____ ?

   A: You spell it : C-O-M-M-U-N-I-C-A-T-E.

5. Q: _____ ?

   A: *Strategy* means an action or actions you take to learn English.

## Exercise 14

Error correction. Rewrite the sentences below correctly.

1. Is he read books?
2. Do they good students?
3. What means *routines*?
4. I watch sometimes TV.
5. How often you listen to native speakers of English?
6. Does he studies in the library?
7. What does the class on Mondays?
8. How you say, "not correct"?
9. I am never make mistakes.
10. Why you feel embarrassed to speak English?

# Activities

### Activity 1

In your group, think of what a good language learner does. Think of at least 15 questions for a questionnaire.

> **EXAMPLES:** Do you avoid English?
>
> Do you listen to English?
>
> Do you feel bad about your mistakes in English?

Compare your questions with the questions from other groups. Choose the 15 best questions. Write a class questionnaire for students in a different class. Ask the students in the other class to fill out the questionnaire. Then, compare their answers to your answers.

### Activity 2

Find a Roommate. You are a student at an American university. You want to share an apartment with another student. What kind of person do you want? What kind of person do you not want? What personal questions do you want to ask? Write ten yes/no or *Wh*-questions to ask your classmates. (Refer to Exercise 3 for help.) Find a "roommate" in your class.

> **EXAMPLES:** Do you smoke?
>
> How often do you have parties?
>
> What time do you get up?
>
> When do you go to bed?

**Activity 3**

Work with a partner. Ask each other yes/no and *Wh*-questions in the simple present tense. Find five ways in which you are the same and five ways in which you are different. Write your questions and answers and then report to the class.

> **EXAMPLES:** Do you eat breakfast?
>
> What do you eat for breakfast?

**Activity 4**

Choose one of the countries represented by your classmates. What do you want to know about this country? Write at least six questions about customs, habits, etc. Interview a classmate from the country and write the answers.

> **EXAMPLES:** Do children go to school on Saturdays?
>
> What do people do on weekends?
>
> How do people celebrate their birthdays?
>
> Do waiters and waitresses receive tips?

# 13

# Imperatives

*Task*

Match each statement to a picture.

1.

2.

3.

4.

5.

6.

**Picture #**

**(a)** "Please give me change for a dollar, Sir." _____

**(b)** "Have a piece of cake with your coffee, Mary." _____

**(c)** "Don't talk to me. My boyfriend's very jealous!" _____

**(d)** "Don't throw your litter on the street. Pick it up!" _____

**(e)** "Go straight down 8th Ave. and turn left at the bakery." _____

**(f)** "Watch out!" _____

# *Focus 1*

## Affirmative and Negative Imperatives

- Imperative sentences are different from all other English sentences.
  - They usually have no subject. The subject "you" (singular/plural) is understood, but you don't need to say it.
  - They do not show tense.
- To form an affirmative imperative, use the **base form** of the verb.
  - **(a)** Have a piece of cake with your coffee, Mary.
- To form a negative imperative, use *do not* or *don't* in front of the base form of the verb.
  - **(b)** Don't throw your litter on the street!
- To make an imperative more polite, use *please* at the beginning or end of the imperative sentence.
  - **(c) Please** give me change for a dollar.
  - **(d)** Give me change for a dollar, **please.**
  - **(e) Please** don't do that again.
- Note: The speaker's tone of voice is also important in imperatives. The tone of voice can make the speaker sound either angry or polite.

## *Exercise 1*

Go back to the statements in the Task. Underline all the affirmative and negative imperatives.

USE

# Functions of Imperatives

USE

- Imperatives have different functions or purposes. Look at the pictures and corresponding imperatives. Study the function of each imperative in context.

A.

B.

C.

D.

E.

F.

| | Functions |
|---|---|
| **A.** "Don't drink so much beer every night, Kurt." | giving advice or making a suggestion |
| **B.** "Be careful!" | giving a warning when there is danger |
| **C.** "Make a right at the corner." | giving directions or instructions |
| **D.** "Please give me some aspirin, Mom." | making a polite request |
| **E.** "Have some coffee, dear." | politely offering something |
| **F.** "Don't come home drunk again!" | giving an order |

## Exercise 2

Look back at the pictures in the Task. Write the number of the picture that corresponds to each function. The first one has been done for you.

| Use | Picture # |
|---|---|
| **A.** giving advice | 2 |
| **B.** giving an order | |
| **C.** giving a warning when there is danger | |
| **D.** making a polite request | |
| **E.** politely offering something | |
| **F.** giving directions | |

## Exercise 3

Read the text below. Underline all the affirmative and negative imperative forms.

**Caution:** Keep away from heat and flame. Open windows and doors when you paint. If you have headaches or feel dizzy, get more fresh air or cover your mouth and nose. If you feel sick, leave the room. Close paint container after each use. Avoid contact with skin. Do not swallow. Keep out of the reach of children.

Circle the correct answer.

1. Where was this text?
   **a.** on a container of milk
   **b.** on a can of house paint
   **c.** on a jar of children's paint

2. What is the purpose of this text?
   **a.** politely offering
   **b.** politely requesting
   **c.** warning

**149**

# Exercise 4

Choose an appropriate verb from the list below and fill in each blank with an affirmative or negative imperative.

| use | keep | drink | be | drive |
| wear | obey | leave | look | use |

To avoid accidents, learn to drive cautiously.

1. _____ prepared to stop.

2. _____ ahead.

3. _____ your rearview mirrors.

4. _____ the speed limit.

5. _____ space between your car and the car in front of you. (Do not "tailgate.")

6. _____ your seat belt.

7. _____ if you are very tired, or are on medication.

8. _____ and drive.

9. _____ your horn to warn other drivers of danger.

10. _____ your car in good condition.

1. Where was this text?
   a. in a magazine about health
   b. in a driver's manual
   c. in a toy car

2. What is the purpose of this text?
   a. giving instructions
   b. making a polite request
   c. offering

# Exercise 5

Work with a partner. Read each statement on the left. Your partner gives an appropriate response from the right.

1. I don't like my landlord.
2. I have a headache.
3. I am overweight.
4. I have the hiccups.
5. I have a toothache.
6. I don't have any friends here.
7. I feel tired every morning.
8. I miss my family.
9. I worry too much.
10. I smoke a pack a day.

a. Go on a diet.
b. Make an appointment to see the dentist.
c. Make friends with your classmates.
d. Move to a different apartment.
e. Call home.
f. Go to bed early.
g. Don't buy cigarettes.
h. Hold your breath for two minutes.
i. Take it easy.
j. Take some aspirin.

**1.** What is the function of the statements on the right?
   **a.** giving advice
   **b.** giving orders
   **c.** offering

Work with a partner. State three problems you each have, and then respond to each other's problems.

# Exercise 6

The following are examples of common English expressions that are imperatives.

Choose an appropriate verb from the box below. Write affirmative and negative imperatives on the two separate lists. Discuss the meanings of these expressions. The first one has been done for you.

| talk | keep | give | take | cry | be |
| rock | go | leave | drink | have | do |

**Affirmative**

1. _____Give_____ me a break.

2. _____ careful.

3. _____ it easy.

4. _____ ahead.

5. _____ a good day.

6. _____ in touch.

7. _____ me alone.

8. _____ the best you can.

**Negative**

1. _____ the boat.

2. _____ to strangers.

3. _____ over spilled milk.

4. _____ and drive.

**151**

# *Focus 3*

## Using Imperatives Appropriately

USE

- It is appropriate to use imperatives as orders when:
    - the speaker has the right or authority to order the listener to do something.
        - **(a)** (police officer to woman): "Pick that up!"
    - the speaker and listener are equals, working together.
        - **(b)** (a teacher to a teacher): "Pass me that book, please."

## *Exercise 7*

Check "Yes" if the imperative is appropriate in the situation. Check "No" if it is not. Check "It Depends" if you think the imperative is appropriate under specific circumstances.

| Situation | Imperative | Yes | No | It Depends |
|---|---|---|---|---|
| **1.** A student says to a teacher: | "Give me my paper." | | | |
| **2.** A worker says to his boss: | "Don't bother me now, I'm busy." | | | |
| **3.** A man stops you on the street. He says: | "Tell me the time." | | | |
| **4.** A student says to a classmate: | "Wait for me after class." | | | |
| **5.** You get into a taxi and say: | "Take me to the airport, fast!" | | | |
| **6.** One roommate says to the other: | "Turn off that music. I hate it!" | | | |

# Activities

## Activity 1

Look around your neighborhood or your home. Find imperatives in public or household notices. Bring the notices to class. Discuss the meaning of the notices.

**EXAMPLE:**

BE AWARE!
BE WATCHFUL!
PROTECT
YOUR BELONGINGS!

THE QUEENS LIBRARY JOINS WITH YOUR LOCAL LAW ENFORCEMENT AGENCIES TO HELP YOU AVOID BEING A VICTIM!

**WHAT YOU CAN DO IN THE LIBRARY**

- Don't leave handbags, briefcases, coats or other personal belongings unattended or out of your sight

- Inform the library staff if you see someone loitering

- Report thefts immediately to those in charge and to the police

PROTECT YOURSELF FROM PICKPOCKETS

BE ALERT!
BE AWARE!

Queens Borough
Public Library

## Activity 2

Work in a group. Create an information pamphlet to give advice to new students in the United States. Choose from some of the ideas below or decide on an idea with your group.

How to Learn English
How to Find an Apartment
How to Find a Job
How to Meet People
How to Do Well in School

## Activity 3

Read the following entry from a student's journal. (Please note that the grammar in this journal entry is not correct! Do not correct it.) Write a response to this student, giving him advice.

I open the English books and see the letters in a book. The English words get in my head. What on earth is the English ? Why don't I know? I study English, but I don't understand. I am very difficult to make sentence.

## Activity 4

Prepare a list of "Do's and Don't's" for people who plan to travel to your country or a country you know well.

**EXAMPLES:** In Japan, do not tip the waiters.

In Saudi Arabia, do not wear shorts.

# 14

# Prepositions of Direction

## *Task*

Read the paragraph on the next page and follow Sandy's route on the map.

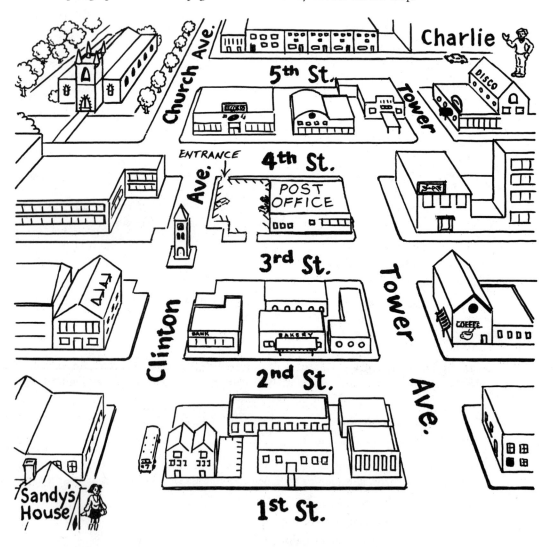

Sandy walks out of her house and goes to the corner. She gets on the #7 bus. She gets off the bus at Church Avenue and 5th Street. She walks down 5th Street to Tower Avenue. She walks across Tower Avenue and goes into the building on the corner of 5th and Tower. She takes the elevator up to the 5th floor. She leaves there at 3:00 A.M.

Where does Sandy go on Saturday evening?_____

What do you think she does?_____

Charlie does something different on Saturday evening. Read the paragraph below and trace his route on the map.

At 10:00 P.M., Charlie gets into his car and drives down Tower Avenue. Sometimes he drives past the coffee shop between 2nd and 3rd Streets, but sometimes he stops and buys a cup of coffee. He turns right on 2nd Street and makes another right on Clinton Avenue. He drives past the tower and into the parking lot on the corner of 3rd Street. He gets out of his car, walks across the parking lot and into the building. He leaves there at 6:00 A.M.

Where does Charlie go on Saturday evening?_____

What does Charlie do on Saturday evening?_____

# Focus 1

## Form of Prepositions of Direction

**FORM**

- The prepositions in Unit 7 are prepositions of location. Use these prepositions to talk about position or place. They usually combine with position verbs (*be, live, work, wait*).
  - **(a)** The disco is **at** 45 Tower Avenue.
  - **(b)** Sandy lives **on** the second floor of an apartment building.
- Prepositions of direction are different. They combine with verbs of motion (*go, get, drive, fly, move, run, walk*). They can be one word or two words.
  - **(c)** Sandy walks **out of** her house.
  - **(d)** She gets **off** the bus.

## Exercise 1

Go back to the Task and circle all the prepositions of direction. Underline the verbs of motion in the two paragraphs that describe where Sandy and Charlie go.

**EXAMPLE:** Sandy <u>walks</u> (out of) her house to the corner.

# Focus 2

## MEANING

### To, Away From, On(to), Off (of), In(to), Out Of

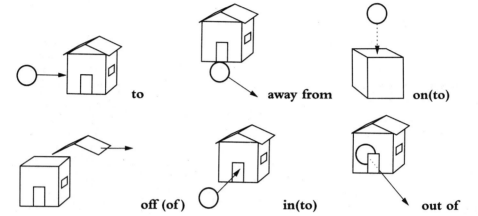

to  away from  on(to)

off (of)  in(to)  out of

- Note: For cars and taxis, use *in(to)* and *out of*:

**(a)** He gets **in(to)** the car.  **(b)** He gets **out of** the taxi.

For bicycles and public transportation, use *on* and *off*:

**(c)** She gets **on** her bicycle.  **(d)** They get **off** the plane.

## Exercise 2

Here is a story about the hard life of a mouse. Look at the pictures and write the correct preposition of direction in the blank.

1. The mouse comes _____ his hole.

2. The cat jumps _____ the table.

3. The mouse runs _____ the cheese.

 **4.** The cat jumps _____ the table and chases the mouse.

 **5.** The mouse runs _____ the cat.

 **6.** The mouse runs _____ his hole.

## Focus 3

MEANING

# Up, Down, Across, Along, Around, Over, Through, Past

MEANING

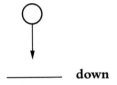 up

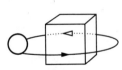 down

 across

 along

 around

 over

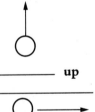 through

 past

## Exercise 3

Here is a story about the hard life of a cat. Look at the pictures and write the correct preposition of direction in the blank. Use one of the prepositions from the previous page.

1. The cat sees the dog. He runs _____ the field.

2. He runs _____ the grass.

3. He runs _____ the bridge.

4. He climbs _____ the tree.

5. The dog barks. He runs _____ the tree.

6. The dog's owner arrives and puts a leash on the dog. The cat

   climbs _____ from the tree.

7. The cat walks _____ the dog.

8. He walks _____ the road with a smile on his face.

158

## Exercise 4

Sally is a truck driver. She makes several pickups and deliveries on Mondays. Follow the route she usually takes on the map and complete the passage with the correct prepositions.

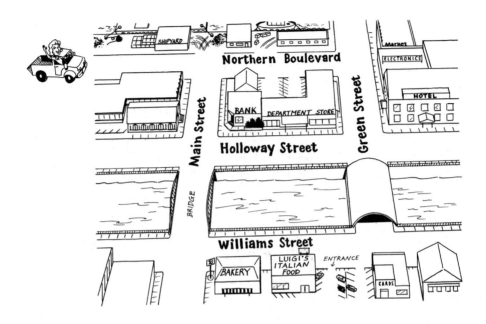

Sally gets (1) _____ her truck and drives (2) _____ the shipyard. At the shipyard, she puts some

boxes (3) _____ the truck, and she drives (4) _____ the department store. Then she drives

(5) _____ the bank and then (6) _____ the bridge. After that, she drives (7) _____ the

river and (8) _____ the restaurant parking lot. She eats dinner and then walks (9) _____ the

restaurant. On the return trip, she usually takes a shortcut and drives (10) _____ the tunnel.

When she gets (11) _____ the tunnel, she drives (12) _____ the hotel. Her last stop is the

market next to the electronics store. At the market, she gets (13) _____ her truck and takes the

remaining boxes (14) _____ the truck.

# *Focus 4*

# Giving Directions

- Prepositions of direction can be used for giving directions.
- Look at the map below and read the conversation.

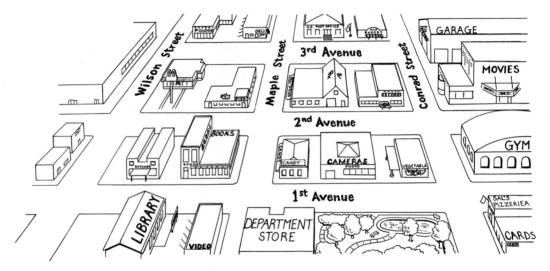

(Person A is at the bakery.)

A: "Excuse me, how do I get to the department store?"

B: "Walk **down** Conrad Street until you get to First Avenue. Then turn **right** at the corner. Go **straight.** Walk one block. The department store is on the corner on the left."

## Exercise 5

Refer to the map in Focus 4. Read the directions. Trace the path on the map. Then answer the questions.

1. You are in the bakery. Walk down Conrad Street and make a right on to Second Avenue. Go straight and make a left on Maple Street. Walk across the street. Where are you?

   _____.

2. You are coming out of McDonald's. Walk down Second Avenue and go two blocks. Turn right on Conrad Street. Go straight until you get to First Avenue. Make a left. Walk into the building on your right. Where are you? _____.

3. You are at the library. Walk up Wilson Street. Make a right on Third Avenue. Go straight for two blocks. Then make a left on Conrad Street. Go across the street from the bakery. Where are you? _____.

## Exercise 6

With a partner, take turns asking for and giving directions to different places, using the map in Focus 4. State where you are and ask for directions on how to get from there to your destination.

## Exercise 7

Mime the commands below. Show how they are different.

1. Step off the bus.
   Step onto the bus.

2. Put your hand into your pocket.
   Take your hand out of your pocket.

3. Walk to the blackboard.
   Walk away from the blackboard.

4. Put a pencil into the desk drawer.
   Put a pencil on the desk.

5. Climb up a mountain.
   Climb down a mountain.

6. Walk on the grass.
   Walk through the tall grass.

7. Walk away from the teacher.
   Walk around the teacher.

8. Walk past a group of people.
   Walk through a group of people.

9. Jump across the room.
   Jump over a chair.

# Exercise 8

Read the dialogues and fill in the blanks with the correct preposition of direction.

1. Woman (in car talking to police officer): Excuse me, officer. What's the quickest way to

   midtown?

   Officer: Go _____ the tunnel. It costs $2.50, but it's fast!

2. Elevator Operator: Step _____ the elevator, ladies and gentlemen. Be

   careful!

3. Mother (shouting to son Billy): Billy! Don't run _____ the street. There's a lot of

   traffic.

4. Sarah (talking to a girlfriend): I usually walk (a) _____ the store with $50 and I

   always walk (b) _____ the store with 50 cents!

5. Girlfriend (talking to boyfriend): Don't walk _____ me when I'm talking to you.

   Stay here and answer me!

6. Husband: On our next vacation, let's go (a) _____ the Caribbean. I want to walk

   (b) _____ the beach and sleep (c) _____ the stars.

   Wife: And I want to jump (d) _____ a sailboat and dive (e) _____

   the blue water. Let's go now!

# Activities

## Activity 1

In small groups, talk about the route you take to and from school every day. Use prepositions of direction.

> **EXAMPLE:** "I get out of school every day at 3:00. I walk across the street and go to the subway."

## Activity 2

Work in a group to write all the prepositions of direction from this unit on separate cards. Place the cards upside down in the center of your group. Pick up a card and give a command to another classmate, using the preposition on the card. The other student must do the action. Another student then continues the activity by choosing the second card. Continue in this way until you have gone through all the cards.

> **EXAMPLE:**

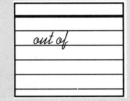

_out of_

You say: "Walk out of the classroom."

## Activity 3

Work with a partner. Write five sentences using prepositions of direction and position and then mime the sentences. Have the class guess the sentences from what you mime. For each sentence the class guesses, you get one point. The pair with the most points wins.

> **EXAMPLE:**
> 1. Walk along the sidewalk.
> 2. Stop at the corner.
> 3. Take a pack of cigarettes out of your pocket.
> 4. Smoke a cigarette and throw it down on the ground.
> 5. Walk across the street.

## Activity 4

Work in a group to prepare a treasure hunt. Hide items around the school and write directions leading another group to the items. The group that finds all the items wins.

# 15

# Direct Objects and Object Pronouns

## Task

Look at the pictures and read the story. Then answer the two questions by circling **a**, **b**, or **c**.

1.
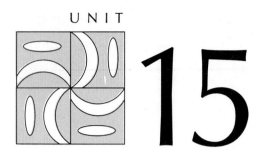

2.

3.

4.

5.

6.

."Pom Pom Perry" plays the guitar in a jazz club every night. He loves his job. But Pom Pom Perry has a problem. He sometimes sees spots before his eyes. These spots really worry him. Finally, one day, Perry visits his eye doctor. He describes his problem. "Please help me, doctor," he says. The doctor examines Perry carefully. He uses all his instruments. He tests Perry's vision. Perry reads all the letters on the eye chart. He doesn't see spots before his eyes now. The doctor is puzzled. He doesn't understand the problem. He shrugs his shoulders in confusion. "I can't help you, Perry," he says. So Perry takes his hat and his guitar and sadly starts for home.

Questions: Circle the correct answer.

1. Why does Perry see spots before his eyes?
   a. because Perry's eyes are tired.
   b. because his hat has pom poms on it.
   c. because he needs glasses.
2. Why can't the doctor solve Perry's problem?
   a. because he's not a good doctor.
   b. because he's a young doctor and he doesn't have any experience.
   c. because he doesn't know about Perry's hat.

# Focus 1

FORM

## Noun Phrases as Direct Objects

FORM

- The basic word order in an English sentence is

| Subject | Verb | Object |
|---------|------|--------|
| Perry | has | a problem. |

- The **direct object**:
  - can be a noun phrase
  - comes immediately after the verb
  - answers the question *what* or *whom*

|     | Subject | Verb | Object |  |
|-----|---------|------|--------|--|
| (a) | Perry | sees | spots. | (*Spots* is the direct object. It tells us **what** Perry sees.) |
| (b) | The doctor | examines | Perry. | (*Perry* is the direct object. It tells us **whom** the doctor examines.) |

## Exercise 1

Read these sentences about the story. Circle the direct object.

1. Pom Pom Perry plays the guitar.
2. He loves his job.
3. He sees spots before his eyes.
4. Finally, one day, he visits his eye doctor.
5. The doctor examines Perry.
6. He tests Perry's vision.
7. Perry reads the chart.
8. The doctor doesn't understand the problem.
9. The doctor never sees Perry's hat.
10. Perry takes his hat and his guitar and goes home.

## Focus 2

FORM

# Object Pronouns

FORM

- The direct object can also be a pronoun. A pronoun takes the place of a noun phrase.

| Subject | Verb | Object |
|---|---|---|
| The doctor | examines | Perry. |
| The doctor | examines | him. |

| Subject Pronouns | Object Pronouns | Subject Pronouns | Object Pronouns |
|---|---|---|---|
| I | me | we | us |
| you | you | you | you |
| he | him | they | them |
| she | her | | |
| it | it | | |

## Exercise 2

Read the interview between the doctor and Perry. Fill in the correct subject or object pronouns.

**1. Doctor:** How often do you see these spots before your eyes?

    **Perry:** (a) _____ see (b) _____ every time I go outside.

**2. Doctor:** I have some drops here. (a) _____ can put (b) _____ in your eyes.

    **Perry:** No, (c) _____ don't need (d) _____. My eyes are fine when I'm inside.

3. **Doctor:** Hmmm. Do you want to try sunglasses?

   **Perry:** No, (a) _____ never wear sunglasses. (b) _____ don't like

   (c) _____.

4. **Doctor:** Are you nervous about your job these days, Perry?

   **Perry:** Of course, I'm not nervous about my job. (a) _____ love

   (b) _____.

5. **Doctor:** Perry, are there any, uh, any problems between you and your wife?

   **Perry:** No, doctor. My wife is wonderful. (a) _____ adore

   (b) _____.

6. **Doctor:** Does she know about the spots?

   **Perry:** Yes, she does. (a) _____ is worried about (b) _____ too.

   But she is strong. (c) _____ always tries to help

   (d) _____.

7. **Doctor:** You're a lucky man, Perry. But this problem is serious. (a) _____

   just don't understand (b) _____. (c) _____ really puzzles

   (d) _____.

   **Perry:** So, doctor?

   **Doctor:** Let me think. Here are some pills. I want you to take (e) _____ tonight

   and call (f) _____ in the morning!

   **Perry:** O.K. doctor, but please help (g) _____. (h) _____ am

   very concerned.

167

# Exercise 3

Work with a partner and choose the part of either Perry or the doctor. Role-play the dialogue in Exercise 2.

# Exercise 4

This is a story about a love triangle. Ted has a steady girlfriend, Alice. He also has another girlfriend named Maggie.

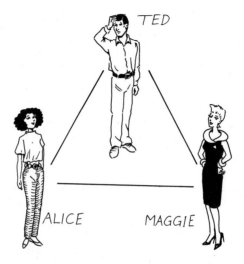

Read the text below and underline the incorrect pronouns. Then write the correction above the pronoun.

Ted loves his girlfriend Alice. He also likes Maggie. Alice doesn't know about she. Maggie works with Ted. She sees he every day. He sometimes invites she to dinner. He likes to talk with she. He doesn't love Maggie, but she loves he. She thinks about he all the time. Ted doesn't want to leave Alice. He can't tell she about Maggie. Ted cares for both Alice and Maggie. He doesn't know what to do. He doesn't want to hurt they. He says to himself, "What's the matter with me? Alice loves I and I love she. I must end my relationship with Maggie!"

# *Focus 3*

## USE
## Using Object Pronouns
## for Reference

USE

- Use object pronouns to refer to a noun phrase in an earlier part of the text. It is important to make a clear connection between the object pronoun and the noun phrase it refers to.

Maggie is in love with Ted. She thinks about **him** all the time.

## *Exercise 5*

Pom Pom Perry is confused. He is talking to himself on his way home. Look at the underlined object pronouns. Draw an arrow from each object pronoun to the noun phrase it refers to and circle the noun phrase.

"I don't understand (these spots). I am really worried about <u>them</u> now. It's strange. Sometimes I see

<u>them</u> and sometimes I don't see <u>them</u>. My eyes are fine. The doctor checked <u>them</u>. My vision is good.

The doctor tested <u>it</u>. The doctor's a good doctor. I can't be angry at <u>him</u>. Maybe it's my hat. When I

wear <u>it</u>, I see the spots. When I don't wear <u>it</u>, I don't see <u>them</u>. That's it! It's my hat! I'm allergic to

my hat! I must discuss this with the doctor. I'll call <u>him</u> tomorrow."

## *Exercise 6*

Alice finds out about Maggie. She talks to Ted on the phone when he comes home late one night. Fill in the correct object pronouns.

1. **Alice:** Hello, Ted. Do you remember (a) _____?

   **Ted:** Of course I remember (b) _____, Alice. You're my girlfriend!

2. **Alice:** I know about Maggie, Ted.

   **Ted:** What? You know about (a) _____?

3.   **Alice:** That's right, Ted. I know everything about you and (a) _____.

   **Ted:** How do you know?

   **Alice:** Your secretary, Ted. I meet (b) _____ for lunch sometimes. She knows about (c) _____ and Maggie.

4.   **Alice:** She can't come between (a) _____, Ted.

   **Ted:** I know, Alice. Don't worry. I don't love (b) _____.

   **Alice:** Do you love (c) _____?

   **Ted:** Of course, I love you, Alice! I want to marry (d) _____!

5.   **Alice:** You can't see (a) _____ again, Ted.

   **Ted:** O.K., Alice. O.K. Trust (b) _____.

## Exercise 7

Using the following cues, ask a partner questions with *how often*. Your partner answers using object pronouns.

> **EXAMPLE:**     You: How often do you call your parents?
> Your Partner: I call them once a week.

1. call your parents?
2. do your laundry?
3. visit the dentist?
4. wash your car?
5. read the newspaper?

6. brush your teeth?
7. wash your hair?
8. see your friends?
9. drink coffee?
10. do the shopping?

# Activities

### Activity 1

Write down the names of three people you respect. Then write the reasons why you respect them. Share your answers with a partner. Your partner will ask questions about your choices.

> **EXAMPLE:** You: I respect my father.
>
> Your partner: Why do you respect him?
>
> You: People like him. He's very generous. He always helps his friends.

### Activity 2

Write down the names of ten occupations on ten pieces of paper. Choose one of the pieces of paper and make sentences for the class so they can guess the profession. You get one point for each sentence you make. When the class guesses the profession, another student picks a piece of paper. The person with the most points in the end wins.

> **EXAMPLE:** (You choose "firefighter")
>
> You say: This person wears a hat.
>
> He or she drives a vehicle.
>
> He or she saves people.

### Activity 3

Each person in the class writes down a personal habit—good or bad. Then each person reads his or her statement to the class. The class asks questions to find out more information. (Possible habits: play with your hair, tap your feet, wash your hair every day.)

> **EXAMPLE:** You : I bite my fingernails.
>
> Class: Why do you bite them?
>
> You : Because I'm nervous!

### Activity 4

Think of the different things people have. Then give clues so that your classmates can guess the object.

> **EXAMPLE:** Clues: The Japanese make a lot of them.
>
> We drive them. What are they?
>
> Answer: Cars!

# 16

## Can versus Know How To; And/But

## Task

Part I. Write the appropriate expression under each picture.

use a word processor       play a musical instrument
cook       dance
sing       swim
drive a car       speak many languages
touch your toes       draw

_____   _____   _____   _____   _____

_____   _____   _____   _____   _____

Part II. Who is the most versatile member of your class? Who can do **all** of the things in the pictures? Put a check next to all the things that you can do. Count one point for each activity. The student with the highest score wins the contest.

     Your score: _____.

# Focus 1

FORM ● MEANING

## The Modal *Can*

- *Can* is a modal verb that expresses ability. Place it before the base form of the main verb.
  - Do not use *to* after *can*.
    - **(a)** I **can speak** French.
      NOT: I can to speak French.
  - When you use *can*, do not add an *s* to the main verb in the 3rd person singular.
    - **(b)** She **can play** tennis.
      NOT: She can plays tennis.
- To make negative statements, use *cannot*, or the contraction *can't*.

| Affirmative | | Negative | | Negative Contraction | |
|---|---|---|---|---|---|
| I<br>You<br>He<br>She<br>It<br>We<br>You<br>They | can speak<br>English. | I<br>You<br>He<br>She<br>It<br>We<br>You<br>They | cannot speak<br>Chinese. | I<br>You<br>He<br>She<br>It<br>We<br>You<br>They | can't speak<br>French. |

## Exercise 1

Go back to the Task. With a partner, take turns making statements aloud about what you can/cannot do.

**EXAMPLES:** "I can't play a musical instrument."
"I can cook."

## Exercise 2

Use the pictures and cues below to make affirmative or negative statements. The first one has been done for you.

**EXAMPLE:**

1. He / hear his mother
   *He can't hear his mother.*

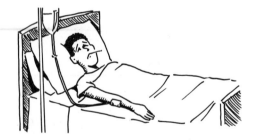

2. She / swim

3. They / eat with chopsticks

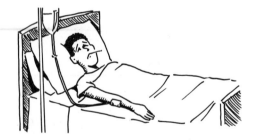

4. She / open the jar

5. He / walk

6. He / go to work

7. They / see the screen

8. They / speak English

## Exercise 3

What can you do in English? On the self-assessment grid below, check **yes** for things you can do and **no** for things you can't do. Then exchange papers with a partner. Tell the class what your partner can and cannot do in English.

**EXAMPLE:** My partner can introduce someone.

| Self-Assessment Grid | Yes | No |
|---|---|---|
| 1. I can introduce someone. _____ | | |
| 2. I can ask about the price of an object. _____ | | |
| 3. I can describe people and places. _____ | | |
| 4. I can make a polite request. _____ | | |
| 5. I can give directions. _____ | | |
| 6. I can give advice. _____ | | |
| 7. I can ask for information about English. _____ | | |

# Focus 2

FORM

## Yes/No Questions with *Can*

FORM

- To make questions, put *can* in front of the subject. Use *can* and *can't* in short answers. Do not use *do* or *does* with *can* or *can't*.

  **(a) Can** you use a word processor?    Yes, I **can.**
  No, I **can't.**

  **(b) Can** he cook?    Yes, he **can.**
  No, he **can't.**

      NOT: Does he can cook?

# Exercise 4

Write yes/no questions with *can*. Remember, these questions with *can* are about ability. Then, under *Your Response,* check yes/no to give your own opinion about each question. Leave the columns under *Total* blank for now.

| | Your Response | | Total | |
|---|---|---|---|---|
| | Yes | No | Yes | No |
| 1. a woman / work as a fire fighter _____ ? | | | | |
| 2. women / be good combat soldiers _____ ? | | | | |
| 3. a man / be a good nurse _____ ? | | | | |
| 4. men / teach kindergarten children _____ ? | | | | |
| 5. women / be mounted police officers _____ ? | | | | |
| 6. a woman / be a construction worker _____ ? | | | | |
| 7. a man / work as a housekeeper _____ ? | | | | |
| 8. a woman / be President of a country _____ ? | | | | |

# Exercise 5

Go back to Exercise 4. Take turns reading the questions aloud. Do a survey by counting how many students say yes and how many say no to each question. Write the total number of yes and no answers in the appropriate column. How does your opinion compare to your classmates' opinions? Give reasons for your answers.

**EXAMPLE:** Women can be mounted police officers. They can ride horses. They can fight crime. They can use guns.

## Exercise 6

Test your knowledge. Make yes/no questions using the cues below. Then discuss your answers.

1. people / live without food for six months
2. a computer / think
3. smoking / cause cancer
4. an airplane / fly from New York to Paris in four hours
5. a person / run 25 miles an hour
6. a river / flow uphill
7. we / communicate with people on other planets
8. a person / learn a language in a week
9. cars / run on alcohol
10. you / think of any more questions

## Focus 3

MEANING

# Expressing Ability:
# *Can* versus *Know How To*

**MEANING**

- To express **learned ability**:
  - Use *can* / Use *know how to*
    - **(a)** I can speak French.
    - **(b)** She knows how to cook.
    - **(c)** He doesn't know how to do the laundry.
    - **(d)** Can you fix a car?      Yes, I can.
                                       No, I can't.
    - **(e)** Do you know how to type?   Yes, I do.
                                          No, I don't.
- To express **natural ability:**
  - Use *can* / Do not use *know how to*
    - **(f)** I can breathe
             NOT: I know how to breathe.
    - **(g)** I can see.
             NOT: I know how to see.

## Exercise 7

Make affirmative or negative statements aloud using the cues below. Make one statement with *can* and one with *know how to* to express learned ability. Make only one statement with *can* to express natural ability.

1. A blind person / see
2. A dog / live for twenty years
3. Infants / walk
4. A deaf person / hear
5. Fish / breathe on land
6. Mechanics / fix cars
7. Men / take care of babies
8. A man / have a baby
9. Doctors / cure some diseases

# Focus 4

FORM  ●  MEANING

## Sentence Connectors
## And / But

FORM
MEANING

- To connect two sentences and show similarity (A is the **same** as B), use *and*. If the subject is the same for the two verbs, it is not necessary to repeat the subject or *can*.

  **(a)** I can rollerskate **and I can** ski.

  **(b)** I can rollerskate and ski.

- To connect two sentences and show contrast (A is the **opposite** of B), use *but*. Use a comma to separate sentence A from *but*.

  **(c)** I can rollerskate, **but I can't** ski.

  **(d)** I can read a short story, but I can't read a novel.

## Exercise 8

How skilled are you? Make statements about yourself using *can/know how to* with *and/but*.

   **EXAMPLE:** I *can* use a typewriter, *but I can't* use a word processor.

1. use a typewriter / use a word processor
2. rollerskate / rollerblade
3. drive a car / drive a stick shift car
4. take a photograph / make a video tape

5. use the telephone / use an answering machine
6. swim / dive
7. cook / bake
8. record a television show on videotape / program my VCR

Now make two statements of your own:
9. ...
10. ...

# Focus 5

## Communication Strategy

USE

- When you are not sure your English is correct, check by asking: **Can I say, "She doesn't can to whistle" in English?**
- When you don't know how to say something in English, get help by asking: **How can I say "..." in English?**

To explain what you can't say, you can **mime the word:**

Use your hands
to show "tremendous."

Use facial expressions
to show "sour."

Use your body to show actions
like "sweeping."

## Exercise 9

Look at the pictures. First mime each action and then ask your classmates questions to find out how to say each word.

1.    2.    3.

4.    5.    6.

**179**

# Activities

## Activity 1

What abilities do you need to do each of the five jobs below? Write the job(s) next to each ability. Then make statements aloud about the abilities you have. The class or group will decide which job is good for you.

### JOBS

**A.** nurse
**B.** teacher
**C.** superintendent
**D.** secretary
**E.** hotel manager

### ABILITIES

1. follow directions: *nurse, secretary*

2. type: _____

3. explain things clearly: _____

4. help people: _____

5. fix a leaky faucet: _____

6. work under pressure: _____

7. solve problems: _____

8. work irregular hours: _____

9. get along with people: _____

10. file: _____

11. keep a building clean: _____

**Activity 2**

Read the following job advertisement from the classified ad section of the newspaper. This is an ad for a babysitter. Write eight questions using *can / know how to* or simple present tense that you would use to interview applicants for the job.

> WANTED: Babysitter
> Responsible, mature,
> flexible woman.
> Full time work five days a week,
> 8:00–5:00, some evenings
> and weekends.
> Must speak English
> and be able to drive.
> Laundry, light housekeeping,
> and cooking required.
> Experience with young children
> necessary. References requested.

> **EXAMPLE:** Do you know how to cook?

**Activity 3**

What can you do that your parents or other people you know cannot do? What can other people do that you can't do? Write five sentences about this.

> **EXAMPLES:** My mother can't ride a bicycle, but I can.
>
> My mother can sew, but I can't.

**Activity 4**

Do you think it's better to be a man or a woman? Give as many reasons as you can for your opinion.

> **EXAMPLE:** It's better to be a woman. A woman can have children...

**Activity 5**

Ask yes/no questions for each box.

> **EXAMPLE:** Can you touch your toes?

If the person says "yes," write his/her name in the box. Then go to another student and ask another question. If the person says "no," ask the other questions until he or she says "yes." Then write his or her name in the box. At the end of the activity, each student who answered "yes" must perform the action in the box!

| touch his or her toes | dance | draw a horse | whistle |
|---|---|---|---|
| sing a rap song | make a braid | say "Hello" in four languages | pronounce the word "Psychology" |
| tell a joke in English | win an arm wrestle | divide 36 by 9 | juggle |

# 17

# Adverbs of Manner

## *Task*

This is the Long-Life Insurance Company's Accident and Health Record for one of their clients, Bill Rogers. Look at his record and then read the sentences below. Check either Yes, No, or I Don't Know in the columns.

---

### *Long-Life Insurance Company*
### *Health and Accident Record*

| | | | |
|---|---|---|---|
| Name: | Bill Rogers | Sex: | Male |
| Date of Birth: | 9/20/58 | Marital Status: | Single |
| Height: | 5'7" | Weight: | 350 lbs. |

Smoking: Started Smoking 1975 — Smokes 2 packs/day

Offenses: Ticket for speeding:   5/19/82, 8/15/86
Ticket for going through red light:   7/14/87, 9/20/88, 12/31/90
 7/4/92
Arrested for drunk driving:   2/14/89 (license revoked 6 months)
Crashed into fire hydrant:   3/17/90

---

| | Yes | No | I Don't Know |
|---|---|---|---|
| **1.** Bill is a careful driver. | | | |
| **2.** He eats moderately. | | | |
| **3.** He drives slowly. | | | |
| **4.** He's a heavy drinker. | | | |
| **5.** He works hard. | | | |
| **6.** He drives carelessly. | | | |
| **7.** He is a big eater. | | | |
| **8.** He drives fast. | | | |
| **9.** He dresses neatly. | | | |
| **10.** He is a heavy smoker. | | | |

# Focus 1

## Adjectives and Adverbs of Manner

FORM
MEANING

- Look at these two sentences:
  **(a)** He is a **careful** driver.
  **(b)** He drives **carefully**.
- In sentence **(a)**, *careful* is an adjective. It describes the noun *driver*. Place the adjective before the noun.
- In sentence **(b)**, *carefully* is an adverb of manner. It describes the verb *drive*; in other words, the action of the sentence. The adverb answers the question "how." When you ask, "How does he drive?" the answer is "carefully." Place the adverb after the verb or, if there is an object, after the object.
  **(c)** He drives his car **carefully.**
  NOT: He drives carefully his car.

## Exercise 1

Go back to the sentences in the Task and underline all the adjectives and circle all the adverbs.

  **EXAMPLE:** Bill is a <u>careful</u> driver.
  He eats (moderately).

# Focus 2

## Spelling

FORM

- Many adverbs are formed from adjectives by adding *-ly*. Sometimes the spelling changes.

| Adjective | Rule | Adverb |
|-----------|------|--------|
| slow beautiful | Add *-ly* | slowly beautifully |
| heavy | Adjectives that end in *y*, change *y* to *i* and add *-ly* | heavily |
| terrible | Adjectives that end with *e*, drop *e* and add *-ly* | terribly |
| fantastic | Many adjectives that end with *ic* , add *-ally* | fantastically |

- Some adverbs have the same form as adjectives:

  **(a)** Monique's a **fast** driver.  **(c)** We have an **early** dinner.

  **(b)** She drives **fast**.  **(d)** We have dinner **early**.

  **(e)** We are **hard** workers.  **(g)** We eat a **late** lunch.

  **(f)** We work **hard**.  **(h)** We eat lunch **late**.

- And some adverbs are irregular.

  **(i)** Joel's a **good** cook.

  **(j)** He cooks **well**.

## Exercise 2

The sentences below are written in the pattern *be* + **adjective** + **noun.** Rewrite the sentence, using the adverb.

> **EXAMPLE:** My son is a careful driver.
>
> *My son drives carefully.*

1. Baryshnikov is a graceful dancer.

   _____

2. Ben Johnson is a fast runner.

   _____

3. My father is a heavy smoker.

   _____

4. The President is a good speaker.

   _____

5. Pavarotti is a wonderful singer.

   _____

6. Teachers are hard workers.

   _____

7. Our teacher is a clear speaker.

   _____

8. Some children are slow learners.

_____

9. These painters are sloppy workers.

_____

10. She is a quick reader.

_____

# Focus 3

## Focusing on the Performer or the Activity

USE

- How do you know when to use the adjective or adverb? Look at these two sentences.
  **(a)** Marlon Brando is a good **actor**.
  **(b)** Marlon Brando **acts** well.

When you want to focus on the **performer,** use the adjective.
When you want to focus on the **activity,** use the adverb.

## Exercise 3

Read these sentences and decide if the focus is on the performer or the activity. Check the correct column.

| | Performer | Activity |
|---|---|---|
| 1. Meryl Streep is a fantastic actress. | | |
| 2. My students learn easily. | | |
| 3. Steven dances slowly. | | |
| 4. Karl's a fast runner. | | |
| 5. My children are good cooks. | | |
| 6. Bill Rogers drives carelessly. | | |
| 7. That politician is a bad speaker. | | |
| 8. Marco speaks to his parents impolitely. | | |

**185**

## Exercise 4

Read the statements and fill in the blanks with the most appropriate adverb.

**EXAMPLE:** "Sh, don't say a word," she said quietly.

| politely | sadly | nervously | quickly | shyly |
| incorrectly | impolitely | happily | angrily | kindly |

1. "I just got engaged!" she said _____ .

2. "My dog just died," he said _____ .

3. "I'm in a rush," she said _____ .

4. "I ain't got no mistakes," he said _____ .

5. "May I make a telephone call?" she asked _____ .

6. "Bring me a menu, fast!" he said _____ .

7. "This is the last time I'm telling you! Clean up your room!" she said _____ .

8. "Wwwwwwill yyyyou mmmmmarry mmmmme?" he asked _____ .

9. "Please, don't look at me," she said _____ .

10. "Can I help you?" he asked _____ .

## Exercise 5

Read the following clues and guess which occupation each describes. The choices of occupations are given below.

A. Secretary for the U.N.          D. Artist
B. Lawyer                          E. Emergency Medical Technician or
C. Teacher                             Paramedic

1. I work hard all day.
   I prepare lessons carefully.
   I treat my students respectfully.

   I am a/an _____ .

2. I respond to emergencies very quickly.
   I drive very fast.
   I treat people carefully.

   I am a/an _____ .

3. I solve problems constantly.
   I speak three languages fluently.
   I act diplomatically.

   I am a/an _____ .

4. I draw beautifully.
   I paint well.
   I think creatively.

   I am a/an _____ .

5. I defend my clients well.
   I earn money happily.
   I stay at work late.

   I am a/an _____ .

# Exercise 6

Using adverbs, write sentences to answer the *why* questions below.

1. Why is Carrie a good teacher?

   **(a)** speak/slow *She speaks slowly.*

   **(b)** pronounce words/clear _____

   **(c)** prepare/careful _____

2. Why is Bernice a good secretary?

   **(d)** type/fast _____

   **(e)** answer the phone/polite _____

   **(f)** take messages/accurate _____

3. Why is Mike a good truck driver?

   **(g)** drive/slow _____

   **(h)** respond/quick _____

4. Why is Paula Abdul a good performer?

   **(i)** sing/good _____

   **(j)** dance/fantastic _____

5. Why is Miyuki a good language learner?

**(k)** study/hard _____

**(l)** guess/intelligent _____

**(m)** ask questions/constant _____

## Exercise 7

Read the statements below. Write a sentence that focuses on the performer or one that focuses on the activity.

  **EXAMPLE:** Can you believe it! Jeryl won the marathon!
      *She is a fast runner. She runs fast.*

1. Just look at Joe! He just finished one cigarette and is now smoking another.

  _____

2. My mom cooks a great meal every night. She loves to create new recipes.

  _____

3. Gloria goes to work at 8:00 A.M. and leaves at 6:00 P.M. She never takes a break.

  _____

4. He got another speeding ticket yesterday. That's his third ticket this year!

  _____

5. Bob can sing, dance, act, and even play the piano!

  _____

## Focus 4

MEANING

# Intensifiers with Adjectives and Adverbs of Manner

MEANING

- You can make the focus on the performer or activity stronger by using *very*.
  **(a)** She is a **very** skillful sailor.
  **(b)** Some students don't do **very** well on tests.
- The intensifier *very* goes before the adjective or adverb.

# Exercise 8

Create one or two sentences using *very* + adverb with the information provided in the sentences below.

**EXAMPLES:** I don't want Henry to drive me downtown.
*He doesn't drive very carefully. He drives very fast.*

1. Harold drives 40 miles an hour in a 65-mile-an-hour zone!
2. I can't understand Bruce when he speaks.
3. They just hired Patricia as a head chef for that fancy restaurant uptown.
4. I think Sam deserves the promotion.
5. Rose is a great secretary. She types 100 words a minute.

# Activities

### Activity 1

Work in a group. Each member should choose an adverb of manner (slowly, fast, nervously, happily, busily, etc.). Do not tell the other students in your group the adverb you chose. The students in your group will tell you to do something "in that manner." Mime the action, and the other students will try to guess your adverb.

**EXAMPLE:** (First student chooses the adverb *slowly*.)

**Students in your group say:**
Walk to the door in that manner.
Sit down in that manner.
Drink a cup of coffee in that manner.
Shake my hand in that manner.

### Activity 2

In a group, write sentences using adverbs for a guessing game like the one in Exercise 5. Say your sentences aloud and have another team guess the answer.

### Activity 3

Are you a good student? A good mother? A good friend? A good worker? Write a paragraph explaining why or why not. Use adverbs of manner.

### Activity 4

Remember Bill Rogers from the Task? Do you think he is a good insurance risk? Write five sentences telling why you think he is or is not a good insurance risk.

# 18

# Present Progressive Tense

## Task

Read the story. Match the numbered sentences in the dialogue to the corresponding actions in the picture. Write the numbers next to the actions.

Meet the Harrisons. Regis Harrison is a businessman, and Robin Harrison is a college professor. They have three children—Frankie, Jimmy, and Suzy. Robin teaches three nights a week. She usually stays home and takes care of the children every day. Regis usually works every day and watches the children three nights a week. But today Robin is attending a meeting at the college, so Regis is staying home and taking care of the children. It is 7:30 P.M. and Robin is walking through the door right now...

**Robin:** Hello dear. Is everything under control here?

**Regis:** ...under control? Are you kidding! Everything's going wrong here....

1. The food's burning in the oven.
2. The pots are boiling over on the stove.
3. Suzy's lying in front of the television, hypnotized.
4. The television is blasting, and it's giving me a terrible headache!
5. Frankie and the dog are fighting over a stuffed animal.
6. Frankie is crying.
7. The dog's growling.
8. Jimmy's playing cowboy on my back.
9. His cowboy boots are hurting my stomach!
10. The phone's ringing. I'm going crazy here! Help!

# Focus 1

## FORM

# Affirmative Statements in the Present Progressive

**FORM**

- To form the present progressive tense, use the present tense of the verb *be* + the base form of the verb with an *-ing* ending.

| Subject | *Be* | Base Form of the Verb + *-ing* | |
|---------|------|-------------------------------|---|
| I | am | working | today. |
| You | are | staying | home today. |
| He She It | is | playing. | |
| We You They | are | watching | television. |

- Affirmative Contractions (with *Be*)

| Subject/ *Be* Contraction | Base Form of the Verb + *-ing* | |
|---------------------------|-------------------------------|---|
| I'm | taking | the day off today. |
| You're | staying | home today. |
| He's She's It's | working | now. |
| We're You're They're | staying | home today. |

## Exercise 1

Go back and read the introduction and dialogue in the Task. Circle all the present progressive verbs.

**EXAMPLE:** But today Robin (is attending) a meeting at the college.

# *Focus 2*

FORM

## Spelling of Verbs Ending in *-ing*

FORM

| If the verb: | Rule | Spelling | |
|---|---|---|---|
| **1.** ends in a single *-e* | Drop the final *-e*; add *-ing*. | write | writing |
| **2.** has one syllable with consonant-vowel-consonant | Double the consonant and add *-ing*. | sit<br>swim | sitting<br>swimming |
| (except verbs ending in *-w*, *-x*, or *-y*) | Do not double the final consonant. | show<br>play | showing<br>playing |
| **3.** has more than one syllable, the last syllable = consonant-vowel-consonant and the stress is on the last syllable | Double the final consonant, add *-ing*. | begin<br>forget | beginning<br>forgetting |
| If stress is not on the last syllable | Do not double the final consonant. | listen<br>happen | listening<br>happening |
| **4.** ends in *-ie* | Change the *-ie* to *-y* and add *-ing*. | lie<br>die | lying<br>dying |
| **5.** For all other verbs | Add *-ing* to the base form of the verb. | talk<br>study<br>do<br>agree | talking<br>studying<br>doing<br>agreeing |

## Exercise 2

Complete the sentences by writing the correct spelling of the present progressive form of the verbs in parentheses.

1. Frankie ＿＿＿＿＿＿＿＿ (scream).

2. Frankie ＿＿＿＿＿＿＿＿ (make) a lot of noise.

3. The dog ＿＿＿＿＿＿＿＿ (bite) the stuffed animal.

4. The dog ＿＿＿＿＿＿＿＿ (growl).

**5.** Frankie _____ (sit) on the floor.

**6.** Regis _____ (worry) about dinner.

**7.** Jimmy _____ (choke) his father.

**8.** Regis _____ (get) frustrated.

**9.** Regis _____ (begin) to feel very tired .

**10.** Robin _____ (smile).

**11.** Robin's feet _____ (kill) her.

**12.** She _____ (die) to take her shoes off.

## Focus 3

FORM

# Negative Statements in the Present Progressive

FORM

- To make a negative, put *not* between *be* and the verb + *-ing*.

| Subject *Be* *Not* Verb + *-ing* | Negative Contraction | *Be* Contraction + *Not* |
|---|---|---|
| I  am *not*  cooking dinner. | | I'm  not cooking. |
| You  are *not*  working. | You  aren't working. | You're  not working. |
| He<br>She } is  *not*  listening.<br>It | He<br>She } isn't  listening.<br>It | He's<br>She's } not listening.<br>It's |
| We<br>You } are *not*  smiling.<br>They | We<br>You } aren't smiling.<br>They | We're<br>You're } not smiling.<br>They're |

## Exercise 3

Using negative contractions, say the following sentences aloud.

1. Robin / take care of the children today
2. Robin / prepare dinner tonight
3. Robin / stay home today
4. Regis / have a good day today
5. The children / listen to Regis
6. Suzy / help Regis
7. Regis / answer the phone
8. Regis / pay attention to the dinner in the oven
9. Regis / smile
10. Regis / enjoy fatherhood today

**193**

# Focus 4

## Talking about Actions in Progress

USE

- One use of the present progressive is to talk about an action that is happening now.
  - **(a)** Frankie is screaming.
  - **(b)** Frankie and the dog are fighting over a stuffed animal.
- Use the time expressions below to show that the action is ongoing and not completed:

  now

  right now

  at the moment

## Exercise 4

Look at the cartoon. Use the verbs given to make affirmative or negative statements.

1. Mrs. Bainbridge / have / a party at her house this evening.
2. The guests / talk / in the living room.
3. Mr. and Mrs. Parker / talk/ to the other guests.
4. Mr. and Mrs. Parker / feel / very bored right now.
5. Mr. and Mrs. Parker / enjoy / the party.
6. Mr. and Mrs. Parker / leave / by the front door.
7. Mr. and Mrs. Parker / climb/ out the window at the moment.
8. Mr. and Mrs. Parker / try to escape.
9. Mr. Parker / hold his hat between his teeth.
10. Mrs. Parker / help Mr. Parker climb out the window.

# Focus 5

## Talking about Temporary
## Actions and Changing Situations

USE

- Another use of the present progressive is to talk about an action that is temporary (the action is continuing, but only for a limited period of time), or a situation that is changing.

**(a)** Regis is staying home and taking care of the children today.

**(b)** These days more and more women are working.

- Use the time expressions below to show that the action is temporary.

| today | nowadays | this month |
| these days | this week | this year |

## Exercise 5

Write a sentence for each cue below using the time expressions from Focus 5 (today, these days, nowadays).

**EXAMPLE:** *Nowadays, women are getting more education.*

1. Women / get good jobs _____

2. Women / work outside the home _____

3. Women / earn money _____

4. Men / share household responsibilities _____

5. Husbands / help their wives _____

6. Fathers / spend time with their children _____

7. Family life / change _____

Add three sentences of your own.

# *Focus 6*

## Choosing Simple Present or Present Progressive

USE

- The present progressive and the simple present are used differently.

| Simple Present | Present Progressive |
|---|---|
| • habits and repeated actions<br>   **(a)** Suzy **usually** does her homework in the afternoon.<br>• things that are true in general<br>   **(c)** Robin **usually** stays home with the children. | • actions in progress now<br>   **(b)** Suzy's watching TV **right now.**<br><br>• actions that are temporary, not habitual<br>   **(d)** Robin is teaching at the college **this year**.<br>• situations that are changing<br>   **(e)** **Nowadays** men are spending more time with their children. |

- Review of Time Expressions

| Simple Present | Present Progressive |
|---|---|
| *always* | *at present* |
| *often* | *now* |
| *usually* | *right now* |
| *sometimes* | *at the moment* |
| *seldom* | *today* |
| *rarely* | *this evening* |
| *never* | *this week* |
| *every day* | *this month* |
| *once a week* | *these days* |
| *on the weekends* | *nowadays* |

## Exercise 6

Read each statement. If the statement is in the simple present, make a second statement in the present progressive. If the statement is in the present progressive, make a second statement in the simple present.

**EXAMPLE:** Suzy usually watches soap operas.
*Tonight she is watching cartoons.*

**Simple Present**

1. Robin usually takes care of the children.

2. _____

3. The children usually behave at home.

4. _____

5. Robin usually cooks dinner in the evening.

**Present Progressive**

A. _____

B. Tonight, Robin isn't cooking dinner.

C. _____

D. Suzy is watching TV today.

E. _____

## Exercise 7

Using the verbs below, make one statement in the simple present about something you do regularly. Make another statement in the present progressive showing that you are not doing that activity right now. Connect the two statements with "but."

**EXAMPLE:** smoke / *I smoke every day, but I'm not smoking now.*

1. do my homework
2. write letters home
3. sleep
4. cry
5. sing

6. eat
7. drink coffee
8. read the newspaper
9. daydream
10. cook

## Focus 7

MEANING

# Stative Verbs

MEANING

- Some verbs are not usually used in the present progressive tense. These verbs do not report actions. They describe experiences, conditions, or states, and they are called "stative verbs."

**(a)** Regis **loves** his children.
NOT: Regis is loving his children.

**(b)** Regis **seems** frustrated.
NOT: Regis is seeming frustrated.

- Here are some other stative verbs:

| Emotions | Mental States | Wants | Senses | Possession |
|----------|---------------|-------|--------|------------|
| *like* | *think* | *prefer* | *hear* | *belong* |
| *love* | *believe* | *want* | *see* | *own* |
| *hate* | *understand* | *need* | *smell* | *have* |
| | *seem* | | *taste* | |
| | *forget* | | *feel* | |
| | *remember* | | | |
| | *know* | | | |
| | *mean* | | | |

- Note: The verbs *think, see, feel, have* are commonly used in the present progressive with different meanings.

| Present Simple/State | Present Progressive/Action |
|----------------------|----------------------------|
| **(c)** I **think** you're a good student. (The verb *think* means *believe*.) | **(d)** I **am thinking** about you. (The verb *think* describes an ongoing action or process.) |
| **(e)** I **see** a child in the playground. (*See* is about the visual sense.) | **(f)** **I'm seeing** a wonderful man. (*See* means "dating" here.) |
| **(g)** I **have** two cars. (*Have* means "possession.") | **(h)** **I'm having** a good time. (*Have* is not about possession. It describes an experience.) |

## *Exercise 8*

Fill in the blanks using the present progressive or simple present form of the verb. Read the dialogues aloud, using contractions.

1.  **Regis:** Suzy, I need your help here.

    **Suzy:** But, Dad, you (a) _____ (need) my help every 5 minutes! I

    (b) _____ (watch) TV right now ...!

2. It is 3:00. The telephone rings:

    **Regis:** Hello.

    **Laura:** Hello, Regis. What are you (a) _____ (do) home in the middle of the

    afternoon?

**Regis:** Oh, hi, Laura. I know I (b) _____ (be) never home in the afternoon, but today I (c) _____ (try) to be a househusband!

**Laura:** Did Robin leave you, Regis?

**Regis:** Very funny, Laura! Robin (d) _____ (attend) a meeting at the college.

3. Jimmy interrupts Regis's telephone conversation:

**Regis:** Hold on a minute, Laura...Jimmy (a) _____ (pull) on my leg! Jimmy, I (b) _____ (talk) to Mommy's friend Laura right now. You (c) _____ (know) Laura. She (d) _____ (come) to see Mommy every week. Now just wait a minute, please...

**Laura:** Is everything OK, Regis?

**Regis:** Oh yes, Laura, don't worry. We (e) _____ (do) just fine. Talk to you later. Bye!

4. It is 5:30. The telephone rings:

**Regis:** Hello.

**Robin:** Hi, honey! The meeting (a) _____ (be) over. I (b) _____ (come) home. What (c) _____ (happen)? I hope the children (d) _____ (behave).

**Regis:** They (e) _____ (behave) like wild animals, Robin. I (f) _____ (talk) to them, but they do not listen to a word I say. Please come home soon.

**Robin:** You sound terrible! Can I bring anything home, dear?

**Regis:** Yes, a bottle of aspirin!

## Exercise 9

Work with a partner. You number the pictures below in any order from 1–12. Then describe your picture #1 by making one statement with a stative verb and another statement in the present progressive. Your partner finds the picture you are talking about, and writes the letter of the picture in the blanks. Now repeat the procedure with your partner describing the pictures.

**EXAMPLE:** "In picture #1, a man seems/looks very nervous. He's smoking a cigarette."

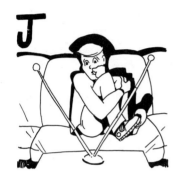  

| PICTURE | LETTER | PICTURE | LETTER |
|---------|--------|---------|--------|
| # 1 | _____ | # 7 | _____ |
| # 2 | _____ | # 8 | _____ |
| # 3 | _____ | # 9 | _____ |
| # 4 | _____ | #10 | _____ |
| # 5 | _____ | #11 | _____ |
| # 6 | _____ | #12 | _____ |

# Focus 8

## Yes/No Questions in the Present Progressive

- To make a question in the present progressive, move the verb *be* in front of the subject.

    Is Frankie crying?

| Yes/No Questions | Short Answers |
|---|---|
| Am  I           studying? | Yes, you are. /  No, you aren't.<br>No, you're not. |
| Are  you         having a good day? | Yes, I am. /   No, I'm not. |
| Is  { he / she / it }  working? | Yes, she is. /   No, she isn't.<br>No, she's not. |
| Are  { you / we / they }  watching TV? | Yes, we are. /   No, we aren't.<br>No, we're not. |

## Exercise 10

Choose an appropriate verb. Then make questions and give short answers.

**EXAMPLE:** Suzy / ... / her father

*Is Suzy helping her father? / No, she isn't.*

| | | | | |
|---|---|---|---|---|
| boil over | lose | hurt | bite | walk |
| take care of | burn | help | fight | smile |

1. children / ... / their father
2. Frankie and the dog / ...
3. the pots / ...
4. their dinner / ...
5. Regis / ... / his patience
6. Jimmy / ... / his father
7. the dog / ... / the stuffed animal
8. Robin / ... / through the door
9. Robin / ...
10. men and women / ... / their children together nowadays?

# Focus 9

## *Wh*-Questions in the Present Progressive

| Question Word | *Be* | Subject | Verb + *-ing* |
|---|---|---|---|
| What | am | I | doing? |
| When<br>Where<br>Why<br>How | are | you | going? |
| Who(m)<br>Who | is<br>is | she | meeting?<br>having a hard day? |

## Exercise 11

Read the answers. Write the questions that ask for the underlined information.

1. Q: _____ ?

   A: Frankie and the dog are fighting <u>because they both want the stuffed animal.</u>

2. Q: _____ ?

   A: Robin is meeting <u>her colleagues</u> today.

3. Q: _____ ?

   A: Robin's thinking that <u>she was lucky to spend the day at work!</u>

4. Q: _____ ?

   A: They're eating peanut butter and jelly sandwiches for dinner <u>because their dinner burned in the oven.</u>

5. Q: _____ ?

   A: <u>Regis</u> is watching the children today.

**203**

6. Q: _____ ?

   A: Regis is taking two aspirins <u>because he has a terrible headache!</u>

7. Q: _____ ?

   A: Robin's meeting is taking place <u>at the college.</u>

8. Q: _____ ?

   A: <u>Robin</u> is walking through the door right now.

9. Q: _____ ?

   A: The children are behaving <u>like wild animals.</u>

10. Q: _____ ?

   A: Regis is feeling <u>very tired</u> right now.

11. Q: _____ ?

   A: <u>The children</u> are making a lot of noise.

# Exercise 12

Error Correction. Rewrite the following sentences correctly.

1. Frankie and the dog are fight.
2. He's having a new TV.
3. The TV is blasts.
4. Why you are working today?
5. Are you needing any help?
6. What Robin is thinking?
7. Is she believing him?
8. Right now, he plays cowboy on his father's back.
9. The soup is smelling bad.
10. Where you are go?

# Activities

## Activity 1

Here's a photo of the Harrisons on their summer vacation. What is going wrong in the picture? Make a list of the things that are wrong.

**EXAMPLE:** Regis is wearing one shoe.

## Activity 2

Your teacher will divide the class into two groups.

Group A should look at the statements in Column A. One student at a time will mime an action. Students in Group B must guess the action. Group B students can ask questions of Group A. Then Group B mimes statements from Column B and Group A guesses the action.

**Column A**

**1.** You are opening the lid of a jar. The lid is on very tight.

**3.** You are watching a very funny TV show.

**5.** You are trying to sleep and a mosquito is bothering you.

**7.** You are crossing a busy street. You are holding a young child by the hand, and carrying a bag of groceries in the other hand.

**9.** You are trying to thread a needle, but you're having trouble finding the eye of the needle.

**Column B**

**2.** You are reading a very sad story.

**4.** You are an expectant father waiting in the delivery room.

**6.** You are sitting at the bar in a noisy disco. At the other side of the bar, there is someone you like. You are trying to get that person's attention.

**8.** You are a dinner guest at a friend's house. Your friend is not a good cook. You don't like the food!

**10.** You are cutting up onions to cook dinner.

## Activity 3

Make up three situations like those above. Write each situation on a separate piece of paper and put all the situations in a hat. Every student will then pick a situation and mime it for the others to guess.

## Activity 4

Bring in photographs of people of different cultures. Give them names, nationalities, occupations, and so on. Write stories about these people using the simple present and the present progressive.

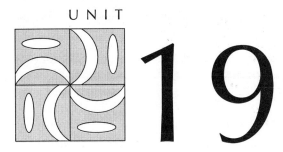

# UNIT 19

# Past Tense of *Be*

## Task

People all over the world know the story "Cinderella." Place the numbers of the appropriate words under each picture from the story.

1. Cinderella
2. the Duke
3. the Fairy Godmother
4. the invitation
5. the Prince
6. the glass slipper
7. the ball
8. the palace
9. the stepmother
10. the stepsisters
11. the magic wand
12. the palace steps

A. _____ _____

B. _____

C. _____

D. _____ _____ _____

E. _____ _____

F. _____ _____

**207**

Using your knowledge of the story "Cinderella," the pictures, and the text below, underline the correct information in parentheses.

Once upon a time, there was a girl named Cinderella.

1. Cinderella was . . . (rich and ugly / <u>poor and beautiful</u>).

2. Her stepmother was . . . (kind / mean).

3. Her stepsisters were . . . (sweet and pretty / spoiled and ugly).

4. One day there was . . . (an invitation to the Prince's ball in the mail / a letter from Heinle and Heinle in the mail).

5. The Prince was . . . (handsome and charming / ugly and nasty). Everyone was excited about the ball.

6. Cinderella was busy all day . . . (with her stepsisters / with the Prince). The stepsisters were dressed and ready, thanks to Cinderella.

7. But when it was time for the ball, Cinderella . . . (was ready / was not ready). She was sad.

8. Cinderella's fairy godmother was there to help her. With her . . . (finger / magic wand) she cast a spell and Cinderella spent a wonderful evening at the ball with the Prince.

9. But at midnight, the spell was broken. Cinderella ran out of the palace. One tiny glass slipper was on her foot; the other glass slipper was . . . (on the palace steps / in her hand).

10. The next day, the Duke was busy around town . . . ("Whose foot was in this tiny glass slipper last night?" / "Whose foot was in this sneaker last night?") he asked.

11. The glass slipper was . . . (the stepmother's / Cinderella's).

12. The Prince was in love with . . . (Cinderella's stepmother / Cinderella).

Soon, Cinderella and the Prince were married. They lived happily ever after. . . .

# *Focus 1*

## Affirmative Statements with *Be* in the Simple Past

FORM

| Subject | Verb | |
|---------|------|---|
| I | was | happy. |
| You | were | jealous. |
| He<br>She<br>It | was | sad. |
| We<br>You<br>They | were | excited. |
| There | was | a prince in the story. |
| There | were | good and bad people in the story. |

- Note: There are no contractions for *be* in the simple past affirmative.

  He was handsome.

  NOT: He's handsome.

## *Exercise 1*

Write the correct form of the verb.

1. Cinderella ＿＿＿＿＿＿＿＿ poor.

2. Cinderella ＿＿＿＿＿＿＿＿ beautiful.

3. Her stepmother ＿＿＿＿＿＿＿＿ mean.

4. There ＿＿＿＿＿＿＿＿ two stepsisters in the story.

5. The stepsisters ＿＿＿＿＿＿＿＿ jealous of Cinderella.

6. The Prince ＿＿＿＿＿＿＿＿ handsome.

7. There ＿＿＿＿＿＿＿＿ a ball at the castle.

8. The fairy godmother and the Duke ＿＿＿＿＿＿＿＿ helpful to Cinderella.

9. The Prince and Cinderella ＿＿＿＿＿＿＿＿ in love.

## Exercise 2

Complete the sentences with the correct form of the verb *be*.

Dear Grandma and Grandpa:
    Here we are in Florida. What a place!
Yesterday we (1) _____ at Disneyworld
all day. The sun (2) _____ really strong,
and it (3) _____ very hot. The lines (4)
_____ long, but the rides and the shows
(5) _____ fun. Disneyworld (6) _____
crowded, but all the people (7) _____ friendly
and polite. Our favorite place (8) _____
Cinderella's castle! The fireworks at night (9)
_____ beautiful. It (10) _____ great
for us, but Dad _____ really tired at the end
of the day!
    We miss you! See you soon.
                Love,
        Melanie and Michele

# Focus 2

FORM

## Negative Statements with *Be* in the Simple Past

**FORM**

- To form a negative statement with the verb *be*, use *not* after the verb.

| Subject | *Be + Not* | | Negative Contractions | | |
|---------|------------|------|------|------|------|
| I | was not | happy. | I | wasn't | happy. |
| You | were not | nasty. | You | weren't | nasty. |
| He<br>She<br>It | was not | sad. | He<br>She<br>It | wasn't | sad. |
| We<br>You<br>They | were not | excited. | We<br>You<br>They | weren't | excited. |
| There | was | no witch. | There | wasn't | any time to say goodnight. |
| There | were | no children at the ball. | There | weren't | any journalists at the ball. |

**210**

## Exercise 3

Read the statements below about the characters in "Cinderella." Make each statement negative. Then make a true affirmative statement.

> **EXAMPLES:** The fairy godmother was mean.
>
> *The fairy godmother wasn't mean. / She was helpful.*
>
> *The fairy godmother wasn't mean. / The stepmother was mean.*

1. Cinderella was rich and ugly.
2. Her stepmother was kind.
3. Her stepsisters were sweet and pretty.
4. The Prince was ugly and nasty.
5. The glass slipper was the stepmother's.
6. The Prince was in love with Cinderella's stepsister.
7. There was a ball at Cinderella's house.
8. There were two princes at the ball.

## Exercise 4

How do Michael and Carol remember their trip to Disneyworld? Write the appropriate affirmative or negative statements with *be*. Then read the dialogue aloud.

**Alice:** Oh, hi, Michael. Hi, Carol. How _____ your trip to Disneyworld?

**Carol:** Hi, Alice. Oh, it _____ fun.

**Michael:** Fun! That vacation _____ (not) fun, it _____ terrible!

**Carol:** But Michael, how can you say that? I think the children and I _____ very satisfied with our vacation.

**Michael:** Carol, the weather _____ boiling hot.

**Carol:** It _____ (not) boiling hot, it _____ very comfortable.

**Michael:** The food _____ (not) very good . . .

**Carol:** The food _____ fine, Michael . . .

**Michael:** The people _____ (not) friendly.

**Carol:** Of course they _____ friendly . . .

**Michael:** The kids _____ a pain in the neck . . .

**Carol:** The kids _____ (not) a pain in the neck, Michael. Come on, they _____ great. Maybe you and I _____ (not) on the same vacation!

## Exercise 5

Read this modern version of the story "Cinderella." Fill in the affirmative or negative form of *be*.

Once upon a time in a big city, there (1) _____ a girl named Cinderella.

Cinderella's parents (2) _____ divorced, so her life (3) _____ difficult.

Cinderella (4) _____ a teenager. She (5) _____ very smart,

but she (6) _____ very neat. Most of the time, her hair (7) _____

combed, and her clothes (8) _____ sloppy. Her poor mother (9) _____

happy about this. She and Cinderella (10) _____ often angry at each other. They

(11) _____ both unhappy. So, Cinderella (12) _____ in therapy.

One day, Cinderella (13) _____ in the waiting room at her psychologist's

office. There (14) _____ a young man in the waiting room. The young man

(15) _____ sloppy too! For Cinderella, this (16) _____ a good sign.

His long hair (17) _____ combed. His jeans (18) _____ torn, and his

sneakers (19) _____ dirty. Cinderella (20) _____ really interested in

him!

When the young man saw Cinderella, he knew he (21) _____ in love.

They (22) _____ made for each other. He (23) _____ very ner-

vous, but his mind (24) _____ made up. "Marry me," he said to Cinderella.

"What???!!!" she said. She (25) _____ in shock. She (26) _____

only a teenager. She (27) _____ ready for marriage. But this young man

(28) _____ pretty attractive!

Just then, the Doctor called his name. "Prince Messie." He (29) _____ a

prince! This (30) _____ unbelievable! Cinderella (31) _____ so happy!

"Yes," she said quickly.

Soon, they (32) _____ married.

They lived happily ever after...

# Focus 3

## Yes/No Questions with *Be* in the Simple Past

FORM

- The verb *be* in simple past questions is like *be* in simple present questions. Put *be* in front of the subject. Do not use *do/does*.

| Yes/No Questions | | | Short Answers | |
|---|---|---|---|---|
| **Verb** | **Subject** | | **Affirmative** | **Negative** **Negative Contraction** |
| Was | I | messy? | Yes, you were. | No, you were not. No, you weren't. |
| Were | you | excited? | Yes, I was. | No, I was not. No, I wasn't. |
| Was | he she it | sad? | Yes, she was. | No, she was not. No, she wasn't. |
| Were | we | happy? | Yes, you were. | No, you were not. No, you weren't. |
| Were | you | satisfied? | Yes, we were. | No, we were not. No, we weren't. |
| Were | they | neat? | Yes, they were. | No, they were not. No, they weren't. |
| Was | there | a big parking lot at Disneyworld? | Yes, there was. | No, there wasn't. |
| Were | there | long lines at Disneyworld? | Yes, there were. | No, there weren't. |

# Exercise 6

Using the cues, make yes/no questions about "Cinderella." Give short answers to the questions.

1. (Cinderella / lucky)
2. (the stepmother / happy at the end of the story)
3. (the end of the story / fair)
4. (the story "Cinderella" / important to you when you were a child)
5. (fairy tales / popular when you were a child)

# Exercise 7

Use the cues to make yes/no questions about the famous people below. Give short answers. If your answer is negative, make a true affirmative statement. The first one has been done for you.

**EXAMPLE:** 1. Gandhi / a famous political leader in England

          *- Was Gandhi a famous political leader in England?*

          *- No, he wasn't.*

          *- He was a famous political leader in India.*

2. Marilyn Monroe / a famous American actress

3. the Marx Brothers / well-known German Communists

4. Mao / a political leader in The People's Republic of China

5. the Beatles / famous hairdressers in the 60s

6. John Kennedy / President of the U.S. in the 60s

7. Martin Luther King / a well-known African leader

8. Nelson Mandela / a prisoner in South Africa

# Exercise 8

Detective Furlock Humes is questioning a police officer about a crime. Using the cues below, write the correct questions with *there* and the verb *be* in the simple past.

**Police Officer:** The body was here, Detective Humes.

**Furlock:** _____ a weapon?

**Police Officer:** Yes, _____ a gun next to the victim's body.

**Furlock:** _____ any fingerprints on the gun?

**Police Officer:** No, Sir, _____ .

**Furlock:** _____ any motive for this crime?

**Police Officer:** We don't know, Sir.

**Furlock:** How about witnesses? _____ any witnesses to the crime?

**Police Officer:** Yes, Sir. _____ one witness—a neighbor upstairs heard screaming in the apartment.

**Furlock:** Where is she ? Bring her to me. . . .

214

# Focus 4

## Past Time Expressions

MEANING

- Use past time expressions with the simple past of *be*.
- Use *but* to contrast past and present meaning.
  - *But* can connect two sentences—one in the past, one in the present.

```
        ┌──────────but──────────┐
  sentence 1              sentence 2
```

Cinderella was a poor girl before. Now she's a princess.
Cinderella was a poor girl before, but now she's a princess.

| Time Expressions | | | | | |
|---|---|---|---|---|---|
| **Past** | | | **Present** | | |
| yesterday | yesterday morning | last time | today | this morning | this time |
| last night | last year | before | tonight | this year | now |

## Exercise 9

Fill in an appropriate time expression. Then read the dialogues aloud.

**The stepsisters are talking to Cinderella.**

1. **Stepsister 1:** Cinderella, where's my dress for the ball?

   **Cinderella:** It was in your closet _____.

   **Stepsister:** I know it was in my closet _____ but it isn't there _____.

2. **Stepsister 2:** Cinderella, where are my jewels? They're not in the drawer.

   **Cinderella:** They were under your bed _____.

   **Stepsister:** Well, they aren't there _____.

**The Prince is thinking about Cinderella.**

3. **The Prince:** Where is that beautiful woman? She was at the palace _____ but she isn't

   here _____.

**Cinderella is worrying about her slipper.**

4. **Cinderella:** Where is that slipper? It was on my foot _____ but it isn't there

   _____.

# Focus 5

## *Wh-*Questions with *Be* in the Simple Past

FORM

| *Wh-*Question Word | Verb *(be)* | Subject |
|---|---|---|
| What | was | the Prince's problem? |
| When | were | Cinderella and the prince together? |
| Where | was | the ball? |
| Why | were | the stepsisters disappointed? |
| How | was | the ball? |
| Whose slipper | was | it? |
| Who* | was | mean in this story? |

*Remember, *who* is the **subject** of this question.

## Exercise 10

Read the argument between Joan and Jim. Use the cues to fill in the blanks. Answer the two questions on p. 217. Then pretend you are Joan and John and role-play the dialogue.

Jim: _____ (*wh*-question/you) yesterday afternoon, Joan?

Joan: What do you mean where was I yesterday afternoon? I _____ (be) in class!

Jim: Oh no you _____ (not/be). I _____ (be) in class and you

_____ (not/be) there!

Joan: OK, Jim. The truth is I _____ (be) in the library.

Jim: In the library? _____ (*wh*-question/you) in the library?

Joan: To study for a test.

Jim: _____ (*wh*-question) with you in the library?

Joan: Well, Larry _____ (be) with me.

Jim: And _____ (wh-question word) idea was it to study together in the library?

Joan: It _____ (be) Larry's idea, Jim.

Jim: And _____ (wh-question word) was studying with Larry?

Joan: It _____ (be) fine, Jim. Larry's smart. But don't worry, he's just a friend!

1. What was the relationship between Jim and Joan?
   a. brother and sister
   b. girlfriend and boyfriend
   c. friends

2. Who was jealous in this conversation?
   a. Jim
   b. Joan
   c. Larry

## Exercise 11

Error Correction. Rewrite the following sentences correctly.

1. Do were her stepsisters beautiful?
2. Her stepsisters was mean.
3. Was lucky Cinderella?
4. Where her glass slipper was?
5. Why the Prince was in love with Cinderella?
6. Was popular the story "Cinderella" in your country?
7. No was any shade at Disneyworld.
8. There was no children at the ball.

# Activities

## Activity 1

Write each of the following time expressions on index cards or slips of paper. Add other time expressions if you can. Put all the cards in a pile. Pick a card and write a statement about yourself comparing your life in the past with your life now.

| | | |
|---|---|---|
| yesterday morning | yesterday | in the summer of 1990 |
| last weekend | last night | in the winter of 1980 |
| last summer | last winter | in the 1960s |

> **EXAMPLES:** *Last year I was a doctor in the Philippines, but this year I'm an ESL student in the United States.*
>
> *When I was a child I was lonely, but now I have many friends.*

## Activity 2

Use the questions below and any other questions you can think of to find out about places your classmates know. Report your information to the class.

> **QUESTIONS:** Where were you?
>
> When were you there?
>
> Why were you there?
>
> What was special about this place?
>
> How was the weather? Was it cold?
>
> Were the people friendly?
>
> How was the food?

## Activity 3

Pretend you are a story writer. You write different kinds of stories:

children's stories (folktales or fairy tales like Cinderella)

love stories

horror stories

murder mysteries / detective stories

ghost stories

other

Choose 3 types of stories from above. How do the stories begin? With a partner, write the first few sentences of the stories using the simple past of *be*. When everyone has finished, read your story beginnings aloud.

The other students will try to guess each story type.

> **EXAMPLES:** It was midnight on a cold, rainy night. Sally was on a dark road. The road was wet and muddy. Sally's car was stuck, and she was really scared. . . . (horror story)
>
> Last night we were all around the campfire. Everybody was sleepy. Suddenly, there was a noise from the trees. . . . (ghost story)

# 20

# Past Tense

## Task

Be a Detective. Read the mini mystery, then study the "Questions to Help You Solve the Mystery." Discuss your solutions to this crime in class. (You will find the answer in Exercise 5!)

### VOCABULARY

| | | |
|---|---|---|
| language lab | semester | videotapes |
| budget cuts | VCR | robbery |

### THE CASE OF THE MISSING VCR

Many students thought Ms. Ditto was the best ESL teacher in the English Language Center. Three years ago, she began to use a VCR in her classes. She brought in videotapes every semester. She taught the students a lot. They enjoyed her classes and really liked her.

Only one student, Harry, didn't like Ms. Ditto. Harry hated her because he failed her course twice. Last summer, he got a job in the language lab because he needed money to register for her class again this semester. Yes, Harry felt angry at Ms. Ditto.

Two weeks ago, just before the new semester started, the Director of the English Language Center heard about budget cuts in the university. The university didn't have money to pay the teachers, so they didn't rehire Ms. Ditto. Everyone was sad, including the Director. Harry just laughed!

Yesterday morning was the first day of the new semester. Professor Paul wanted to use the VCR. He asked Harry to open the language lab. But when Harry opened the door to the lab, the VCR was not there. In its place, there was a typewritten note with a signature on it. The note said:

> Today, I very sad. I no can work in English Language Center because there no have money to pay me. What I can do now? How I can live? I take this VCR because I have angry. Please understand my. I sorry . . .

*Miss Ditto*

Harry immediately reported the robbery to the Director, and gave her the note.

**QUESTIONS TO HELP YOU SOLVE THE MYSTERY:**

1. Did Harry like Ms. Ditto?
2. Did Harry work in the language lab?
3. Did Ms. Ditto write the note?
4. What happened to the VCR? How do you know?

## *Focus 1*

FORM ● USE

# Spelling of Regular Past Tense Verbs

FORM
USE

- Use the simple past tense to talk about completed actions in the past.
- There is only one simple past tense of a verb for all subjects. To form the simple past of **regular verbs,** add *-ed* to the base form of the verb.

| Subject | Simple Past Base Form + *-ed* |
|---------|-------------------------------|
| I<br>You<br>He<br>She<br>It<br>We<br>You<br>They | **started** 3 years ago. |

- However, **regular verbs** can change spelling in the simple past tense.

| If the verb ends in: | Spelling Rule: |
|---|---|
| Vowel + -y<br>**enjoy**<br><br>Two consonants<br>**want**<br><br>Two vowels and one consonant<br>**need** | Add -*ed* to the verb<br>**enjoyed**<br><br><br>**wanted**<br><br><br>**needed** |
| Consonant + -e<br>**place** | Add -*d*<br>**placed** |
| Consonant + -y<br>**study** | Change the -*y* to -*i* and add -*ed*<br>**studied** |
| One vowel and one consonant<br>• One-syllable verbs: **stop**<br><br>• Two-syllable verbs (with the stress on the last syllable): **occur**<br><br>• Two-syllable verbs (with the stress on the first syllable): **listen**<br><br>• Note: Do not double -*x* or -*w* | Double the Consonant and add -*ed*<br>**stopped**<br>Double the consonant and add -*ed*<br>**occurred**<br>Do not double the consonant, just add -*ed*<br>**listened**<br>show = showed<br>fix = fixed |

## Exercise 1

Go back to the Task and underline all the regular past tense verbs.

## Exercise 2

Use the given verbs to complete the statements. Check your spelling!

1. Ms. Ditto _____ (enjoy) teaching.

2. She _____ (use) interesting videotapes in her classes.

3. She _____ (help) her students understand the tapes.

4. The students _____ (study) new vocabulary.

5. They _____ (learn) about American life.

6. They _____ (discuss) the tapes in class.

7. Many students _____ (register) for her class.

8. The students _____ (like) her.

9. Ms. Ditto _____ (stop) teaching because the university didn't have money to pay her.

10. Ms. Ditto's students _____ (cry).

11. One day, a robbery _____ (occur) at the English Language Center.

12. A VCR _____ (disappear).

# Focus 2

## Pronunciation of the -*Ed* Ending

FORM

| GROUP I | When the verb ends with a voiceless sound (the sounds of the letters s, k, p, f, sh, ch, x), the final -*ed* is pronounced /t/. **(æskt)** |
|---|---|
| GROUP II | When the verb ends with a voiced sound (the sounds of the letters b, g, l, m, n, r, v, z), the final -*ed* is pronounced /d/.<br>Remember that all vowels are voiced. Therefore, when a verb ends in a vowel sound (play), the final -*ed* is pronounced /d/. **(pleyd)** |
| GROUP III | When the verb ends in *t* or *d*, the final -*ed* is pronounced /ɪd/. **(pointɪd)** |

## Exercise 3

Read the story about Bookworm Benny. Put each verb in the simple past and read each sentence aloud. Put a check in the column that shows the pronunciation of each verb. Then number the pictures in the correct order.

| t | d | Id |
|---|---|---|
|   |   |    |
|   |   |    |
|   |   |    |
|   |   |    |
|   |   |    |
|   |   |    |
|   |   |    |
|   |   |    |
|   |   |    |
|   |   |    |
|   |   |    |
|   |   |    |
|   |   |    |
|   |   |    |
|   |   |    |
|   |   |    |
|   |   |    |

Bookworm Benny was an excellent student.

1. Teachers always _____ (like) Bookworm Benny.

2. He _____ (work) hard in school.

3. He always _____ (finish) his work first.

4. The teacher always _____ (call) on him.

5. He always _____ (answer) questions correctly.

6. He _____ (remember) all his lessons.

7. He never _____ (talk) out of turn.

8. The other students _____ (hate) Benny.

9. One day, they _____ (decide) to get back at him.

10. They _____ (roll) a piece of paper into a ball.

11. They _____ (wait) for the teacher to turn his back.

12. They threw the paper ball at the teacher. It _____ (land) on the teacher's head.

13. The teacher was really angry. He _____ (yell) at the class.

14. "Who did that?" he _____ (ask).

15. All the students _____ (point) to Benny.

16. But the teacher _____ (trust) Benny.

17. The teacher _____ (punish) the other students.

## Exercise 4

Using the cartoons, retell Bookworm Benny's story.

## Exercise 5

You will find the solution to the Ms. Ditto story in this exercise. Choose from the following verbs. Fill in the correct verb in each sentence. Put the verbs into the past tense and then read the story aloud.

discuss     look     remember     learn     notice
confess     ask      believe      lock      suspect

When the Director of the English Language Center (1) _____ about the robbery, she was

sad. She (2) _____ Ms. Ditto was an honest person. But she (3) _____ Harry.

    To solve the mystery, the Director (4) _____ herself in her office alone. She

(5) _____ the problems between Harry and Ms. Ditto. Then, the Director (6) _____

at the note again. She (7) _____ all the grammar mistakes! And the signature on the note

was not Ms. Ditto's signature.

    The Director (8) _____ Harry to come into her office. She (9) _____ the

problem with him. Finally, Harry (10) _____ to stealing the VCR, typing the note, and

signing Ms. Ditto's name.

## Focus 3

FORM

# Affirmative Statements with Irregular Past Tense Verbs

FORM

- Many verbs are irregular in the past tense.
- There is only one form of the verb for each subject. There is no special form for third person singular subjects (he, she, it).

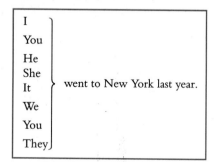

- You can learn irregular past tense forms in groups.

| Base Form | Simple Past |
| --- | --- |
| • Base Form has / I / sound. | |
| • Simple Past has / æ / sound. | |
| begin | began |
| drink | drank |
| ring | rang |
| sing | sang |
| sink | sank |
| swim | swam |

| Base Form | Simple Past |
| --- | --- |
| • past tense: ought / aught | |
| buy | bought |
| bring | brought |
| catch | caught |
| fight | fought |
| teach | taught |
| think | thought |

| Base Form | Simple Past |
| --- | --- |
| • The past form is the same as the base form. | |
| cost | cost |
| cut | cut |
| hit | hit |
| hurt | hurt |
| put | put |
| shut | shut |
| let | let |

| Base Form | Simple Past |
| --- | --- |
| • The base form of the verb ends in -d. | |
| • The past tense form ends in -t. | |
| lend | lent |
| send | sent |
| spend | spent |
| bend | bent |
| build | built |

| Base Form | Simple Past |
| --- | --- |
| • The base form has the / iy / sound. | |
| • The past tense form has the / ε / sound and often ends in -t. | |
| feel | felt |
| keep | kept |
| leave | left |
| meet | met |
| read | read |
| sleep | slept |

| Base Form | Simple Past |
| --- | --- |
| • The base form has ow. | |
| • The past tense has ew. | |
| blow | blew |
| grow | grew |
| know | knew |
| throw | threw |

| Base Form | Simple Past |
| --- | --- |
| • There is a vowel change in the past tense form. | |
| become | became |
| come | came |
| dig | dug |
| fall | fell |
| forget | forgot |
| get | got |
| give | gave |
| hold | held |
| hang | hung |
| run | ran |
| sit | sat |
| win | won |

| Base Form | Simple Past |
| --- | --- |
| • The past tense has the / ō / sound. | |
| break | broke |
| choose | chose |
| sell | sold |
| tell | told |
| speak | spoke |
| steal | stole |
| drive | drove |
| ride | rode |
| wake | woke |
| write | wrote |

| Base Form | Simple Past |
| --- | --- |
| • Miscellaneous | |
| be | was |
| bite | bit |
| do | did |
| eat | ate |
| find | found |
| go | went |
| have | had |
| hear | heard |
| lose | lost |
| pay | paid |
| say | said |
| see | saw |
| stand | stood |
| take | took |
| tear | tore |
| wear | wore |

## Exercise 6

Go back to the Task. Circle the irregular past tense verbs.

## Exercise 7

Lisa and Kate had a "Dream Vacation" in New York. Fill in the past tense of the verbs given.

1. Lisa and Kate _____ (fly) to New York on Sunday, November 4.

2. They _____ (find) many interesting things to do in the city.

3. They _____ (eat) great food every day.

4. They _____ (go) to the Statue of Liberty and the Museum of Natural History.

5. They _____ (take) the ferry to the Immigration Museum at Ellis Island.

6. They _____ (stand) at the top of the World Trade Center.

7. They _____ (spend) an evening in a jazz club.

8. Lisa _____ (buy) gifts for her friends in Finland.

9. They _____ (see) the Matisse Exhibit at the Museum of Modern Art.

10. They _____ (meet) a nice woman at the museum.

11. They _____ (speak) English with her all afternoon.

12. They _____ (think) New York was a beautiful, friendly city.

## Exercise 8

Monique and Daniel are from France. They were in New York at the same time as Lisa and Kate. However, their vacation was very different. Read about their "Nightmare Vacation." Fill in the past tense of the verbs given.

1. On Sunday, November 4, Monique and Daniel's flight from Paris to New York was late, so they _____ (sit) in the airport for four hours.

2. The airline company _____ (lose) all their luggage.

3. On Monday, they _____ (go) shopping for new clothes.

4. On Tuesday, they _____ (get) stuck in the subway when their train _____ (break) down.

5. On Wednesday, they _____ (pay) $89 to rent a car, and _____ (drive) to the Aquarium.

6. They _____ (leave) the car on the street and _____ (get) a parking ticket.

7. A thief _____ (throw) a rock through the car window and _____ (steal) Monique's camera.

8. On Thursday, they _____ (buy) a new camera.

9. On Friday, they _____ (go) ice skating. Monique had the new camera around her neck.

10. Monique _____ (fall) on the ice.

11. She _____ (hurt) her knee.

12. The camera _____ (break).

13. Monique was wet and frozen. She _____ (catch) a cold.

14. On Saturday night, they _____ (drink) a lot of champagne to forget about their nightmare vacation.

15. On Sunday, they _____ (leave) for home.

# Focus 4

## MEANING

# Time Expressions

**MEANING**

- Time expressions specify the definite time in the past at which an action was completed. Here are some examples of past time expressions:

| | | | |
|---|---|---|---|
| yesterday | last night | an hour ago | in 1988 |
| yesterday morning | last week | two days ago | on Sunday |
| yesterday afternoon | last month | 6 months ago | at 6:00 |
| yesterday evening | last year | a year ago | the day before yesterday |

- Time expressions are usually placed at the end of the sentence, but they can also be placed at the beginning. A comma is used after the time expression when it is placed at the beginning of the sentence.

**(a)** Lisa and Kate took a trip to Spain two years ago.

**(b)** Yesterday morning, a VCR disappeared from the English Language Center.

# Exercise 9

Think back to Monique and Daniel's nightmare vacation in New York. Use *yesterday, last, on,* or *ago* to complete the following sentences.

1. It is Monday, November 12th. _____ week, Monique and Daniel were in New York.

2. Exactly a week _____ , they went shopping for new clothes in New York.

3. _____ Tuesday, they got stuck on the subway.

4. _____ Wednesday, a thief stole Monique's camera.

5. Monique caught a cold three days _____ .

6. They drank a lot of champagne _____ .

7. They slept late _____ Sunday morning.

8. _____ evening, they left for Paris.

# Exercise 10

Make statements about yourself using the time expressions in Focus 4.

**EXAMPLE:** *Two months ago, I took a trip to the Yucatan Peninsula in Mexico.*

# Focus 5

## *Did* in Negative Statements with Past Tense Verbs

FORM

- Use the auxiliary verb *did* to make negative statements in the past. Use *did not* and the contraction *didn't* for all subjects. After *did*, use the base form of the verb.

| Subject | Auxiliary *did* + *not/didn't* | Base Form of the Verb |
|---------|-------------------------------|------------------------|
| I | | |
| You | **did not** | trust Harry. |
| He | | |
| She | | |
| It | | |
| We | | |
| You | **didn't** | understand the story. |
| They | | |

## Exercise 11

Use the cues below about the people in this unit to make affirmative or negative statements aloud.

1. The other students / like / Bookworm Benny
2. The teacher / trust / Benny
3. The students / try / to get Benny into trouble
4. The students' plan for Benny / succeed
5. Lisa and Kate / lose / their luggage
6. Lisa's camera / break
7. Lisa and Kate / speak / English in New York
8. Lisa and Kate / get / stuck on the subway
9. Harry / notice / the grammar mistakes in his note
10. Ms. Ditto / sign / the note
11. Harry / steal / the VCR
12. The Director / suspect / Ms. Ditto
13. Monique and Daniel / spend / an evening in a jazz club
14. Monique and Daniel / visit / the United Nations
15. Monique and Daniel / enjoy / their vacation in New York.

# Focus 6

## *Did* in Yes/No Questions with Past Tense Verbs

FORM

- To make a question, put the auxiliary verb *did* in front of the subject, and use the base form of the verb after the subject.

| Auxiliary | Subject | Base Verb | Short Answers |
|---|---|---|---|
| Did | they | visit the U.N.? | Yes, they did. |
| Did | they | get a parking ticket? | No, they didn't. |

## Exercise 12

Ask a partner *yes/no* questions using the following cues and the subject "you." Answer each other's questions.

1. like / the Ms. Ditto story
2. enjoy / being a detective
3. think / Ms. Ditto was guilty
4. guess / that Harry was the thief

5. find / the grammar mistakes in Harry's note
6. correct / the mistakes in the note
7. feel / sorry for Harry
8. want / to give Harry any advice

## Exercise 13

Look at the cartoon about *Jinxed Jerry,* a man with very bad luck. He went on a cruise and his ship ran into a bad storm. Using the cues, ask a partner questions. The pictures will help you answer each other's questions. Remembering that Jerry has very bad luck, how do you think the story ends?

1. Jerry's cruise ship / sink
2. Jerry / know how to swim
3. Jerry / die
4. he / find an island
5. he / have enough food
6. he / make tools
7. he / build a boat

**PREDICTIONS**

8. Jerry's luck / get better
9. the story / have a happy ending
10. Jerry / find his way back home

# Focus 7

FORM

## *Wh*-Questions with Past Tense Verbs

**FORM**

- To make *Wh*-questions, use the pattern:

| *Wh*-word | Auxiliary (*did*) + | Subject | Base Form of the Verb | |
|---|---|---|---|---|
| **(a)** What | did | they | do | last summer? |
| **(b)** When | did | she | make | her vacation plans? |
| **(c)** Where | did | you | go | last summer? |
| **(d)** Why | did | you | go | there? |
| **(e)** How | did | you | get | there? |
| **(f)** How long | did | they | stay | there? |
| **(g)** How long ago | did | they | come | home? |
| **(h)** Who(m) | did | Lisa and Kate | meet | in New York? |

- When *who* or *what* (or other *Wh*-words, such as *which* or *whose*) is the subject of the question, do not use the auxiliary *did*.

| **(i)** What | happened | to Jerry's ship? |
|---|---|---|
| **(j)** Who | had | a nightmare vacation? |

## Exercise 14

Use the cues below to write *Wh*-questions about Jinxed Jerry. Then write the answers to the questions. The first one has been done for you.

1. Jerry / go

    Q: Where *did Jerry go?*

    A: *He went on a cruise.*

2. Jerry's ship / sink

   Q: Why _____ ?

   A: _____ .

3. Jerry / do after the ship sank

   Q: What _____ ?

   A: _____ .

4. Jerry / find on the island

   Q: What _____ ?

   A: _____ .

5. Jerry / eat there

   Q: What _____ ?

   A: _____ .

6. Jerry / build the boat

   Q: How _____ ?

   A: _____ .

7. Jerry / put on the boat

   Q: What _____ ?

   A: _____ .

8. Jerry / feel

   Q: How _____ ?

   A: _____ .

9. the story / end

   Q: How _____ ?

   A: _____ .

# Exercise 15

Using *who* and *whom*, write questions for the information that is underlined. The first one has been done for you.

1. <u>Lisa</u> went to New York with Kate.

   *Who went to New York with Kate?*

2. Lisa and Kate had lunch <u>with a nice woman</u> at the museum.

   _____ ?

3. They bought gifts <u>for their friends</u> in Finland.

   _____ ?

4. <u>Ms. Ditto</u> was the best ESL teacher in the English Language Center.

   _____ ?

5. <u>Harry</u> worked in the language lab.

   _____ ?

6. <u>Harry</u> typed the note.

   _____ ?

7. <u>Harry</u> signed the note.

   _____ ?

8. Harry gave the note <u>to the Director</u>.

   _____ ?

9. Harry hated <u>Ms. Ditto</u>.

   _____ ?

# Exercise 16

Information Gap. This is the story of a remarkable woman named Doina. Here are two incomplete texts about Doina's life. Each text has different information. Working with a partner, ask each other questions to get the missing information.

**TEXT A:**

1. Doina grew up in Romania.

2. She got married to _____. (whom)

3. She had a daughter in 1976.

4. She had another daughter in _____. (when)

5. Doina was unhappy because she was against the government in Romania.

6. She thought of _____. (what)

7. She taught her children how to swim.

8. On October 9, 1988, she and her children swam across the Danube River to _____.

   (where)

9. The police caught them.

10. Doina and her children went _____. (where)

11. They made a second attempt to escape several months later.

12. In their final attempt, they left Romania _____ in the middle of the night. (how)

13. They flew to New York in 1989.

14. Doina went to school _____. (why)

15. She wrote the story of her escape from Romania.

**TEXT B:**

1. Doina grew up in _____. (where)

2. She got married to a government official.

3. She _____ in 1976. (what)

4. She had another daughter in 1978.

5. Doina was unhappy _____. (why)

6. She thought of ways to escape.

7. She taught her children _____. (what)

8. On October 9, 1988, she and her children swam across the Danube River to Yugoslavia.

9. _____ caught them. (who)

10. Doina and her children went to jail.

11. They made a second attempt to escape _____. (when)

12. In their final attempt, they left Romania on foot in the middle of the night.

13. They flew to _____ in 1989. (where)

14. Doina went to school to learn English.

15. She wrote _____. (what)

## Exercise 17

Error Correction. Rewrite the following sentences correctly.

1. This morning, I waked up early.
2. I saw him yesterday night.
3. Harry didn't was sad.
4. They don't met the Mayor of New York City last week.
5. What Harry wanted?
6. Harry didn't noticed his mistakes.
7. Who did signed the note?
8. What did the Director?
9. What did happen to Harry?
10. Where Lisa and Kate went on vacation?
11. Who did go with Lisa to New York?
12. How Jerry built a boat?
13. They no had dinner in a Greek restaurant.
14. Whom did suspect the Director?

# Activities

### Activity 1

Write your own individual ending for the story about Jinxed Jerry. Then compare your endings and discuss them. When you have finished, look at the cartoons at the end of this unit that tell the end of Jerry's story. Write the ending you see in the cartoon. How does this story make you feel?

### Activity 2

The story you are about to complete is called a Mad Lib. Only one person can see this story as it is being written. Do not tell the story to the other members of the class before it is finished. Ask the class for nouns, verbs, adjectives, and so on to complete the blanks. Ask them to give you funny or unusual words. When all the blanks are complete, read the story to the class.

**WANTED!**

A very (1) _____ (adjective) criminal escaped from prison yesterday morning. His name

is (2) _____ (name of a male in the class). He was in jail because he (3) _____

(verb/past tense) a (4) _____ (noun). He has (5) _____ (adjective/color) hair and

(6) _____ (adjective/color) eyes. He is a/an (7) _____ (adjective) man with a/an

(8) _____ (adjective) face.

    This morning, he (9) _____ (verb/past tense) a prison guard before he escaped at about

4:30 A.M. At 6:00 A.M., he (10) _____ (verb/past tense) a bank and (11) _____

(verb/past tense) $10,000. Someone saw him around (12) _____ (name of a place). He had

a (13) _____ (noun) on him.

    If you have any information about this criminal please call (14) _____ (name of a person

in the room) at (15) _____ (telephone #).

    There is a reward of (16) _____ (sum of money) for the person who helps us find this

criminal.

Thank you.

THE FBI

## Activity 3

Interview a partner about a vacation he or she has taken. Ask as many *wh*-questions as you can. Report back to the class about your partner's last trip. Use the questions below to help you.

Where did you go?

When did you go there?

How did you get there?

What did you do there?

How long did you stay?

With whom did you go?

Why did you go there?

## Activity 4

*To Tell The Truth.* Working in groups of three, each one of you tells a true story about yourself. As a group, choose the best story. Then each of you pretends that this story is your own story. Learn as much as you can about the story. Then face the class. One of you reads the story. Your classmates will ask all of you questions. They will try to find out whose story this really is.

> **EXAMPLE:** You say, "When I was 10 years old, I went on a cruise."
>
> The class asks, "Where did you go?"
>
> "With whom did you go?", etc...

## Activity 5

Pretend you are a reporter. Write a newspaper article telling the story of the missing VCR. Remember, a reporter answers the questions: who, what, when, where, why, and how.

## Activity 6

JEOPARDY GAME: Divide the class into 2 teams. Choose one student to be the Master of Ceremonies (MC). If you are the MC, ask Team 1 to choose a category and an amount. Then you look in the box corresponding to the category and the amount chosen and read the answer in the box aloud. Team 1 has one minute to ask a question. If they do not ask the question correctly, Team 2 gets a chance to ask a question. There may be more than one correct question for the answers. The team with the most money wins.

**EXAMPLE:**  Team 1 chooses    "People for $10."

                   Team 1 asks,       "Who lost her job?"

                                      "Whom did Harry hate?"

|  | CATEGORY 1 <br> PEOPLE | CATEGORY 2 <br> *WH*-QUESTIONS | CATEGORY 3 <br> YES/NO QUESTIONS |
|---|---|---|---|
| $10 | Ms. Ditto | a VCR | Yes, she did. |
| $20 | Harry | two weeks ago | Yes, he did. |
| $30 | The Director | in the language lab | No, she didn't. |
| $40 | Professor Paul | because he needed to register for the course again this semester | No, he didn't. |
| $50 | The students | She noticed grammar mistakes in the note. | Yes, they did. |

## Activity 7

The stories in this unit are about unfair or unlucky things that happen to people. Think about a time when something unfair or unlucky happened to you. Write your story and tell the class what happened. Your classmates may ask you questions.

## CONCLUSION TO EXERCISE 13

# Indirect Objects
# with *To*

## *Task*

You need to give a gift to the people on your list below. Look at the gifts you bought and decide which gift you want to give to each person.

### People

1. a single 35–year–old athletic male friend
2. your teenage nephew
3. your 63–year–old grandmother
4. your friend's 4–year–old daughter
5. an artistic 27–year–old friend
6. your mother
7. your music-loving boyfriend/girlfriend
8. a newlywed couple

### Gifts

A.

B.

C.

D.

E.

F.

G.

H.

# Focus 1

## Direct and Indirect Objects

MEANING

- Some verbs take a direct object:
  **(a)** John sends flowers.    *Flowers* is the direct object. It tells us what John sends.
- Some verbs are followed by two objects:
  **(b)** John sends flowers to his girlfriend.    *His girlfriend* is the indirect object. It tells us who he sends flowers to.

# Exercise 1

Write sentences telling what you gave to each of the people in the Task. Underline the direct object and circle the indirect object in each sentence. Then tell why you decided to give that item to that person.

> **EXAMPLE:** I gave <u>the toaster</u> to (the newlyweds.) They are just starting a household together.

# Focus 2

FORM

## Placement of the Indirect Object

FORM

- Almost all verbs that take indirect objects can follow Pattern A.

  Pattern A:

  | Subject | Verb | Direct Object | Indirect Object |
  |---------|------|---------------|-----------------|
  | I | gave | the toaster | to the newlyweds. |

- Some verbs can also follow Pattern B below. In this pattern, you can move the indirect object before the direct object and omit *to*.

  Pattern B:

  | Subject | Verb | Indirect Object | Direct Object |
  |---------|------|-----------------|---------------|
  | I | gave | the newlyweds | the toaster |

- These are some verbs that follow both Pattern A and B.

  | give | send | pass | mail |
  | write | bring | read | offer |
  | show | hand | lend | pay |
  | tell | sell | teach | throw |

**240**

## Exercise 2

Using the sentences that you wrote in Exercise 1, make one sentence using Pattern A and one using Pattern B.

> **EXAMPLE:** "I gave the flowers to my grandmother."
>
> "I gave my grandmother the flowers."

## Exercise 3

Read the statements below about American customs. Rewrite the sentences following Pattern B with the indirect object before the direct object.

> **EXAMPLE: Valentine's Day**
>
> Husbands give flowers to their wives.
>
> *Husbands give their wives flowers.*

### Birth

1. Friends give flowers to the mother.

   _____

2. The father gives cigars to his friends.

   _____

3. The couple sends birth announcements to their friends.

   _____

### Engagement/Marriage

4. The man gives a diamond ring to his girlfriend.

   _____

5. Friends give household gifts to the woman at a "shower."

   _____

6. At the wedding, the guests give money or gifts to the couple.

   _____

### Death

7. People send condolence cards to the family.

   _____

8. Some people send contributions to charities.

   _____

9. Some people send flowers to the family.

   _____

## Exercise 4

Make two sentences about the customs in your country for each of the life events from Exercise 3. Discuss the customs with a partner.

# Focus 3

USE

## Position of New Information

USE

- Look at these two sentences:
  **(a)** I gave a beautiful gift to my mother.
  **(b)** I gave my mother a pair of diamond earrings.
- In English, new information comes at the end of the sentence. In sentence (a) the emphasis is on **who** you gave a gift to. So "to my mother" comes at the end of the sentence.
- In sentence (b) the emphasis is on **what** you gave her, so *a pair of diamond earrings* comes at the end of the sentence.

## Exercise 5

Answer the following questions. The new information is in parentheses ( ).

1. Who(m) did you give a present to? (my co-worker)
2. What did you give your parents for their anniversary? (tickets to a play)
3. Who(m) did you tell the joke to? (my friend)
4. What did you send to your sister? (some new recipes)
5. Did you lend the money to Jerry or Pam? (Pam)
6. Which story did you read to the children—"Cinderella" or "Snow White"? (Cinderella)
7. Who(m) did you mail the application to? (the admissions office)

## Exercise 6

Decide which choice is more appropriate:

1. You are waiting for a friend in front of a restaurant. She is late. You forgot your watch. You want to know the time. You see someone coming toward you. You ask him:
   **(a)** Could you please tell me the time?
   **(b)** Could you please tell the time to me?
2. You are alone at a restaurant and have just finished eating. You see the waiter. You ask him:
   **(a)** Could you please give the check to me?
   **(b)** Could you please give me the check?

3. You are celebrating someone's birthday with a group of friends. You are all finished. You want to be sure **you** pay the check. You tell the waiter:

(a) Please give the check to me.

(b) Please give me the check.

4. Two friends are talking:

Jill: What did Tom give Nancy on her birthday?

Jane: (a) He gave her an engagement ring.

(b) He gave an engagement ring to her.

5. You are at a friend's house for dinner. The food tastes a little bland. You ask:

(a) Please pass me the salt.

(b) Please pass the salt to me.

6. You have just realized you do not have money for the bus. You ask your friend,

(a) "Could you lend a dollar to me?"

(b) "Could you lend me a dollar?"

7.     Jane: "Is Nancy happy?"

Margaret: "Yes."

    Jane: "Why?"

(a) "... because her sister gave her a toy."

(b) "... because her sister gave a toy to her."

8. You are speaking to the Director of the English Language Center. You want to apply to the City University. You have the application form in your hand.

Director: (a) Please, send the application form to the City University.

(b) Please, send the City University the application form.

# Focus 4

FORM

# Indirect Object Pronouns

FORM

- A pronoun can take the place of the indirect object:

  (a) I gave a pair of diamond earrings **to my mother.**

  (b) I gave a pair of diamond earrings **to her.**

- A pronoun can also be used when the indirect object is before the direct object (Pattern B).

  (c) I gave **my mother** a pair of diamond earrings.

  (d) I gave **her** a pair of diamond earrings.

- When there are two pronouns, do not put the indirect object before the direct object.

  (e) I gave **them to her.**
      NOT: I gave her them.

## Exercise 7

Read the conversation. Circle the direct object and put an **X** over the indirect object in the underlined sentences.

**Karen:** I'm so happy Christmas is over. Gift-giving can be very stressful!

**Joel:** What did you give to your mom?

**Karen:** (1) I gave her a pair of diamond earrings.

**Joel:** Wow! And your dad? Did you give him that wool scarf you bought?

**Karen:** (2) No, I gave the scarf to my uncle. (3) I gave my dad a set of golf clubs.

**Joel:** And what did you give your brother out in California?

**Karen:** (4) I sent him some mystery novels and a subscription to *Money Magazine*.

**Joel:** It's too bad that your boyfriend is still in Europe on business. What did you give him?

**Karen:** (5) Well, I wrote him a long letter. I told him about all the presents I have for him!

**Joel:** You gave so many gifts, Karen. And what did you get?

**Karen:** (6) Oh, my bank sent me a huge credit card bill!

## Exercise 8

Change the underlined names or nouns to pronouns.

1. I gave my father golf clubs.
2. Paul wrote Julie a letter.
3. The salesman sold George and Martha a bad car.
4. We owed my brother-in-law money.
5. The department store sent my husband and me the wrong stereo.
6. The postman handed my husband a package.
7. The teacher read the students the story.
8. I told Susan the problem.
9. Karen mailed a check to the bank.
10. Our children wrote my husband and me a beautiful letter.

# Focus 5

## Verbs that Cannot Omit *To* with Indirect Objects

- Remember, many verbs can follow both Pattern A and Pattern B.
  - **(a)** My mother read a story to me. (Pattern A)
  - **(b)** My mother read me a story. (Pattern B)
- However, with some verbs, it is not possible to omit *to* and move the indirect object before the direct object . These verbs can only take Pattern A.
  - **(c)** She explained the problem to me.
    NOT: She explained me the problem.
- The following verbs follow Pattern A only:

| | | |
|---|---|---|
| *explain* | *describe* | *repeat* |
| *introduce* | *report* | *say* |

## Exercise 9

Read the following pairs of sentences or questions aloud. Circle any sentence that is not possible. In some of the pairs, both patterns are possible.

| **Pattern A** | **Pattern B** |
|---|---|
| 1. Sarah passed the potatoes to me. | Sarah passed me the potatoes. |
| 2. George sold his car to Mary. | George sold Mary his car. |
| 3. Can you describe your hometown to me? | Can you describe me your hometown? |
| 4. The doctor explained the problem to the patient. | The doctor explained the patient the problem. |
| 5. She reported the accident to her insurance company. | She reported her insurance company the accident. |
| 6. He read a story to his little brother. | He read his little brother a story. |
| 7. He wrote a love letter to his girlfriend. | He wrote his girlfriend a love letter. |
| 8. She introduced her boyfriend to her parents. | She introduced her parents her boyfriend. |
| 9. Cynthia gives her old clothes to the church. | Cynthia gives the church her old clothes. |
| 10. The teacher repeated the instructions to the class. | The teacher repeated the class the instructions. |

# Activities

### Activity 1

Play this game in groups of four. Make 12 PEOPLE CARDS by writing each person below on a card. Deal the cards so that each student in your group has three cards. Decide who plays first. Then follow the instructions below:

### PEOPLE CARDS

1. Your 63-old aunt.
2. Your husband/wife.
3. Your 5-year-old niece.
4. Your boss.
5. Your co-worker.
6. Your father.
7. Your mother.
8. A friend recently married.
9. A 40-year-old bachelor.
10. Your teacher.
11. Your mother-in-law.
12. Your classmate.

### INSTRUCTIONS

1. Roll the die and land on a gift.
2. Give that gift to one of the people on your cards. Tell the group which person you give this gift to.
3. If the group thinks that is an appropriate gift for that person, turn the card upside down.
4. If the group challenges your decision, defend your choice. Give reasons why you made that choice.
5. The group makes the final decision about the gift's appropriateness. The group can also vote if they cannot agree.

> **How to Win:** The object of the game is to find gifts for the three people you have cards for. The first person who has turned over all three cards wins the game!

> **EXAMPLE:** (You land on the gift **walkman** and one of your cards says "63-year-old aunt".)
>
> **You say:** I want to give the walkman to my 63-year-old aunt. She loves classical music.
>
> **Your group says:** That's ridiculous! Your aunt is 63 years old. She doesn't need a walkman.
>
> **You respond:** Of course, she needs it. She often takes long bus trips, and a walkman can help make the trip go faster.
>
> **Your group says:** Well, o.k. We guess she can use the walkman on a bus. You can turn over your card.

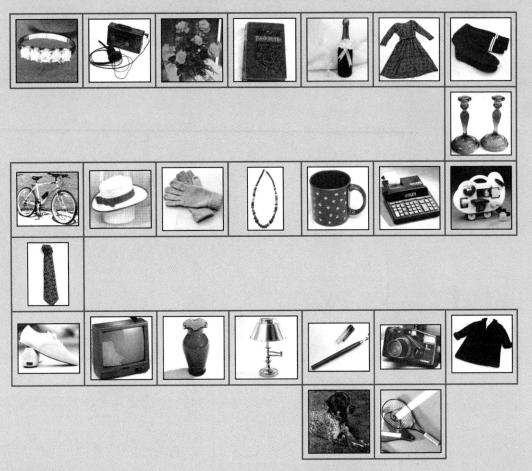

## Activity 2

Work in a small group. On small slips of paper write the numbers 1 to 16 and put them in an envelope. One person picks a number from the envelope and must follow the command in the grid below. Then someone else in the group has to say what the person did.

| **1.** Whisper a secret to the person across from you. | **2.** Give a penny to the person on your left. | **3.** Write a funny message to someone in your group. | **4.** Hand your wallet to the person on your right. |
|---|---|---|---|
| **5.** Send a paper airplane to another group. | **6.** Tell a funny joke to someone. | **7.** Lend some money to a person in your group. | **8.** Describe your boyfriend/girlfriend to someone. |
| **9.** Explain indirect objects to the person across from you. | **10.** Tell your age to the person on your right. | **11.** Introduce the person on your left to the person on your right. | **12.** Offer a cigarette to someone of the opposite sex. |
| **13.** Call up the police and report a crime to them. | **14.** Teach the imperative to your group. | **15.** Throw your pen to the person across from you. | **16.** Pass a secret message to one person in your group. |

**Activity 3**

Here is a culture wheel with major life events. Go around the classroom and ask your classmates about customs in their countries or countries they know. Write a sentence for each event. Compare your culture wheel with a partner's wheel.

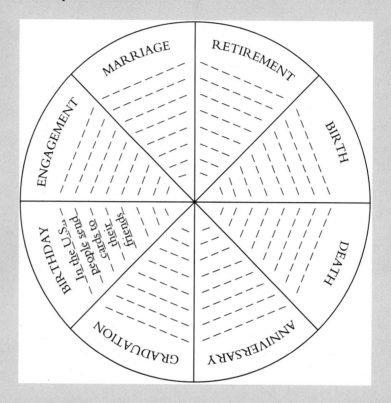

## Task

Read the letters to "Dear Betty" in Part A and match them to the letters of advice in Part B. Write the name of the person who wrote the letter in the space provided in Part B. Compare your answers with a partner.

### Part A: Letters to Dear Betty

1. Dear Betty,
   I'm trying to be a super-woman. I work full-time. I have two small children. I take care of the house, do all of the cooking, and pay the bills. I am very tired and very unhappy. Please help!
   > "Supermom"

2. Dear Betty,
   My wife and I never go out anymore. We just had a baby, and my wife doesn't want to get a baby sitter. I'm going crazy here! Can you help me?
   > "Crazy Man"

3. Dear Betty,
   I'm 50 pounds overweight and I have trouble breathing. My cholesterol level is 278, and I smoke a pack of cigarettes a day. The doctor says I must lose weight and stop smoking. But I love to eat and smoke. Do you have an answer?
   > "Overweight"

4. Dear Betty,
   My mom and dad got divorced last month. They fought a lot and finally my dad moved out. Maybe I wasn't a good daughter to them. Maybe I caused the break-up. What do you think?
   > "Guilty"

### Part B: Letters of Advice

A. Dear _____,
   Don't blame yourself. You did not cause the problems. This is your parents' problem.

B. Dear _____,
   Explain how you feel to her. Tell her you want to go out once a month. Tell her life is too short. Go out and enjoy yourselves!

C. Dear _____,
   You need to do something special for yourself. Go out with your friends once in a while. Buy yourself a new dress.

D. Dear _____,
   Follow your doctor's advice. Take care of yourself. Go on a diet. You're only hurting yourself when you smoke, so quit!

**249**

# Focus 1

## Reflexive Pronouns

FORM
MEANING

- Reflexive pronouns refer to the subject of the sentence. If the subject and the object are the same, use the reflexive pronoun as the object.

    **(a) Sara** bought **herself** a new car.
    NOT:  Sara   bought Sara    a new car.

- In imperative sentences, the reflexive pronouns refer to the subject *you,* which is understood:
    **(b)** (Singular *you*) Take care of **yourself.**
    **(c)** (Plural *you*) Go out and enjoy **yourselves.**

| Examples | Reflexive Pronouns |
|---|---|
| **(d)** I bought **myself** a new stereo. | myself |
| **(e)** You're hurting **yourself** by smoking. | yourself |
| **(f)** He doesn't take care of **himself.** | himself |
| **(g)** She blames **herself** for the accident. | herself |
| **(h)** A cat licks **itself** to keep clean. | itself |
| **(i)** We enjoyed **ourselves** at the theater. | ourselves |
| **(j)** There's plenty of food. Help **yourselves.** | yourselves |
| **(k)** The children behaved **themselves** at the party. | themselves |

## Exercise 1

Go back to the letters in the Task and circle all the reflexive pronouns.

## Exercise 2

Write the correct reflexive pronoun in the spaces provided in the dialogues below.

1. **Bill:** I could just kick (a) _____ for losing my wallet. I know I had it in my

    back pocket.

    **Mary:** Don't be so upset with (b) _____ . It's only a wallet and you can replace

    everything in it.

2. Monica: Thanks for such a lovely evening, Gloria. We really enjoyed (a) _____ .

   Gloria: Well, thanks for coming. And the children were just wonderful. They really behaved

   (b) _____ the whole evening. I hope you can come back soon.

3. Patty & Kevin: We can't believe that our parakeet flew away! We forgot to close the cage

   yesterday!

   Margaret: Don't blame (a) _____ . He's probably happier now. He's getting

   a taste of freedom!

4. Cynthia: What's the matter with Bobby? Why is he limping?

   Enrique: He hurt (a) _____ at the soccer game last night.

# Focus 2

## Using Reflexive Pronouns after Certain Verbs

USE

- There are some verbs in English that are commonly followed by reflexives: *amuse, blame, cut, dry, enjoy, hurt,* and *introduce.*

  **(a)** Mary: Oh, I slipped on the ice yesterday.
     Bob: Did you hurt yourself?

- When talking about routine actions that people obviously do themselves, you can omit the reflexive pronoun. For example, some routine action verbs like *dress, shave,* and *wash* often refer back to the subject, so we don't need to use a reflexive pronoun. We assume that the subject is doing the action to himself or herself if no other object is mentioned.

  **(b)** Sara: It's 8:00! Let's hurry! The party is at 9:00.
     Carl: Oh, I have to shave and get ready.

- When talking about actions that people do not necessarily do themselves, use *by* + reflexive pronoun to emphasize that they are doing it alone.

  **(c)** I sometimes go to the movies by myself.

**251**

## Exercise 3

Write a sentence for each picture. The verbs will help you:

look at/admire   cut     dry    enjoy
shave      clean/lick   hurt    talk to

1. _____

2. _____

3. _____

4. _____

5. _____

6. _____

7. _____

8. _____

# Focus 3

## Reciprocal Pronouns

MEANING

- The reciprocal pronoun *each other* is different in meaning from a reflexive pronoun.

**(a)** John and Ann blamed themselves
for the accident.

**(b)** John and Ann blamed each other
for the accident.

## Exercise 4

Draw two pictures to describe the differences in meaning between the following sentences.

**(a)** The football players poured beer on themselves after they won the game.

**(b)** The football players poured beer on each other after they won the game.

## Exercise 5

Act out the following sentences to show the difference between reciprocal pronouns and reflexive pronouns.

1. You and your classmate are looking at yourselves in the mirror.
2. You and your classmate are looking at each other.
3. You and your classmate are talking to yourselves.
4. You and your classmate are talking to each other.
5. You're playing ball with a friend, and you just broke a neighbor's window. Blame yourself for the accident.
6. You're playing ball with a friend, and you just broke a neighbor's window. Blame each other for the accident.

**253**

## Exercise 6

Circle the correct word in the "Dear Betty" letter below.

Dear Betty,

(I, My, Mine) boyfriend is very vain. (He, His, Him) is very proud
of (he, him, himself). He always looks at (he, him, himself) in store
windows when he passes by. (Himself, He, Him) only thinks about (his,
himself, him). He never brings (my, me, myself) flowers. The last time
he told (my, me, myself) that he loved me was two years ago. He never
lends me (him, himself, his) car. He says that the car is (himself, him,
his), and he doesn't want me to use it. Do (yourself, your, you) have
any suggestions?

"Frustrated"


Dear "Frustrated":

(You, Your, Yourself) boyfriend is very self-centered. (You, Your,
Yourself) can't really change (he, himself, him). Get rid of (he, himself, him)! Find (you, yourself, yours) a new guy!

Betty

## Exercise 7

Error Correction. Rewrite the following sentences correctly.

1. I hurt me.
2. They're looking at theirselves in the mirror.
3. I shave myself every morning.
4. I have a pen pal in Poland. We write to ourselves every month.
5. We enjoyed us at the circus.
6. Larry blamed Harry for the accident. Harry blamed Larry for the accident. They blamed themselves for the accident.
7. He did it hisself.

# Activities

## Activity 1

Read the following riddle and try to figure it out. Discuss it with a partner. (The answer is at the end of the unit.)

A prison guard found a prisoner hanging from a rope in his cell. Did he hang himself or did someone murder him? There was nothing else in the cell but a puddle of water on the floor.

## Activity 2

Who is the most independent person in your class? Make up a survey with ten questions. Then go around to all the students in your class and ask your questions. Make a list of the students who are independent.

> **EXAMPLE:** Do you like to be by yourself?
> Do you usually study by yourself?
> Do you ever go to the movies by yourself?

## Activity 3

Interview another classmate, using the questions below.

1. Do you believe in yourself?
2. When you go shopping for clothes, do you like to look at yourself in the mirror?
3. Do you ever compare yourself to other people?
4. Do you ever buy yourself a present?
5. In a new relationship, do you talk about yourself or try to learn about the other person?
6. Do you ever talk to yourself?
7. Do you cook for yourself?
8. Do you blame yourself for your problems or do you blame others?
9. Do you take care of yourself? (Do you eat well? Do you get enough sleep?)
10. Do you ever get angry at yourself?

(**Answer to Activity 1**) The prisoner stood on a block of ice with the rope around his neck. When the ice melted, his feet didn't touch the ground, so he hanged himself.

# Future Time
## *Will* and *Be Going To*

## *Task*

Wanda the Fortune Teller is making predictions. Match the predictions to the person/people she is talking to.

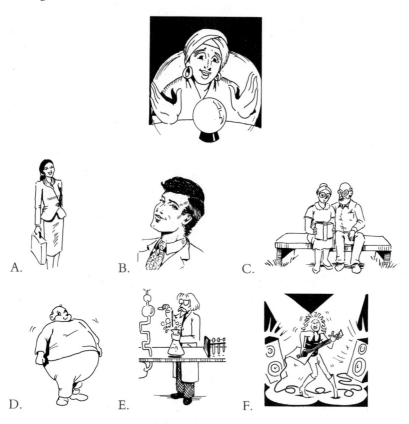

A.      B.      C.

D.      E.      F.

G.

H.

I.

J.

K.

L.

1. "You will find a cure for cancer." ———————

2. "You will find $1,000 on the sidewalk." ———————

3. "You will meet a tall, dark, beautiful stranger." ———————

4. "You will suddenly grow hair on your head." ———————

5. "You are going to get a raise at work." ———————

6. "You will rescue someone and win a medal." ———————

7. "You will stay in power for 50 more years." ———————

8. "You and your boyfriend are going to get married." ———————

9. "You're going to produce a new movie and get rich." ———————

10. "You and your husband will have 10 grandchildren." ———————

11. "You're going to lose 50 pounds in 2 weeks!" ———————

12. "You will become a rock star. Hundreds of
girls will fall in love with you." ———————

# *Focus 1*

## Predicting Future Events

MEANING
USE

- Use both *will* and *be going to* to predict future events—to express what we think will happen in the future.

| *Will* | *Be Going To* |
|---|---|
| • is more formal | • is more informal |
| • is more hypothetical, less dependent on the present situation | • is more concrete, more dependent on the present situation. Use it when there is something in the present situation that makes you feel sure of what will happen in the near future. |
| **EXAMPLE:**<br><br>(a) You will stay in power for 50 more years. | **EXAMPLES:**<br><br>(b) Look at those big black clouds. It's going to rain.<br>NOT: It will rain.<br><br>(c) I have a terrible headache. I'm going to have a bad day today.<br>NOT: I will have a bad day today. |

# *Focus 2*

## FORM

# The Modal *Will*

**FORM**

- *Will* is called a modal verb. The simple future is formed with *will* and the **base form** of the main verb. *Will* never changes form with different subjects.

| Affirmative Statements | Contractions |
|---|---|
| **(a)** She will get a raise at work. | She'll get a raise at work. |
| **(b)** They will travel to the Bahamas. | They'll travel to the Bahamas. |
| **Negative Statements** | **Contractions** |
| **(a)** He will not become rich and famous. | He won't become rich and famous. |
| **(b)** They will not have children right away. | They won't have children right away. |
| **Yes/No Questions** | **Short Answers** |
| **(a)** Will I find a job? | Yes, you will. |
| **(b)** Will Wanda's predictions come true? | No, they won't. |
| ***Wh-*Questions** | **Answers** |
| **(a)** When will the scientist discover a cure? | In 12 years. |
| **(b)** Who will get a medal? | The lifeguard. |
| **(c)** How long will she be away? | For 2 months. |
| **There +*be*** | **Contractions** |
| **(a)** There will be peace in the world. | There'll be peace in the world. |
| **(b)** There will not be any more wars. | There won't be any more wars. |

# *Exercise 1*

Think about the people in the Task. Try to remember the predictions for each person without looking back at the Task. Say the predictions aloud.

**EXAMPLE:** The scientist will find a cure for cancer.

# *Exercise 2*

How will our lives be different in 20 years? Look at the possible changes. Make affirmative or negative statements aloud, using *will* or *won't*. Discuss your predictions.

**PHYSICAL CHANGES:**

1. The weather _____ get warmer.

2. Pollution _____ get worse.

3. Staying in the sun _____ be more dangerous.

**ECONOMIC CHANGES:**

4. Poor people_____ become richer.

5. All countries _____ share the world's wealth equally.

6. People _____ need money.

**SOCIAL CHANGES:**

7. The traditional family _____ disappear.

8. People of different races _____ learn to love each other.

9. Women _____ earn more money than men.

10. People _____ work only 4 days a week.

11. Scientists _____ discover a cure for AIDS.

**TECHNOLOGICAL CHANGES:**

12. Cars _____ run on solar power.

13. People _____ live to be 110 years old.

14. We _____ communicate with beings on other planets.

**POLITICAL CHANGES:**

15. We _____ produce weapons.

16. We _____ fight wars.

17. A woman _____ become Prime Minister of Australia.

18. We _____ have three political parties in the United States.

## Exercise 3

Think about your own future. Use *will/won't* to complete the following statements about yourself. If you are not sure, you can also say, "Maybe I will..." or "Maybe I won't...."

**EXAMPLE:** *I'll* try to do something important in my life.
*Maybe I'll* go back to my country. I *won't* stay single.

1. I _____ try to do something important in my life.

2. I _____ finish my education.

3. I _____ quit school and get a job.

4. I _____ stay single.

5. I _____ get married.

6. I _____ have children.

7. I _____ go back to my country.

8. I _____ learn to speak English fluently.

9. I _____ be successful.

10. I _____ be happy.

Add two statements of your own.

## Exercise 4

Janice Williams is one of Wanda's steady clients. Janice is asking Wanda a lot of questions. Wanda is looking into her crystal ball for the answers. Pretend you are Janice Williams. Use the cues to ask yes/no and *wh*-questions with *will* to get the following information:

**Wanda's Crystal Ball:**

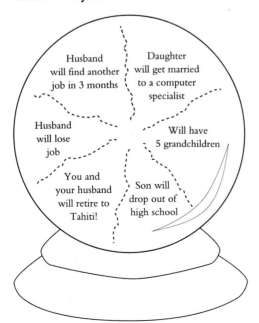

Husband will find another job in 3 months

Daughter will get married to a computer specialist

Husband will lose job

Will have 5 grandchildren

You and your husband will retire to Tahiti!

Son will drop out of high school

**Janice's Questions:**

1. my husband/lose his job?
2. my husband/find another job?
3. when/my husband/find another job?
4. my daughter get married?
5. who(m)/she/marry?
6. I/have/grandchildren?
7. how many grandchildren/I/have?
8. my son/go to college?
9. what/he/do?
10. my husband and I/retire?
11. where/we/retire?

## Exercise 5

Look at the list below. Will there be any poverty in 50 years? Will there be any crime? Discuss your ideas. Give reasons.

| | There will be: | There won't be: |
|---|---|---|
| 1. poverty | | |
| 2. crime | | |
| 3. pollution | | |
| 4. weapons | | |
| 5. borders | | |
| 6. discrimination | | |
| 7. a common language | | |

# Focus 3

FORM

# Be Going To

FORM

- To express the future with *be going to*, use the correct form of the verb *be* + *going to* + the base form of the main verb.

| Affirmative Statements | Contractions |
|---|---|
| **(a)** I am going to lose 50 pounds.<br>**(b)** She is going to look for a new job.<br>**(c)** We are going to visit France. | I'm going to lose 50 pounds.<br>She's going to look for a new job.<br>We're going to visit France. |
| **Negative Statements** | **Contractions** |
| **(a)** I am not going to wait.<br>**(b)** He is not going to call.<br>**(c)** They are not going to come with us. | I'm not going to wait.<br>He isn't/He's not going to call.<br>They aren't/They're not going to come. |
| **Yes/No Questions** | **Short Answers** |
| **(a)** Are you and your family going to take a vacation?<br>**(b)** Is your son going to go with you? | Yes, we are.  No, we aren't.<br>          No, we're not.<br>Yes, he is.  No, he isn't.<br>          No, he's not. |

| *Wh*-Questions | Answers |
|---|---|
| **(a)** When are you going to leave? | In two weeks. |
| **(b)** Where are you going to go? | To Colorado. |
| **(c)** What are you going to do there? | We're going to go on a rafting trip. |
| **(d)** How are you going to get there? | By plane. |
| **(e)** How long are you going to be away? | For two weeks. |
| **(f)** Who's going to steer the raft? | My husband and I. |

- *Going to* is often pronounced "gonna" in everyday speech. "Gonna" is not used in writing unless it's in a dialogue or a quote.

  I'm $\begin{Bmatrix} gonna \\ going\ to \end{Bmatrix}$ have a wonderful time.

# *Exercise 6*

Look at the pictures. Then fill in the blanks in the captions with the affirmative or negative form of *be going to.*

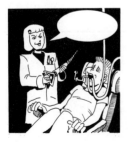

1. "Watch out! You _____ hit him!"

2. "Hurry up! We _____ miss the bus."

3. "This _____ hurt you one bit!"

4. "I am exhausted! I _____ take a nap."

5. "They _____ have a baby."

6. George: O.K. I _____ have just
one more doughnut.

Woman: That's what you always say,

George. You _____ lose
weight this way!

7. "Watch her, Jack! She _____ fall
into the pool!"

8. Husband: Good night, honey. I

_____ go to bed.

Wife: OK, Matt. I _____
watch the news for a while.

## Exercise 7

Make statements about yourself. Use *be going to*.

1. Next week, _____ .

2. Next summer, _____ .

3. The day after tomorrow, _____ .

4. I _____ soon.

5. Tomorrow night, _____ .

## Exercise 8

Read the responses. Write an appropriate question with *be going to*.

1. Q: _____ ?

   A: To the beach.

2. Q: _____ ?

   A: Tomorrow.

3 Q: _____ ?

   A: At 8:00 in the morning.

4. Q: _____ ?

   A: By car.

5. Q: _____ ?

   A: With my friends.

6. Q: _____ ?

   A: Go swimming and get a suntan.

7. Q: _____ ?

   A: About $10.

8. Q: _____ ?

   A: Yes, we are!

## Exercise 9

Use your imagination to answer these questions about the people from the Task. Use *be going to* in your answers. Compare your answers with your partner's.

1. What is the poor person going to do with the $1,000?
2. Where is the young bachelor going to meet the tall, dark, beautiful stranger?
3. Who is the lifeguard going to save?
4. What kind of movie is the director going to make?
5. How many children are the young couple going to have?
6. Is the old couple going to be happy? What's going to happen to them?
7. How is the overweight man going to lose 50 pounds?
8. What kind of music is the young boy going to sing?
9. How much of a raise is the executive going to get?

## Focus 4

# Future Time Expressions

**MEANING**

- Place future time expressions at the beginning or at the end of the sentence. When you place the time expression at the beginning of the sentence, use a comma to separate it from the rest of the sentence.

**(a)** I'll speak to you **tomorrow evening.**

**(b)** **A month from now,** Wanda will be on a tropical island.

| tomorrow | morning<br>afternoon<br>evening<br>night | next | week<br>month<br>year<br>summer<br>Monday | soon<br>later<br>the day after tomorrow<br>a week from today<br>a month from now |
| --- | --- | --- | --- | --- |

## Focus 5

MEANING

# Prepositions of Time

**MEANING**

- Prepositions can also be used to refer to future time.

**(a)** I'll be there  for two days.
                 in three weeks.
                 in September.
                 on Thursday.

**(b)** I'll be there  at 3:00.
                 after 3:00.
                 until 3:00.

- *Until* shows that at a specific time in the future, the action will change.

**(c)** I'll be there **until** 3:00. = At 3:00, I will leave. I will not be there after 3:00.

**(d)** I won't be there **until** Monday. = Before Monday, I won't be there. After Monday, I'll be there.

**(e)** I won't see you **until** next week. = I'll see you next week, but not before.

## Exercise 10

Anthony and Sally are planning a vacation in Europe. They are going to visit four countries in seven days. Sally is telling Anthony their itinerary. Fill in the blanks with prepositions of time: *in, on, at, for,* or *until.*

1. We'll arrive in London (a)_____ 6:00 P.M. (b)_____ Sunday.

2. We'll stay in London _____ two days.

3. Then, we'll fly to Paris _____ Tuesday morning.

4. We'll stay in Paris _____ late Wednesday afternoon.

5. Then, we'll fly to Rome _____ the evening.

6. We won't leave Rome _____ Friday morning.

7. _____ 10:00 A.M. on Friday morning, we'll fly to our final destination, Athens, Greece!

8. We'll stay in Greece _____ three whole days.

9. We'll return home _____ Sunday.

## Exercise 11

Look at Wanda's calendar below. Imagine it is now 2:00 P.M. on Wednesday, April 10, 1993. Read the sentences about Wanda's plans and write the appropriate time expression or preposition of time in the blanks. For some of the sentences there is more than one possible answer.

| Sunday | Monday | Tuesday | Wednesday | Thursday | Friday | Saturday |
|---|---|---|---|---|---|---|
| APRIL | 1 | 2 | 3 | 4 | 5 | 6 |
| 7 | 8 | 9 | 10 *last client 6:00 pm* | 11 *polish crystal ball* | 12 *deposit money in bank* | 13 |
| 14 | 15 | 16 *buy cards* | 17 | 18 *secretary goes on vacation* | 19 *Annual Convention* | 20 |
| 21 | 22 | 23 | 24 | 25 | 26 | 27 |
| 28 | 29 | 30 | | | | |

| Sunday | Monday | Tuesday | Wednesday | Thursday | Friday | Saturday |
|---|---|---|---|---|---|---|
| MAY | | | 1 | 2 | 3 | 4 |
| 5 | 6 *Place ad in newspaper* | 7 | 8 | 9 | 10 | 11 |
| 12 | 13 | 14 | 15 | 16 | 17 | 18 |
| 19 | 20 | 21 | 22 | 23 | 24 | 25 |
| 26 | 27 | 28 | 29 | 30 | 31 | |

*Still To Do:*
*— "How to Make Predictions" arrives on June 10th*
*— Retire - 1999!*
*— Write autobiography - 2005*

268

1. Today, Wanda is going to see her last client _____ .

2. She's going to attend the Annual Convention of Fortune Tellers _____ .

3. She's going to polish her crystal ball _____ .

4. She's going to deposit all her money in the bank _____ .

5. Her secretary is going to go on vacation _____ .

6. She is going to buy a new deck of fortune-telling cards _____ .

7. She's going to put an ad in the newspaper to advertise her services _____ .

8. She will receive her first issue of *How to Make Predictions* magazine _____ .

9. She will retire to a tropical island _____ .

10. She will write a book called *How to Be a Successful Fortune Teller in 10 Easy Lessons*

_____ .

# *Focus 6*

USE

## Expressing Intentions or Prior Plans

USE

- Use *will* and *be going to* to talk about our future intentions and plans.

| Will | Be Going To |
|------|-------------|
| • is used when you decide to do something at the time of speaking. | • is used when you have already decided, planned, or arranged to do something. |
| **EXAMPLE:**<br>Mother: That's the phone, kids!<br>Child: I'll get it, Mom! | **EXAMPLE:**<br>Mother: Where are you going?<br>Daughter: I'm going to take a drive with Richard tonight. Remember, Mom? You said it was okay. . . .<br>Mother: I did? |

## Exercise 12

Work with a partner. You read the first five statements in Column A aloud. Your partner chooses the appropriate response from Column B. After the first five, have your partner read from Column A and you choose the response from Column B.

| Column A | Column B |
|---|---|
| 1. Christine just called. She's coming over for dinner. | A. Great! I'll cook. |
| | B. Great! I'm going to cook. |
| 2. What are you doing with that camera? | A. I'll take your picture. |
| | B. I'm going to take your picture. |
| 3. Do you need a ride home today? | A. No, thanks. Jason will take me home. |
| | B. No, thanks. Jason's going to take me home. |
| 4. We don't have a thing to eat in the house. | A. I'll call up and order a pizza. |
| | B. I'm going to call up and order a pizza. |
| 5. Hi, honey. Guess what? The car's stuck again! | A. Calm down. Don't move. I'll be right there. |
| | B. Calm down. Don't move. I'm going to be right there. |
| 6. Why are you meeting June in the library tonight? | A. She'll help me with my homework. |
| | B. She's going to help me with my homework. |
| 7. Look, there's a robbery in progress over at the bank! | A. I'll call the police. |
| | B. I'm going to call the police. |
| 8. Mom, can you brush my hair? | A. I'll do it in a minute, sweetie. |
| | B. I'm going to do it in a minute, sweetie. |
| 9. Are you off the phone yet, dear? | A. I'll be off in a minute, Harry! |
| | B. I'm going to be off in a minute, Harry! |
| 10. Why did Trudy break the date for Saturday night? | A. Her parents will take her away for the weekend. |
| | B. Her parents are going to take her away for the weekend. |

# Activities

### Activity 1

On December 31st, New Year's Eve, many people make resolutions about what they will or will not do the next year. Imagine it's New Year's Eve. Write down three resolutions. Go around the room and share your resolutions with the other students. Find someone else that has the same resolution(s) as you.

    **EXAMPLE:** I will give up smoking.
                 I will lose weight.

## Activity 2

What do you think the world will be like in the year 2050? Think about physical, technological, economic, political, and social changes. With your group, write down 10 changes. Compare your group's ideas with those of the rest of the class.

**ENVIRONMENTAL CHANGES**

The weather will be warmer.

**ECONOMIC CHANGES**

Credit cards will replace cash.

**SOCIAL CHANGES**

All people will get married three or four times.

**TECHNOLOGICAL CHANGES**

Cars will run on solar power.

**POLITICAL CHANGES**

People all over the world will have more freedom.

## Activity 3

Sit in a circle with 5 or 6 people. On the top of a blank piece of paper write:

On_____/_____ in the year 2015, _____:
       month/day                  (your name)

Pass your sheet of paper to the person on your left. This person completes the sentence by writing a prediction of what she or he thinks you will be or do on this date in the year 2015. After completing the sentence, she or he passes the paper to the left for the next person to write a prediction. When your original paper comes back to you, read the predictions your classmates have made and circle the ones you like the best. Share your favorite ones with the class.

> **EXAMPLE:** On _____/_____ in the year 2015, Mario:
>          month/day
> 1. will be a famous rock star.
> 2. will have ten children.
> 3. will be President of a large corporation.

## Activity 4

Make a weekly calendar and fill in your schedule for next week. Write different activities for each day. Then ask your partner questions about his or her future plans using *going to*.

> **EXAMPLE:** "What are you going to do on Sunday?"
> "I'm going to go jogging in Central Park."

## Activity 5

You and your partner have just won $1,000 on a game show. You have one day to spend it. What are you going to do together? Be sure to give details of your activities. For example, if you rent a car.... what kind of car are you going to rent? a sports car, a convertible, a limousine?

Share your plans with the class. Decide which pair has the most interesting plans.

## Activity 6

What will you need in 100 years? What won't you need? Make a list of items and discuss why you think these things will be necessary in the future or not.

> **EXAMPLES:** We won't need cash. People will use credit cards.
> We will need computers.

271

## Task

This is a chart of what Billy, Bobby, and Brad usually eat for breakfast every day. The chart also indicates the number of calories and the amount of fat and cholesterol in all the foods they eat. Answer the questions below based on the chart.

**Calories** are the amount of heat or energy a food will produce in the body. To lose weight, we need to reduce our calorie intake.

**Fat** is a substance found in foods like dairy products and red meat.

**Cholesterol** is a substance in the body and in foods like eggs and butter. High cholesterol can cause heart disease.

| | Calories | Fat (grams) | Cholesterol (milligrams) |
|---|---|---|---|
| **Billy** | | | |
| eggs (3) | 140 | 9.8 | 399 |
| sausages (2) | 180 | 16.3 | 48 |
| muffin | 170 | 4.6 | 9 |
| milk (whole) | 165 | 8 | 30 |
| **Bobby** | | | |
| cereal | 80 | 1.1 | 0 |
| orange juice (1 glass) | 80 | 0 | 0 |
| milk (skim) | 85 | 0 | 0 |
| bananas (1) | 130 | less than 1 | 0 |
| **Brad** | | | |
| pancakes (3) | 410 | 9.2 | 21 |
| vanilla milkshake | 290 | 1.3 | 10 |
| doughnuts (2) | 240 | 20 | 18 |

1. How many pancakes does Brad usually eat?
2. How much juice does Bobby drink?
3. How many eggs does Billy usually have?
4. How much cholesterol is there in three pancakes?
5. How much cholesterol is there in a bowl of cereal?
6. Which drink has a lot of calories?

7. How much fat is there in a muffin?
8. How many calories are there in Bobby's breakfast? In Billy's? In Brad's?
9. How much cholesterol is there in each breakfast?
10. Which foods have a little cholesterol?
11. Which foods have a lot of cholesterol?
12. Which foods don't have any cholesterol?
13. Who has the healthiest breakfast?

# Focus 1

## Review of Count and Non-Count Nouns

FORM

- If a noun is viewed as a count noun
  - *a* or *an* can be used in front of it:
  - it has a plural form:
  - it can be used in a question with *how many*:
  - a number can be used before it:
  - a singular or plural verb can be used before it:

**(a)** **an** egg, **a** muffin
**(b)** Brad likes **pancakes**.

**(c)** **How many eggs** does Billy eat?
**(d)** **Three** eggs.

**(e)** There **is** a fast-food restaurant near here.
**(f)** There **are** a lot of calories in a milkshake.

- If a noun is viewed as a non-count noun
  - *a/an* cannot be used in front of it:
  - it does not have a plural form:
  - it can be used in a question with *how much*:
  - a number isn't used in front of it:

  - it always takes a singular verb:

**(g)** **Cereal** isn't fattening.
**(h)** He eats a muffin with **butter**.
**(i)** **How much cholesterol** does it have?

**(j)** It has **a little** cholesterol.
NOT: It has 200 cholesterol.
**(k)** Milk **is** good for you.

## Exercise 1

Go back to the food items in the Task and make a list of the count and non-count nouns.

# Focus 2

# Quantifiers

- Quantifiers are words or phrases that modify nouns and show how many things or how much of something you are talking about. Certain quantifiers are used with count nouns and others with non-count nouns. Some quantifiers are used for both.

| Affirmative |
| --- |
| **Count** |
| There are **many eggs** in the fridge. |
| **a lot of** apples. |
| **some** bananas. |
| **a few** potatoes. |
| **Non-Count** |
| There is **a lot of** milk in the fridge. |
| **a lot of** cheese. |
| **some** juice. |
| **a little** cake. |

| Negative |
| --- |
| **Count** |
| There aren't **many** potatoes. |
| There are **few** tomatoes. |
| There aren't **any** onions. |
| There are **no** onions. |
| **Non-Count** |
| There isn't **much** cake. |
| There is **very little** coffee. |
| There isn't **any** jam. |
| There is **no** jam. |

- Note: In American English, *much* does not normally occur in the affirmative with non-count nouns in everyday speech. We use *a lot of* instead of *much*.

## Exercise 2

Match the picture to the statement by writing the corresponding letter next to each statement.

A.
Community Bank
• January 31 Account # 536 •
• •
• Debits : $325.00 Credits : $325.00 •
• Balance : $___.00 •

B.
Community Bank
• January 31 Account # 289 •
• •
• Debits : $312.80 Credits : $412.80 •
• Balance : $100.00 •

C.
Community Bank
• January 31 Account #741 •
• •
• Debits : $458.31 Credits : $958.31 •
• Balance : $500.00 •

D.
Community Bank
• January 31 Account #125 •
• •
• Debits : $7,096.10 Credits : $12,096.10 •
• Balance : $5,000.00 •

E.

F.

G.

_____ 1. Carlos has a lot of money in the bank.

_____ 2. François has a little money in the bank.

_____ 3. Kim has no money in the bank.

_____ 4. Lee has some money in the bank.

_____ 5. The Greens have a lot of plants in their home.

_____ 6. The Smiths don't have any plants.

_____ 7. The Taylors have a few plants.

## Exercise 3

Read these statements and draw pictures to represent each one.

1. Jean has a few friends.
2. Sally has no friends.
3. Mary has a lot of friends.

4. Bill has a lot of hair.
5. Jim doesn't have any hair.
6. Albert has a little hair.

## Exercise 4

Read the sentences below. In each one there is a quantifier whose form is not correct. Cross out the incorrect quantifier.

1. Middletown has $\left\{\begin{array}{l}\text{a lot of} \\ \text{a little} \\ \text{a few}\end{array}\right\}$ pollution.

2. The teacher gave us $\left\{\begin{array}{l}\text{some} \\ \text{many} \\ \text{a little}\end{array}\right\}$ homework.

3. Billy has $\left\{\begin{array}{l}\text{a little} \\ \text{a few} \\ \text{many}\end{array}\right\}$ girlfriends.

4. Mario speaks $\left\{\begin{array}{l}\text{much} \\ \text{several} \\ \text{a few}\end{array}\right\}$ languages.

5. Majid has $\left\{\begin{array}{l}\text{a lot of} \\ \text{a little} \\ \text{many}\end{array}\right\}$ money.

## Exercise 5

Write five true statements and five false statements from the chart in the Task. Then work with a partner and read your statements aloud. Your partner must say if the statement is true or false.

| **EXAMPLES:** | There are a lot of calories in a muffin. | False |
| | There's a little cholesterol in scrambled eggs. | False |
| | There isn't any fat in a glass of orange juice. | True |

# Focus 3

FORM

## Questions with Quantifiers

FORM

- **Count Nouns**
  - **(a)** Are there any eggs in the fridge?
  - **(b)** Are there a lot of potatoes in the fridge?
  - **(c)** How many eggs are there?

  Yes, there are. There are a lot of eggs.
  No, there aren't. There are only a few.
  About ten.

- **Non-Count Nouns**
  - **(d)** Is there any milk in the fridge?
  - **(e)** Is there much cake?
  - **(f)** How much coffee is there?

  Yes, there is. There's a lot of milk.
  No, there isn't. There's just a little.
  There's about a quarter of a pound.

276

## Exercise 6

Information Gap. Your partner gave you recipes for French potato salad and gazpacho, but you spilled some water on the paper and cannot read it. You look only at the incomplete recipes and ask your partner for the quantities. Your partner answers your questions by looking at the complete recipe.

**EXAMPLE:** How many potatoes do I need?

How much bacon do I need?

### INCOMPLETE RECIPES

1. French potato salad

potatoes
bacon
onions
vinegar
olive oil
salt and pepper
parsley

2. Gazpacho

| tomatoes | tomato juice |
| red peppers | eggs |
| onions | cayenne pepper |
| cucumbers | salt and pepper |
| vinegar | dill |
| olive oil | |

### COMPLETE RECIPES

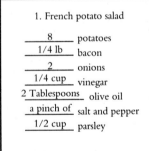

1. French potato salad

8 potatoes
1/4 lb bacon
2 onions
1/4 cup vinegar
2 Tablespoons olive oil
a pinch of salt and pepper
1/2 cup parsley

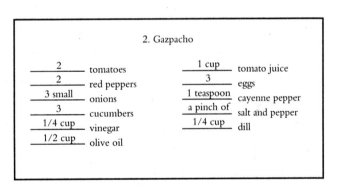

2. Gazpacho

| 2 tomatoes | 1 cup tomato juice |
| 2 red peppers | 3 eggs |
| 3 small onions | 1 teaspoon cayenne pepper |
| 3 cucumbers | a pinch of salt and pepper |
| 1/4 cup vinegar | 1/4 cup dill |
| 1/2 cup olive oil | |

# Focus 4

## A Few/Few
## A Little/Little

MEANING

- The quantifiers *a few/a little* and *few/little* have different meanings. *A few* and *a little* have a positive meaning. They mean "some" or "more than zero." *Few* and *little* have a negative meaning. They mean "not very much," "not many," or "almost zero." Look at the sentences in the chart below.

|  | Count | Non-count |
|---|---|---|
| **Positive Meaning** | a few<br><br>**(a)** I have **a few** friends. =<br>I have **some** friends. | a little<br><br>**(b)** I have **a little** time. =<br>I have **some** time. |
| **Negative Meaning** | few<br><br>**(c)** I have **few** friends. =<br>I **don't have many** friends. | little<br><br>**(d)** I have **little** time. =<br>I **don't have much** time. |

- Note: The negative form "I don't have many friends," is more common than "I have few friends."

## Exercise 7

Linda and Janice both went abroad to live in Europe for a year. They had very different experiences. Fill in the blanks with *few/a few* or *little/a little*.

1. Linda was very lonely and desperate. She had _____ friends and she had _____ money.

2. Janice's experience living in Europe was great. She was able to speak _____ languages after a year.

3. Linda got a job as a baby sitter. She hated it. She had _____ patience for it.

4. Linda felt the people were unfriendly. She asked the people for help, but they had _____ time for her.

5. Janice went to school and made _____ very good friends. She worked hard, but she always had _____ time to go out and enjoy herself.

# Focus 5

## Measure Words

MEANING

- Measure words can change the way a noun is viewed. Non-count nouns can be viewed as count nouns if measure words are used in front of them.
    - Container-based measure words

        a **can** of tuna    a **jar** of jam     a **box** of cereal
        a **bottle** of beer   a **tube** of toothpaste   a **bag** of sugar
    - Portion-based measure words

        a **slice** of pizza    a **pinch** of salt    a **pint** of ice cream
        a **piece** of pie     a **quart** of milk   a **cup** of coffee
        a **pound** of sugar
    - Specific-quantity measure words

        a **cup** of flour     a **quart** of milk    a **yard** of cloth
        a **pint** of ice cream   a **pound** of sugar
    - Other measure words

        a **head** of lettuce   a **loaf** of bread   a **sheet** of paper
        an **ear** of corn     a **roll** of film    a **bar** of soap
- Container and specific-quantity measure words can also be used before count nouns:

    a **bag** of apples
    a **pound** of onions
    a **dozen** eggs       NOT: a dozen of eggs
    **five thousand** people    NOT: five thousands of people

## Exercise 8

Here is Maggie at the checkout counter. Re-create her shopping list below. Use measure words.

### Shopping List

**a pound of** coffee          _____ oil

_____ milk               _____ soda

_____ rice               _____ bread

_____ soup             _____ soap

_____ toothpaste     _____ lettuce

_____ candy           _____ toilet paper

_____ beer              _____ beef

_____ butter          _____ peanut butter

## Exercise 9

Error Correction. Rewrite the following sentences correctly.

1. Jane: Can I talk to you for a minute?
   Kevin: Sure, I have little time.
2. John has much friends.
3. How many money do you have?
4. My teacher gave us many homeworks.
5. My hairs are black.
6. Elsie is in great shape. She jogs few miles a day.
7. We don't sell no newspapers here.
8. There are much opportunities in this city.
9. I would like some informations please.
10. My friend gave me many advices.

# Activities

## Activity 1

Test your knowledge about food. Check *true* if you think the statement is true and *false* if you think it is false. Then compare your answers to your partner's answers.

| | True | False |
|---|---|---|
| 1. There's a lot of salt in a McDonald's hamburger. | | |
| 2. There are no calories in beer. | | |
| 3. There's a lot of fat in cheese. | | |
| 4. There are few calories in a small baked potato. | | |
| 5. There's little cholesterol in fish. | | |
| 6. There are few vitamins in orange juice. | | |
| 7. There's some fat in low-fat yogurt. | | |
| 8. There isn't much protein in beans. | | |
| 9. There isn't any sugar in fruit. | | |
| 10. There's a little caffeine in tea. | | |

## Activity 2

Food Habit Survey: Using the cues below, ask "How much" and "How many" questions of three students.

**EXAMPLES:** How much coffee do you drink a day?

How many teaspoons of sugar do you put in your coffee?

|  | Student #1 | Student #2 | Student #3 |
|---|---|---|---|
| coffee or tea/drink/a day |  |  |  |
| teaspoons of sugar/put in tea or coffee |  |  |  |
| meat/eat/a week |  |  |  |
| fish/eat/a week |  |  |  |
| soda/drink/a day |  |  |  |
| money/spend on food/a week |  |  |  |
| alcohol/drink/a day |  |  |  |
| fruit/eat/a day |  |  |  |
| salt/put on food |  |  |  |
| glasses of water/drink/a day |  |  |  |
| eggs/eat/a week |  |  |  |
| meals/have/a day |  |  |  |

Add a few of your own.

## Activity 3

Start a circle game with all the students in the class. Make a statement starting with "I went to the store and bought. . . ." Say an item that begins with the letter *A* and use a measure word. The second student repeats your statement and adds a second item that starts with the letter *B*. The third student does the same and adds on an item with the letter *C* and so on. Use a measure word with each item.

**EXAMPLE:** Student #1: I went to the store and bought a bag of apples.

Student #2: I bought a bag of apples and a bottle of beer.

Student #3: I bought a bag of apples, a bottle of beer, and a head of cabbage.

## Activity 4

Look at a menu from a restaurant. Order lunch, including a drink, from the waitress.

**EXAMPLE:** I'd like a ham sandwich with a few tomatoes and a little lettuce. Put a little mustard and mayonnaise on the bread. I'd also like French fries with a lot of ketchup. To drink, I'd like a large glass of soda.

## Activity 5

Choose a recipe you like and write out the ingredients without writing the amount. The other students ask you questions with *how much* and *how many* to fill in the exact amount. After everyone has finished, compile all the recipes and make a class book of international recipes.

# UNIT 25

# Adjective Phrases

## Task

Read the statements on page 284 and write the letter of the person next to the statement. Then match each person to one of the houses by writing the letter of the person next to the house he or she lives in.

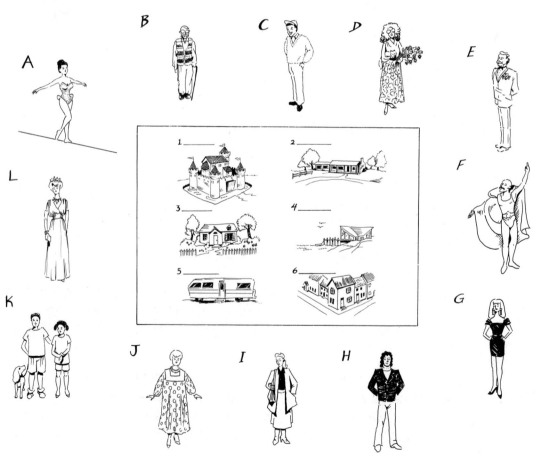

1. The bald man with the mustache has an athletic wife.                          F

2. The man with the medals on his jacket lives in house # 1.                    _____

3. The man in the dark jacket and turtleneck sweater is an accountant and lives in

   house #6.                                                                    _____

4. The woman with the flowers is the occupant of house #3.                      _____

5. The woman with the crown on her head is married to the man in house #1.       _____

6. The retired woman in the polka-dot dress lives in house #2.                   _____

7. The man in the striped vest is married to the retired woman.                  _____

8. The children with the dog live with their parents.                            _____

9. The man with the cap lives in house #4. He has two children.                  _____

10. The woman with the bag over her shoulder is married to the accountant.        _____

11. The woman on the tightrope lives in #5.                                       _____

12. The woman in the high-heeled shoes has two children.                          _____

# *Focus 1*

FORM ● MEANING

## Forming Adjective Phrases

**FORM
MEANING**

- Adjective phrases are groups of words that modify nouns. Adjective phrases follow the nouns they modify.
- An adjective phrase consists of a preposition and a noun, with or without adjectives.
  - **(a)** *The woman* **in the polka-dot dress** is retired.
  - **(b)** *The flowers* **on the table** are beautiful.
- The verb in the sentence agrees with the subject; not with the noun in the adjective phrase.
  - **(c)** *The man* in the dark jacket **is** an accountant.
  - **(d)** *The woman* with the flowers **is** the occupant of House #3.

## Exercise 1

Look back at the sentences in the Task. Put parentheses around the adjective phrases. Underline the subject and the verb in each sentence.

**EXAMPLE:** <u>The bald man</u> (with the mustache) <u>has</u> an athletic wife.

# *Focus 2*

FORM

## More About Forming Adjective Phrases

**FORM**

- An adjective phrase is a combination of two sentences.

  **(a)** The man has medals on his jacket.
  **(b)** The man is a king.

  The man **with the medals on his jacket** is a king.

  **(c)** The man has a mustache.
  **(d)** He's smoking a pipe.

  The man **with the mustache** is smoking a pipe.

  **(e)** The woman is wearing a polka-dot dress.
  **(f)** She's retired.

  The woman **in the polka-dot dress** is retired.

  **(g)** The flowers are on the table.
  **(h)** The flowers are beautiful.

  The flowers **on the table** are beautiful.

# Exercise 2

Each chair below belongs to one of the people on the next page. Match each person to the appropriate chair. Then, using adjective phrases, write sentences. The first one has been done for you.

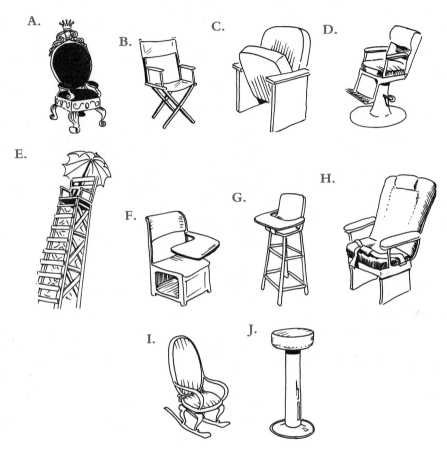

A.

B.

C.

D.

E.

F.

G.

H.

I.

J.

1. MEGAPHONE
2. BOTTLE
3. POPCORN
4. MIRROR
5. SUITCASES
6. CANE
7. CROWN
8. BOOKS
9. ICE CREAM CONE
10. WHISTLE

| | Chair | Person | |
|---|---|---|---|
| 1. | A | 7 | *The man with the crown sits in chair A* . |
| 2. | | | . |
| 3. | | | . |
| 4. | | | . |
| 5. | | | . |
| 6. | | | . |
| 7. | | | . |
| 8. | | | . |
| 9. | | | . |
| 10. | | | . |

## *Exercise 3*

Combine each of the following sentence pairs to write one sentence with an adjective phrase.

**EXAMPLE:** The girl has curly hair. She is my classmate.

The girl *with the curly hair* is my classmate.

### KINDERGARTEN CHAOS

1. The girl has pigtails. She is kicking her partner.

   _____

2. The boy is wearing a baseball cap. He is throwing a paper airplane across the room.

   _____

3. The girls are near the window. They are waving to friends outside.

   _____

4. The boy is wearing a Ninja Turtle suit. He is standing on the teacher's desk.

   _____

5. The boys are fighting. They are in the back of the room.

   _____

6. The boy is reading. He is in the corner.

   _____

7. The girl is crying. She is in the closet.

   _____

8. The girl has a walkman. She is singing.

   _____

9. The man is the new teacher. He has a rope around him.

   _____

10. The man is wearing a suit and tie. He is the principal.

    _____

11. The new teacher will lose his job. The new teacher is in this story.

    _____

# Focus 3

## Questions with *Which*

- Use the question word *which* when there is a choice between two or more things. Use *which* with singular or plural nouns.

| | |
|---|---|
| **(a) Which house** belongs to the accountant? | House #6. |
| **(b) Which houses** have trees around them? | Houses #2, 3, and 4. |

- Substitute the words *one* or *ones* for nouns when reference to the noun is clear in context, and you know the noun(s).

| | |
|---|---|
| **(c)** Which coat do you like, Mom? | I like the black coat. |
| | I like the black **one**. |
| **(d)** Which **one** do you like, Dad? | The red **one**. |

- You can also use adjective phrases after *one* and *ones*:

| | |
|---|---|
| **(e)** Which shoes do you want? | The ones **in the window**. |

**288**

# Exercise 4

Here is a before-and-after picture of Julie's house. Julie has just been robbed. She is talking to her husband on the telephone and telling him about the damage that was done. Working with a partner, say Julie's statements aloud. Your partner asks questions with *which* to find out the specific information.

**EXAMPLE:** You say: The vase is broken.

Your Partner: Which vase is broken?

You say: The one on the dining room table.

**BEFORE**

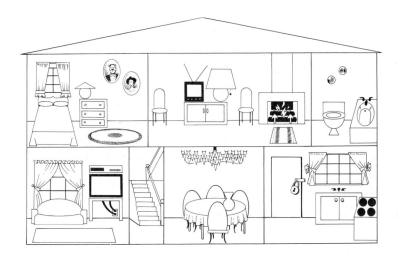

**AFTER**

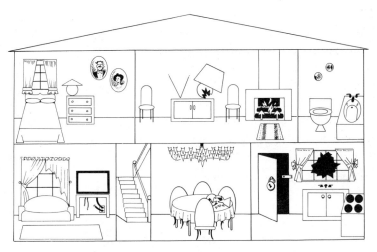

1. The window is broken.
2. The curtains are torn.
3. The TV is missing.
4. The door is open.
5. The lamp is broken.
6. The VCR is missing.
7. The lock is broken.
8. The rug is missing.

# Activities

### Activity 1

In a group, write sentences about ten students in the class, using adjective phrases. Do not use anyone's name. Then read your sentences to the class and have them guess each person you are talking about. You get one point if the class guesses the person on the first guess, two points if they guess on the second guess, three points on the third guess, and so on. The student with the most points at the end of the game wins.

> **EXAMPLE:** The student from Bogotá has pretty eyes.
>
> The student next to Miyuki is wearing glasses.
>
> The student with the biggest smile is from Panama.

### Activity 2

Bring a photograph or drawing of your family or the place you live to class. Write a description of the photograph, using adjective phrases.

> **EXAMPLE:** The house *on top of the hill* is my uncle's house.
>
> The woman *on the left* is my mother.

### Activity 3

Think about different countries and the things they are known for. Then write five sentences about those things. Make a list of the sentences that other people in the class have written.

> The coffee in Brazil is delicious.
>
> The beaches in Puerto Rico are beautiful.

# 26

# Phrasal Verbs

## *Task*

Nervous Nelly is giving a talk on her trip to South America for the first time. She had made some notes on index cards to help herself remember what to do, but she was so nervous that she dropped the cards on the floor. Can you help her put them in order? Number the cards from 1 to 10.

# Focus 1

## FORM
# Phrasal Verbs

**FORM**

- Form phrasal verbs by combining common verbs such as *come, go, make,* and *give* with certain particles such as *up, down, on, off, back,* and *around.* The two words together have a specific meaning.
  - **(a) Stand up** and give the lecture.
  - **(b) Turn on** the slide projector.
- The "particle" in a phrasal verb is different from a preposition. Look at these two sentences:
  - **(c)** I **go to** the bank on Fridays. (verb + preposition)
  - **(d)** You can **stand up** now. (phrasal verb)
- In sentence (c) the verb *go* is followed by the preposition *to.* However, in sentence (d) the verb *stand* is followed by the particle *up.* The verb + particle combination has a particular meaning.

## Exercise 1

Go back to Nelly's notes in the Task and circle all the phrasal verbs.

    **EXAMPLE:** (Stand up) and walk to the table at the front of the room.

# Focus 2

## MEANING ● USE
# The Meaning and Use of Phrasal Verbs

**MEANING USE**

- Sometimes you can tell what a phrasal verb means by combining the meaning of the verb and the particle. For example, in the sentence, "I hung up the picture on the wall," you can understand the meaning of the phrasal verb *hung up* by combining the meaning of the verb *hung* with the particle *up.*

  However, the meanings of phrasal verbs are usually different from the meanings of the words they are made of. For example, the meaning of *call on* is not the combination of *call* and *on.* To *call on* means to visit. Here are a few others:

| Phrasal Verb | Meaning | Example |
|---|---|---|
| **(a)** Hand out | Distribute | Nelly handed out the forms. |
| **(b)** Take off | Remove | She took off her shoes at home. |

- Phrasal verbs are used more frequently than their one-word equivalents in informal spoken English. It is more appropriate in face-to-face conversations to say, "Please throw away that letter," than it is to say, "Please discard that letter."

## Exercise 2

Match each phrasal verb with its one-word equivalent. Try to understand the meaning of each from the context.

1. Don't just stand at the door. *Come in.*
2. Don't be nervous. *Calm down.*
3. I've just pulled the fire alarm. The firemen will be here soon to *put out* the fire.
4. We're going to practice using phrasal verbs. Henry, would you please *hand out* the exercise.
5. I left my assignment book at school. I don't re-member the homework for tonight. I'll *call up* Manny and ask him.
6. I can't talk to you now. *Come back* in 15 minutes.
7. I can't concentrate! Would you please *turn down* the music.
8. I love that new song. Please *turn up* the volume.
9. Aren't you hot? Why don't you *take off* your jacket.
10. Your hands are all sticky. *Throw away* that candy wrapper.

Extinguish

Raise

Remove

Telephone

Relax

Distribute

Discard

Return

Enter

Lower

# Focus 3

FORM

# Separable versus Inseparable Phrasal Verbs

**FORM**

- Some phrasal verbs cannot be separated. They follow the form:

|   | **Verb +** | **Particle +** | **Noun Object/Pronoun Object** |
|---|---|---|---|
| **(a)** I | ran | into | my friends. |
|   |   |   | them. |

- Many phrasal verbs, however, can be separated. A noun object can come between the verb and the particle.

**(b)** I **handed out** the evaluation forms.
  I **handed** the evaluation forms **out**.

- With separable phrasal verbs, the pronoun object always comes before the particle.

**(c)** I handed **them out.**
  NOT: I handed out them.

## Exercise 3

Here are additional notes Nelly wrote. These phrasal verbs are separable. Write the imperatives in the other two ways.

**EXAMPLE:** Take out your notes.
*Take your notes out.*
*Take them out.*

1. Turn on the projector.

_____

_____

2. Turn off the lights.

_____

_____

3. Hand out the evaluations.

_____

_____

4. Take off your jackets.

_____

_____

5. Throw away your gum.

_____

_____

6. Look over your notes.

_____

_____

7. Put out your cigarettes.

_____

_____

## Exercise 4

Here are directions for lab assistants working in the language lab. Fill in the blanks with the correct phrasal verb below:

put away    turn on    pick up    throw away    turn off    pull out

> ### DIRECTIONS FOR LAB ASSISTANTS
> When you leave the language lab, there are several things you must do. First, 1)_____ all the paper from the floor. Then 2)_____ all the equipment — tape recorders, VCRs, etc. In fact, you need to 3)_____ the plugs on the computers. 4) _____all the cassettes that students have returned. 5) _____ any coffee cups or litter students left behind. Finally, 6)_____ the alarm system before you lock the doors.

# Exercise 5

Read the problems on the left to your partner. He or she responds with the appropriate solution on the right.

**Problems**

1. I don't feel like cooking tonight.
2. It's hot in here.
3. It's so quiet in here.
4. I can't read the TV schedule.
5. I need to finish my homework, but the TV is still on.
6. I have a 9:00 meeting in Los Angeles. That's two hours away from here.
7. My feet are killing me.
8. We're driving 75 miles an hour in a 55-mile zone.
9. I'm really upset about our argument today.
10. I'm so tired of sitting on this plane.

**Solutions**

Calm down.

Get up early.

Stand up for a few minutes.

Sit down and rest.

Slow down.

Take off your sweater.

Put on your glasses.

Turn off the TV.

Let's eat out.

Turn on the radio.

# Exercise 6

Fill in the blanks with one of the phrasal verbs below. Change verb to past tense wherever necessary.

call up     hang up     figure out     go over     pick up

I couldn't (1)_____ the homework assignment, so I decided to (2)_____

one of my classmates. I dialed his number. He (3)_____ the receiver after five rings.

We (4)_____ the homework and then kept talking. We didn't (5)_____

till an hour later!

# Exercise 7

Fill in the blanks in the dialogue with one of the phrasal verbs below. Use a pronoun object in the second blank of each dialogue.

**EXAMPLE:** (clean up)

Mother: Danny, don't forget to *clean up* the mess in your bedroom before you go out.

Danny: Mom, I *cleaned it up* this morning!

pick up    hand out    take out    fill out

1. **Counselor:** You need to (a) _____ (b) _____ this application for college.

   **Abdul:** Can I (c) _____ (d) _____ (e) _____ at home?

2. **Susie:** Danny, it's your turn to (a) _____ (b) _____ the garbage.

   **Danny:** I'm (c) _____ (d) _____ (e) _____ right now.

3. **Jackie:** Could you please (a) _____ (b) _____ that paper on the floor for me?

   **Mark:** I'll (c) _____ (d) _____ (e) _____ with pleasure!

4. **Ms. Wagner:** Can you help me (a) _____ (b) _____ these exams, Wang?

   **Wang:** Sure, I'll (c) _____ (d) _____ (e) _____ right now.

## Exercise 8

Sylvia is working late tonight. She's calling her husband Abe to see whether he has done all the things on the list she left him. Role-play the dialogue, following the pattern below.

**Sylvia:** Did you pick up the children at school?
**Abe:**    Yes, dear, I picked them up.

1. pick up our clothes at the cleaners
2. hang up the clean clothes
3. put away the clean laundry
4. take out the dog
5. throw out the garbage

6. pick up something for dinner
7. cook up dinner
8. turn on the movie for the children
9. call up your mother
10. clean up the kitchen

# Activities

### Activity 1

Using the picture below, write your own story or dialogue with these phrasal verbs.

turn off    turn on    get up    wake up    take off    put on

### Activity 2

Work with a partner to create a story or dialogue about the situation below. Role-play the situation for the class. Then the class will write the story.

Situation: It is 11:00 P.M. You are sleeping very soundly. Suddenly, you hear some loud noise coming from the apartment downstairs. Your downstairs neighbor is playing his stereo very loudly.

Phrasal Verbs:    wake up
                  throw out
                  turn down
                  get along
                  turn off
                  turn on

## Activity 3

Work in a group. Put numbers from 1 to 12 in a hat. Pick out a number from the hat. Read the sentence in the grid below that corresponds to the number and then do the action. After the group does all the actions, write sentences about all the things you did.

**EXAMPLES:** *Mario turned on the tape recorder.*

*José wrote a sentence and crossed out the phrasal verb.*

### Phrasal Verb Grid

| | | |
|---|---|---|
| **1.** Put on a piece of a classmate's clothing or jewelry. | **2.** Turn off the light. | **3.** Make up a new name for yourself. |
| **4.** Call up a friend and tell him or her you are sick. | **5.** Draw a picture of yourself on a piece of paper and hang it up on the wall. | **6.** Write a sentence with a phrasal verb and cross out the phrasal verb. |
| **7.** Talk on the phone with someone, have an argument, and hang up. | **8.** Hand your telephone number out to all the people in the group of the opposite sex. | **9.** Take something out of your pocket and throw it away. |
| **10.** Take off an article of clothing and put it on someone else. | **11.** Turn on something electrical (tape recorder, radio, light, etc.) and then turn it off. | **12.** Pretend you find a word whose meaning you don't know. Look it up in the dictionary. |

# Comparison with Adjectives

## Task

Here are two cars you are interested in buying. Look at the descriptions of the cars. Then read the statements below and decide whether they are true or false. Circle the correct answer.

| | | The Mini (2-door) | The Charisma (4-door) |
|---|---|---|---|
| A. | engine size | 1.5 liter | 1.9 liter |
| B. | length | 214.1 in. | 217.3 in. |
| C. | width | 77.0 in. | 79.6 in. |
| D. | height | 56.7 in. | 60.9 in. |
| E. | weight | 1850 lbs | 2460 lbs |
| F. | gas mileage | 30 mpg | 23 mpg |
| G. | warranty | 5 years 50,000 m | 7 years 70,000 m |
| H. | safety features | seat belts | automatic seat belt system & air bags |
| I. | price | $6,950 | $8,750 |

1. The Mini is longer than the Charisma.     T     F
2. The Charisma's engine is bigger than the Mini's.     T     F
3. The Charisma is wider than the Mini.     T     F
4. The Charisma is safer than the Mini.     T     F
5. The Mini is more powerful than the Charisma.     T     F
6. The Charisma is more economical than the Mini.     T     F
7. The Charisma is more expensive than the Mini.     T     F
8. The Mini is heavier than the Charisma.     T     F
9. The Mini is more comfortable than the Charisma.     T     F

Now write the name of one of the cars in the space below:

10. In my opinion, I think the _____ is prettier.

**299**

# *Focus 1*

FORM ● MEANING

## Comparative Form of Adjectives

- One way to compare two things, people, or places is to use the comparative form of adjectives + *than*.

| Adjective | Rule | Example |
|---|---|---|
| Adjectives with One Syllable:<br>**1.** Ending in *-e*<br><br>  *wide*<br><br>  *safe* | Add *-r*. | **(a)** The Charisma is **wider than** the Mini.<br>**(b)** A big car is **safer than** a small one. |
| **2.** Consonant-vowel-consonant<br><br>  *big*<br><br>  *thin* | Double the consonant, and add *-er*. | **(c)** The Charisma's engine is **bigger than** the Mini's.<br>**(d)** She's **thinner than** you. |
| **3.** All others<br>  *tall* | Add *-er*. | **(e)** Joe is **taller than** I (am). |
| Adjectives with Two or More Syllables:<br>**4.** Ending in *-y*<br><br>  *pretty*<br>  *noisy* | Change the *-y* to *-i* and add *-er*. | **(f)** Sara is **prettier than** she (is).<br>**(g)** A motorcycle is **noisier than** a car. |
| **5.** All others<br><br>  *economical*<br><br>  *expensive* | Use *more* or *less* before the adjective. | **(h)** The Mini is **more economical than** the Charisma.<br>**(i)** The Mini is **less expensive than** the Charisma. |

- Note: It is correct to use the subject pronoun after *than* in comparative statements. But in informal spoken English, it is more common to use the object pronoun if no verb form follows.

  **(j)** Joe is taller than me.
  **(k)** Sara is prettier than her.

## Exercise 1

Go back to the Task. List all the comparative forms of the adjectives in the space below. Indicate which rule they refer to.

| Comparative | Rule | Comparative | Rule |
|---|---|---|---|
| 1. longer than | 3. | 7. | |
| 2. | | 8. | |
| 3. | | 9. | |
| 4. | | 10. | |
| 5. | | 11. | |
| 6. | | | |

## Exercise 2

Look at the following adjectives. Indicate how many syllables the adjective has. Then write the comparative form of the adjective.

**EXAMPLE:** interesting    4    more interesting than

| Adjective | # of Syllables | Comparative Form |
|---|---|---|
| 1. large | _____ | _____ |
| 2. enthusiastic | _____ | _____ |
| 3. busy | _____ | _____ |
| 4. exciting | _____ | _____ |
| 5. intelligent | _____ | _____ |
| 6. hot | _____ | _____ |
| 7. nervous | _____ | _____ |
| 8. comfortable | _____ | _____ |
| 9. crazy | _____ | _____ |
| 10. sad | _____ | _____ |

## Exercise 3

You are a marketing specialist. Use the following adjectives to write ads that will sell the products below.

**EXAMPLE:** "Sinful Delight" chocolate cake tastes richer than regular chocolate cake.

1. Product: **Lo-Cal Sinful Delight Chocolate Cake versus Choco-Bake**

Adjectives:   rich, creamy, delicious, moist, sweet, thick, fattening

_____

_____

_____


2. Product: **Suds Plus versus Bubbles Soap**

Adjectives:   strong, effective, expensive, quick

_____

_____

_____

3. Product: **Save-a-Watt Space Heater versus Consumer Space Heater**

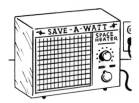 

Adjectives: efficient, safe, reliable, small, easy, economical, practical

_____

_____

_____

# Focus 2

FORM

## Irregular Comparatives

FORM

- Some adjectives have irregular comparative forms:

| | |
|---|---|
| *good* | **(a)** The Charisma's warranty is **better than** the Mini's (warranty). |
| *bad* | **(b)** Cookies are **worse** for you than crackers. |
| *far* | **(c)** The Mini car dealer is **farther** away **than** the Charisma dealer. |

# Exercise 4

Yoko wants to study English in the United States. She knows about an English program in Brattleboro, a small town in Vermont, and one in Los Angeles, a big city in California. She needs to decide where she wants to live. Here is the information she has about the two places.

|  | **Brattleboro, Vermont** | **Los Angeles, California** |
|---|---|---|
| 1. Attractive | (yes)  OK  no | yes  (OK)  no |
| 2. Population | 12,000 | 3 million |
| 3. Cost of a 1-bedroom apartment | $450/mo | $1,000/mo |
| 4. Public Transportation | good  satisfactory  (bad) | good  (satisfactory)  bad |
| 5. Weather | cold in winter<br>hot in summer | warm in winter<br>hot in summer |
| 6. Crime | high  (low) | (high)  low |
| 7. Clean | (good)  satisfactory  bad | good  (satisfactory)  bad |

Now write comparative sentences for each of the categories above using the adjectives in parentheses. The first one has been done for you.

**1.** (attractive)  *Brattleboro is more attractive than Los Angeles.*
*Los Angeles is less attractive than Brattleboro.*

**2.** (populated)

**3.** (cheap/expensive)

**4.** (good/bad)

**5.** (cold/hotter)

**6.** (dangerous/safe)

**7.** (clean/dirty)

# Focus 3

FORM

## Questions with Comparative Adjectives

**FORM**

- *Yes/No* Questions
  - **(a)** Is the Charisma **more expensive than** the Mini?
  - **(b)** Are small cars **better than** big cars?
- *Who, Which, Whose*
  - **(c) Who** is **older**, you or your brother?
  - **(d) Which** is **more difficult**, French or Spanish?
  - **(e) Whose car** is **more comfortable**, yours or hers?

## Exercise 5

Go back to the Task and ask a partner *yes/no* questions about the Mini and the Charisma.

**EXAMPLE:** Is the Charisma more economical than the Mini?

## Exercise 6

Ask your partner *yes/no* questions with the following cues. Answer each other's questions.

> **EXAMPLE:** Question:  Is a theater ticket more expensive than a movie ticket?
>
> Answers:  Yes, I think so. (or) Maybe.

1. a theater ticket/expensive/a movie ticket
2. people in the United States/friendly/people in your native country
3. English grammar/difficult/the grammar of your language
4. an IBM computer/easy to use/a Macintosh computer
5. reading/interesting/watching TV
6. fried chicken/fattening/broiled chicken
7. fast food/good/a homemade meal
8. electric heat/economical/gas heat
9. men/emotional/women
10. a Japanese watch/expensive/a Swiss watch

## Exercise 7

Using the pairs and the adjectives below, ask a partner questions with *who* or *which*. Answer each other's questions.

> **EXAMPLE:** (popular)  Madonna or Tina Turner?
>
> *Who is more popular, Madonna or Tina Turner?*
>
> (practical)  cordless phone or regular phone?
>
> *Which is more practical: a cordless phone or a regular phone?*

| | | |
|---|---|---|
| 1. | (intelligent) | women or men? |
| 2. | (difficult) | speaking English or writing English? |
| 3. | (bad) | ironing or vacuuming? |
| 4. | (cheap) | a city college or private college? |
| 5. | (powerful) | a 4-cylinder car or a 5-cylinder car? |
| 6. | (dangerous) | a motorcycle or a car? |
| 7. | (sensitive) | women or men? |
| 8. | (delicious) | Chinese food or Italian food? |
| 9. | (spicy) | Indian food or Thai food? |
| 10. | (useful) | a typewriter or a computer? |
| 11. | (heavy) | a ton of feathers or a ton of bricks? |

# Focus 4

FORM ● MEANING

## Equatives: Expressing Similarities and Differences

FORM
MEANING

- When you want to say that two things are equal, use the pattern *as* + adjective + *as*:

  **(a)** Mark is **as tall as** Sam.

  **(b)** Tokyo is **as crowded as** New York City.

- You can also express a difference between two things by using a negative equative: *not as* + adjective + *as*:

  **(c)** Steve is taller than Mark. = Mark **isn't as tall as** Steve.

  **(d)** The Mini is cheaper than the Charisma. = The Charisma **isn't as cheap as** the Mini.

## Exercise 8

Here is a dialogue between Tommy and his mother. Tommy wants to buy a motorcycle. His mother doesn't agree with him. She wants him to get a car instead. Write the correct form of the comparative in the blanks. Use *-er, more than,* and *as . . . . . . as.*

**Mother:** Tommy, I don't want you to buy a motorcycle. Why don't you buy a car instead? A

car is (1) _____ (convenient) a motorcycle and it's (2)_____

(practical) too!

**Tommy:** It might be more practical, but a car isn't (3)_____ (economical) a

motorcycle. I can get 50 miles to a gallon with a motorcycle! A motorcycle's

(4)_____ (cheap) a car.

**Mother:** Listen to me. You live in a big city. There are a lot of crazy people out there on the

streets. A car is (5) _____ (safe) a motorcycle.

306

**Tommy:** Mom, I'm a good driver. I'm (6) _____ (good) you are. With a motorcycle, I can see everything around me. I'm (7) _____ (aware) of other people. And besides that, it's (8) _____ (easy) to park a motorcycle in the city than it is to park a car.

**Mother:** Well, you're right about that. But I am still your mother and you live in my house, so you will do as I say! When you are (9)_____ (old), you can do whatever you want.

## *Focus 5*

USE

# Using Negative Equatives

USE

- Look at the following two sentence pairs. Check the statement you think is more polite.
  **(a)** Hamid is shorter than Marco.     **(c)** Nicos is less fluent in English than Spiros.
  **(b)** Hamid is not as tall as Marco.   **(d)** Nicos is not as fluent in English as Spiros.
- Statements **(b)** and **(d)** are negative equatives. They are less direct and softer; therefore, they are more polite.

## *Exercise 9*

Work with a partner. You are "Blunt Betty." Read a statement from Column A. Your statements are very direct and somewhat impolite. Your partner, "Polite Polly," makes a negative equative to make the comparative softer or more polite. Write the negative equative in Column B and then read it aloud.

**EXAMPLE:** Blunt Betty:  Marco is fatter than Jonathan.
Polite Polly:  *Marco is not as thin as Jonathan.*

**A. Blunt Betty**

**B. Polite Polly**

1. London is dirtier than Paris.          _____

2. Science class is more boring than math.  _____

3. Your child is less intelligent than mine.  _____

4. This book is worse than that book.    _____

5. Your apartment is smaller than ours.    _____

6. Miguel's pronunciation is worse than Maria's.    _____

7. American coffee is weaker than Turkish coffee.    _____

## Exercise 10

Use the categories below to write statements comparing yourself to a partner.

> **EXAMPLE:** *My partner's older than I am.* (My partner's older than me.)
> *I'm not as old as he is.* (I'm not as old as him.)

|   |   | Me | My Partner |
|---|---|----|------------|
| A. | Age | 18 | 24 |
| B. | Height |  |  |
| C. | Weight |  |  |
| D. | Hair length |  |  |
| E. | Hair color |  |  |
| F. | Eye color |  |  |
| G. | Personality |  |  |

## Exercise 11

Error correction. Rewrite the following sentences correctly.

1. John is tall than Mary.
2. Tokyo is more safer than New York City.
3. Paul is as selfish than Robert.
4. Mary is not beautiful as Kim.
5. My test scores were more worse than Margaret's.

# Activities

**Activity 1**

How much do the following items cost in your country or a country you know? On a separate sheet of paper, write the average cost (in U.S. dollars) of each item in that country. Then ask three other people in your class the prices of the same items in other countries they know. Present your comparisons to the class.

> **EXAMPLE:** A gallon of gas in Italy is more expensive than in the United States.

Items:    a gallon of gas    a movie ticket    bus fare    a pair of jeans    a cup of coffee

## Activity 2

In a group, write six statements comparing cities, countries, or other places in the world. Make three statements that are true and three that are false. Read your statements to the class. The class must guess if they are true or false.

**EXAMPLE:** New York City is dirtier than Orlando.     (T)

The United States is larger than The People's Republic of China.   (F)

## Activity 3

Rate your personality according to the following adjectives. Then work with a partner and compare your personalities. Write a comparative sentence for each adjective:

**EXAMPLE:** I'm *more talkative than* my partner.

He's *less practical than* I am.

I'm *as moody as* he is.

| | | | | | | |
|---|---|---|---|---|---|---|
| not very talkative | 1 | 2 | 3 | 4 | 5 | very talkative |
| not very extroverted | 1 | 2 | 3 | 4 | 5 | very extroverted |
| not very shy | 1 | 2 | 3 | 4 | 5 | very shy |
| not very neat | 1 | 2 | 3 | 4 | 5 | very neat |
| not very practical | 1 | 2 | 3 | 4 | 5 | very practical |
| not very energetic | 1 | 2 | 3 | 4 | 5 | very energetic |
| not very moody | 1 | 2 | 3 | 4 | 5 | very moody |
| not very lazy | 1 | 2 | 3 | 4 | 5 | very lazy |

## Activity 4

You are looking for an apartment to rent in the San Francisco area. You are a student and you are single. You have a part-time job. Read the following ads and decide which one you want. Compare the apartments. Write a short paragraph explaining your choice and read it to the class.

**Berkeley**, $750, includes utilities. Nicely furnished apartment on 4th floor. No elevator. 1 Bedroom and large kitchen. 5 blocks to public transportation. No children and no pets.

**Oakland**, $550, large studio, unfurnished, needs work. Elevated building. 10 blocks to subway. No pets.

**Sausalito**, $850, 2 Bedrooms, unfurnished. Two baths. Brand-new condition. Near subway.

## Activity 5

Work with a partner to design a new product. Decide on the kind of product you want to sell, the name of the product, and how it will look. Then write a 30-second radio commercial to sell your product.

## Activity 6

Choose a topic below and write a paragraph about it.

1. Compare this country with your native country.
2. Compare men and women.
3. Compare life nowadays with life 20 years ago.
4. Compare your mother and father.
5. Compare prices in the U.S. with prices in your native country.

# 28

# Comparison
# with Adverbs

## Task

Do you think men learn faster than women? Do you think women work harder than men? Read the questions below and put a check if the answer is *yes*, *no*, or *maybe*. Then compare your answers with a partner and discuss them.

|  | Yes | No | Maybe |
|---|---|---|---|
| 1. Do women live longer than men? |  |  |  |
| 2. Do men drive more safely than women? |  |  |  |
| 3. Do women communicate better than men? |  |  |  |
| 4. Do women manage people better than men do? |  |  |  |
| 5. Do men work harder than women? |  |  |  |
| 6. Do women dance more gracefully than men do? |  |  |  |
| 7. Do men think more clearly than women do in emergencies? |  |  |  |
| 8. Do women take care of children more patiently than men? |  |  |  |
| 9. Do women express their feelings more openly than men do? |  |  |  |
| 10. Can women learn languages more easily than men? |  |  |  |
| 11. Can men do math more easily than women? |  |  |  |
| 12. Do women spend money more freely than men? |  |  |  |

# Focus 1

## Comparative Form of Adverbs

FORM

| Adverb | Rule | Example |
|---|---|---|
| • Short adverbs<br>*fast*<br>*long* | Add *-er* | **(a)** Men run **faster than** women (do).<br>**(b)** Women live **longer than** men (do). |
| • Adverbs with 2 or more syllables<br>*safely*<br>*carefully* | Use *more* or *less* + adverb + *than* | **(c)** Do women drive **more safely than** men (do)?<br>**(d)** Do men drive **less carefully than** women (do)? |
| • Adverb of frequency<br>*frequency*<br>*often* | Use *more* or *less* + adverb of frequency + *than* | **(e)** Jerry and Pam eat out **more frequently than** we (do).<br>**(f)** He exercises **less often than** his son (does). |
| • Irregular comparative forms<br>*well*<br>*badly*<br>*far* | | **(g)** Do women cook **better than** men (do)?<br>**(h)** Do women score **worse** on tests **than** men (do)?<br>**(i)** Can a man throw a ball **farther than** a woman (can)?<br>**(j)** I went **further** in school than you (did). |

- Note the use of auxiliary verbs in comparative statements.

    **(k)** Jason **can** climb higher than his brother **can**.

    **(l)** I type faster than my classmate **does**.

    **(m)** We speak Spanish better than they **do**.

    **(n)** She'**ll** do a better job than you **will**.

- In informal English, the object pronoun is commonly used in comparatives. You will often hear:

    **(o)** I run faster than **him**.

    **(p)** He speaks better than **me**.

Go back to the questions in the Task and underline all the comparatives.

**EXAMPLE:** Do women live <u>longer than</u> men?

## Exercise 2

Using a comparative, write a statement to answer the questions in the Task.

**EXAMPLE:** *I think women live longer than men.*

# Focus 2

FORM ● MEANING

## Equatives: Expressing Similarities and Differences

FORM
MEANING

- Express similarities with equatives using the pattern

    **as** + adverb + **as**

    **(a)** A woman can work **as hard as** a man.

    **(b)** A man can work **as hard as** a woman.
- Use **just** to emphasize that the two parts of the comparative are exactly alike.

    **(c)** Women drive **just** as carefully as men.
- Express differences with negative equatives using the pattern

    **not as** + adverb + **as**

    **(d)** He doesn't speak **as clearly as** I (do) = I speak more clearly than he (does).

    = He speaks less clearly than I (do).

## Exercise 3

Sally Strathers and Bill Murphy are applying for a job as director of an art company. You are part of a committee and must decide who is the better candidate for the job. Make five comparative sentences about each candidate.

**EXAMPLES:** *Sally works as hard as Bill.*
*Bill draws more artistically than Sally.*

| WORK HABITS | Sally Strathers | Bill Murphy |
|---|:---:|:---:|
| 1. works hard | √ | √ |
| 2. draws artistically | | √ |
| 3. thinks creatively | √ | √ |
| 4. communicates openly | √ | |
| 5. treats workers fairly | √ | |
| 6. reacts to problems calmly | √ | |
| 7. prepares diligently | | √ |
| 8. thinks through problems carefully | | √ |
| 9. writes clearly | √ | √ |
| 10. works fast | | √ |

## Exercise 4

Pretend you are the president of the art company. Write down some questions to ask the committee to find out about Sally and Bill.

**EXAMPLE:** *Does Sally write as clearly as Bill?*
*Does Bill react to problems more calmly than Sally?*

## Exercise 5

Work with a partner. Say the sentences you wrote about men and women in Exercise 2 aloud. Your partner responds with an equative expression using "as . . ."

**EXAMPLE:** Student 1: I think women live longer than men.
Student 2: I think men live just as long as women do.

313

## Exercise 6

Discuss the pre-reading questions in class. Then read the following paragraphs.

**PRE-READING QUESTIONS:**

1. Do you think boys and girls grow up differently? In what way(s) do they grow up differently?
2. Do you think boys and girls talk differently?
3. Do you think boys and girls play differently?

Boys and girls grow up in different worlds. Research shows that boys and girls have very different ways of acting. For example, boys and girls often play at the same time, but they don't play together. They spend most of their time playing in same-sex groups. Some of their activities are similar, but their favorite games are different. Also, the language they use in their games is different.

Boys usually play outside in large groups. Their groups have a leader. The leader gives orders. Boys also become leaders by telling stories and jokes. Boys' games have winners and losers. Finally, boys frequently boast of their skill and argue about who is the best.

Girls, however, play in small groups or pairs. The center of a girl's social life is her best friend. Intimacy or closeness is very important. In their most frequent games, like jump rope or hopscotch, everyone gets a turn. Many of their activities, such as playing house, do not have winners or losers. Girls don't boast about their skills. They don't give orders. They usually express suggestions. They like to sit together and talk.

## Exercise 7

Based on the article above, check true or false for the statements below:

|  | True | False |
|---|---|---|
| 1. Boys and girls play differently. | | |
| 2. Girls behave more socially than boys. | | |
| 3. Boys and girls usually play in the same group. | | |
| 4. Girls play more competitively than boys do. | | |
| 5. Boys boast about themselves more frequently than girls do. | | |
| 6. Girls talk to each other more intimately than boys do. | | |
| 7. Girls give suggestions more frequently than boys do. | | |
| 8. Boys act more cooperatively than girls do. | | |

## Exercise 8

Use the cues below to make statements about boys and girls with comparatives and equatives. Discuss your answers.

**EXAMPLE:** build / creatively
*Boys build more creatively than girls.*
*Boys build less creatively than girls.*
*Girls build as creatively as boys.*
*Girls don't build as creatively as boys.*

1. score / high on math tests
2. run / fast
3. act / aggressively
4. act / independently

5. learn languages / easily
6. solve problems / creatively
7. make friends / quickly
8. study / hard

# Focus 3

FORM

## Questions with *How*

- *How* is often followed by an adjective, an adverb of manner, or an adverb of frequency:

| Adjective | **(a) How old** are you? | I'm 17. |
| Adverb of manner | **(b) How well** do you speak English? | Very well. |
| Adverb of frequency | **(c) How often** do you come to the United States? | Every year. |

- Questions with *How far* ask about distance in miles, kilometers, blocks, etc. The impersonal pronoun *it* functions as the subject in the question and in the response.

**(d) How far** is **it** from here to the park?     It's (about) 5 blocks.

**(e) How far** is **it** from Baltimore to Washington, D.C.?     It's (about) 70 miles.

- Questions with *How long does it take* ask about time.

**(f) How long does it take** to fly to from New York to Beijing?     It takes about 24 hours.

**(g) How long does it take** you to prepare dinner?     It takes me an hour.

## Exercise 9

Use the cues below to ask a partner questions.

> **EXAMPLES:** how long/do your homework
>
> How long does it take (you) to do your homework?

1. how long/get dressed in the morning
2. how far/live from school
3. how long/get to school
4. how well/cook
5. how fast/drive
6. how far/run
7. how hard/study
8. how long/clean your apartment/house

Add two questions of your own.

## Exercise 10

Answer the following questions about yourself. Then ask a partner the same questions and write the information in the space provided. Compare your answers with a partner's. Finally, write a sentence comparing yourself to your partner.

These adverbs will help you:

| early | late | fast | quickly | slowly | often |
|-------|------|------|---------|--------|-------|
| far | close | hard | well | long | frequently |

|   | Me | My Partner |
|---|-----|-----------|
| 1. What time do you get up in the morning? *I get up earlier than Joseph.* | 6:30 A.M. | 7:30 A.M. |
| 2. What time do you go to bed at night? | | |
| 3. How well do you speak English? | | |
| 4. What time do you usually come to class? | | |
| 5. How high can you jump? | | |
| 6. How many hours a day do you study? | | |
| 7. How many hours a day do you work? | | |
| 8. How fast do you type? | | |
| 9. How far can you jog? | | |
| 10. How often do you eat out? | | |

# Activities

## Activity 1

Using the cues below, compare two cities or places that you know. Write a sentence for each cue.

> **EXAMPLE:** *The trains run more smoothly in Paris than in Montreal.*

1. trains/run smoothly
2. buses/run efficiently
3. people/work hard
4. taxi drivers/drive carelessly
5. traffic/move slowly

6. people/talk loudly
7. people/treat foreigners politely
8. stores/stay open late
9. people act/strangely

Add two of your own:

_____

_____

## Activity 2

Here is a list of adverbs and a list of actions. Write each adverb and each action on a separate card. With a partner, take one adverb card and one action card. Both of you mime the action and the adverb. The class guesses the action and the adverb. Then the class compares the two mimes by making a comparative sentence.

> **EXAMPLE:** | Angrily | Eat spaghetti |
> "Paolo ate spaghetti more angrily than Maria."

| Adverbs | Actions |
|---|---|
| Slowly | Eat spaghetti |
| Sadly | Put on your clothes |
| Nervously | Make the bed |
| Angrily | Dance |
| Fast | Type a letter |
| Carefully | Brush your teeth |
| Seriously | Comb your hair |
| Happily | Paint a picture |
| Loudly | Play tennis |
| Softly | Shake someone's hand |

## Activity 3

Here is a map of the Southwestern part of the United States. You and your friend want to take a three-week vacation and visit the national parks. Depart from Denver and list the order of the places you will go. Then fill in the chart below. Ask questions with *how far* and *how long* to determine the route you will take and the time involved. Remember you will travel by car and the average speed limit is 55 miles per hour.

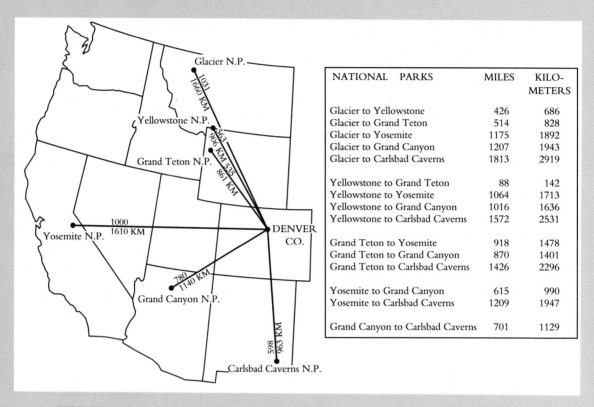

| NATIONAL   PARKS | MILES | KILO-METERS |
|---|---|---|
| Glacier to Yellowstone | 426 | 686 |
| Glacier to Grand Teton | 514 | 828 |
| Glacier to Yosemite | 1175 | 1892 |
| Glacier to Grand Canyon | 1207 | 1943 |
| Glacier to Carlsbad Caverns | 1813 | 2919 |
| | | |
| Yellowstone to Grand Teton | 88 | 142 |
| Yellowstone to Yosemite | 1064 | 1713 |
| Yellowstone to Grand Canyon | 1016 | 1636 |
| Yellowstone to Carlsbad Caverns | 1572 | 2531 |
| | | |
| Grand Teton to Yosemite | 918 | 1478 |
| Grand Teton to Grand Canyon | 870 | 1401 |
| Grand Teton to Carlsbad Caverns | 1426 | 2296 |
| | | |
| Yosemite to Grand Canyon | 615 | 990 |
| Yosemite to Carlsbad Caverns | 1209 | 1947 |
| | | |
| Grand Canyon to Carlsbad Caverns | 701 | 1129 |

| Depart from: | Denver, Colorado | Distance in miles/kilometers |
|---|---|---|
| Stop #1: | | |
| #2 | | |
| #3 | | |
| #4 | | |
| #5 | | |
| | | Total # miles/kilometers _____ |

UNIT

# 29

# Superlatives

## Task

Do you know the answers to the trivia questions below? Work with a partner and try to guess the answers.

1. What is the longest wall in the world?
2. What's the most common contagious disease?
3. What's the most valuable painting in the world?
4. What's the most common language in the world?
5. What's the hottest place on earth?
6. What's the tallest office building in the world?
7. What is the biggest city in the world?
8. What was the most popular movie ever made?
9. What's the most expensive university in the United States?
10. What's the hardest gem?

## Focus 1

FORM ● MEANING

# Expressions with the Superlative

FORM
MEANING

- Use the superlative form to rank a person or thing at the top or bottom of the group in question.
    **(a) The tallest office building in the United States** is the Sears Tower in Chicago.
    **(b) The least expensive item on the menu** is a hamburger.
- At the end of superlative sentences, use adjective phrases that identify the group of people or things to which the one person or thing is being compared.
    **(c)** Dr. Stevens is *the most respected teacher* **at the school.**
    **(d)** M.I.T. is *the most expensive university* **in the United States.**
    **(e)** Rose is *the smartest* **of all the students.**

# *Focus 2*

## Regular and Irregular Superlative Forms

| Adjectives/Adverbs | Rule | Example |
|---|---|---|
| • With one syllable | Use *the* + (adjective + -*est* + noun)<br>Use *the* + (adverb + -*est*) | **(a)** The Great Wall of China is **the longest** wall in the world.<br>**(b)** My grandfather worked **the hardest** of his three brothers. |
| • Consonant-vowel-consonant | Double the final consonant and add -*est* | **(c)** **The hottest** place on earth is in Ethiopia. |
| • Ending in -*e* | add -*st* | **(d)** Jupiter is **the largest** planet. |
| • With two syllables + -*y* | Change -*y* to -*i* and add -*est* | **(e)** **The easiest** subject for me is geography. |
| • With two or more syllables | Use *the* + *most/least* + adjective | **(f)** **The most contagious** disease is the common cold.<br>**(g)** **The least fattening** item on the menu is yogurt. |
| | Use *the* + *most/least* + adverb | **(h)** Of all his friends, he drives **the most carefully**.<br>**(i)** She danced **the least gracefully** of all the students. |

• Like comparatives, some adjectives and adverbs also have irregular superlative forms:

| Adjectives/Adverbs | Comparative | Superlative |
|---|---|---|
| good/well | better | the best |
| bad/badly | worse | the worst |
| far | farther | the farthest (means physical distance) |
| far | further | the furthest (can mean physical or metaphysical distance) |

**(j)** The Guinness Book of World Records has **the best** collection of facts.

**(k)** That was **the worst** movie I saw last year.

**(l)** Pluto is **the farthest** planet from the sun.

**(m)** His explanation was **the furthest** from the truth.

## Exercise 1

Go back to the questions in the Task and circle all the superlative forms.

**EXAMPLE:** What is (the longest) wall in the world?

## Exercise 2

Here are some interesting and amusing facts from *The Guinness Book of World Records*. Write the correct form of the superlative in the spaces provided.

1. _____ (large) cucumber weighed 66 lbs.

2. _____ (popular) tourist attraction in the United States is Disneyworld.

3. _____ (successful) songwriters are Paul McCartney and the late John Lennon.

4. _____ (heavy) baby at birth was a boy of 22 lbs. 8 oz. He was born in Italy in 1955.

5. _____ (fat) person was a man in New York City. He weighed almost 1200 lbs. In 1987, he got stuck in his bedroom doorway and had to be rescued by firemen.

6. _____ (prolific) painter was Pablo Picasso (1881–1973). He produced about 13,500 paintings; 100,000 prints; 34,000 book illustrations; and 300 sculptures.

7. _____ (long) attack of hiccups lasted 67 years.

8. _____ (big) omelet was made of 54,763 eggs with 531 lbs. of cheese in Las Vegas, Nevada in 1986.

## Focus 3

USE

# Using *One of the* + Superlative + Plural Noun

USE

- The expression "*one of the* (superlative) + plural noun" is common with the superlative form.
  **(a)** He's **one of the most interesting people** I have ever met.
  **(b)** Bach was **one of the greatest composers** of all time.

## Exercise 3

Write sentences about the following, using the pattern "*one of the* (superlative) + plural noun."

    **EXAMPLE:** Paris is one of the most beautiful cities in the world.

1. a beautiful city in the world
2. an interesting place (in the city you are living in)
3. a good restaurant (in the city you are in)
4. a dangerous disease in the world
5. a serious problem in the world
6. a bad movie
7. a popular food (in a certain country)
8. a great book

## Exercise 4

Play this jeopardy game in two teams. Team 1 chooses a category and a dollar amount (Example: "Animals for $20"). One person in the class is the host of the game and reads the questions under the CATEGORIES column aloud. Team 1 has one minute to think of the answer. If the answer is correct, they "win" the amount of money they have chosen. If the answer is incorrect, Team 2 gets a chance to answer and win the money. If their answer is incorrect, nobody gets the money. Then it's Team 2's turn and they choose a category and a dollar amount. The team with the most money at the end of the game wins.

    **EXAMPLE:** Team 1: We choose "Animals" for $20.
                   Host: What's the most dangerous animal?
                   Team 1: The mosquitoes (that cause malaria).

|        | **Planets** | **Animals** | **Other** |
|--------|-------------|-------------|-----------|
| **$10** |             |             |           |
| **$20** |             |             |           |
| **$30** |             |             |           |
| **$40** |             |             |           |
| **$50** |             |             |           |

## CATEGORIES

### Planets
| | |
|---|---|
| **$10** | What is the largest planet in the solar system? |
| **$20** | What is the fastest planet? |
| **$30** | What is the hottest planet? |
| **$40** | What is the furthest planet from the sun? |
| **$50** | What is the nearest planet to earth? |

### Other
| | |
|---|---|
| **$10** | What is the most populous city in the world? |
| **$20** | What is the largest desert in the world? |
| **$30** | What is the longest day of the year? |
| **$40** | What is the shortest day of the year? |
| **$50** | What is the highest court in the United States? |

### Animals
| | |
|---|---|
| **$10** | What's the tallest animal? |
| **$20** | What's the most dangerous animal? |
| **$30** | What's the fastest land animal? |
| **$40** | What's the most valuable animal? |
| **$50** | What's the largest and heaviest animal? |

# Exercise 5

Information Gap. Work with a partner. One person looks at Grid A, and the other person looks at Grid B. Ask your partner questions to find out the missing information on your grid. Write the answers in the grid.

**EXAMPLE:** "What is the longest river in Asia?"

**GRID A**

| | North America | South America | Asia | Europe | Africa | The World |
|---|---|---|---|---|---|---|
| long/ river | | The Amazon | | The Volga | | The Nile |
| large/ country | Canada | | The People's Republic of China | | Sudan | |
| populous/ country | | Brazil | | Germany | | The People's Republic of China |
| high/ mountain | Mt. McKinley | | Mt. Everest | | Mt. Kilimanjaro | |
| small/ country | | Grenada | | Vatican City | | Vatican City |

**GRID B**

| | North America | South America | Asia | Europe | Africa | The World |
|---|---|---|---|---|---|---|
| long/ river | The Mississippi | | The Yangtze | | The Nile | |
| large/ country | | Brazil | | France | | The People's Republic of China |
| populous/ country | USA | | The People's Republic of China | | Nigeria | |
| high/ mountain | | Mt. Aconcagua | | Mt. Elbrus | | Mt. Everest |
| small/ country | Bermuda | | Macao | | Seychelles | |

# Activities

## Activity 1

Work in a group. Make up five trivia questions in the superlative form like the ones in the Task to ask the class.

> **EXAMPLES:** What's the most expensive car in the world?
>
> What's the most stubborn animal?
>
> What's the most popular restaurant in your neighborhood?

## Activity 2

Using the superlative form, write ten questions to ask other students in the class about life in their country or a country they know. The adjectives below can help you.

> **EXAMPLES:** What's the most industrial city in Brazil?
>
> What's the most unusual food you know?

| City | Sport | Food |
|------|-------|------|
| big | popular | common dessert |
| crowded | difficult | spicy |
| populated | dangerous | popular dish |
| polluted | expensive | unusual |
| beautiful | | expensive |
| urban | | |
| modern | | |
| industrial | | |
| popular | | |

## Activity 3

In groups, discuss the following statements. Say if you agree or disagree and why.

1. Democracy is the best form of government.
2. AIDS is the worst disease of this century.
3. English is the most difficult language to learn.
4. Baseball is the most boring sport.

## Activity 4

Interview a partner about his or her life experiences. Use the adjectives below to write questions with superlatives. Then write five sentences about your partner's experiences. Tell the class one or two interesting things you learned about your partner.

> **EXAMPLE:** What was the most embarassing moment in your life?

### ADJECTIVES TO DESCRIBE EXPERIENCES:

| | | |
|------|------|------|
| unusual | sad | exciting |
| embarassing | interesting | unexpected |
| happy | dangerous | frightening |

# Factual Conditionals

## *Task*

Match each condition on the left with the appropriate result on the right. Write your answers (number + letter) on the lines provided in the middle.

1. If you spend more money
   than you earn,
   _____  a. you risk having a car accident.

2. If you mix red and white,
   _____  b. you don't smoke.

3. If you drink and drive,
   _____  c. people respect you.

4. If you commit a crime,
   _____  d. you get into financial trouble.

5. If you care about your health,
   _____  e. you become a couch potato.

6. If you eat too much,
   _____  f. you go to jail.

7. If you respect people,
   _____  g. people listen to you.

8. If you read extensively,
   _____  h. you gain weight.

9. If you watch too much TV,
   _____  i. you get pink.

10. If you speak well,
   _____  j. you learn a lot.

# Focus 1

## MEANING

# Expressing Facts

MEANING

- Factual conditionals express relationships—such as those based on physical laws—that are always true and never change. These types of factual conditionals are often used in scientific writing.
  - **(a)** If you don't eat properly, your health suffers.
  - **(b)** If your heart stops, blood is not pumped to the brain.

# Exercise 1

Test Your Knowledge. Work with a partner. Circle the correct result for each condition on the left. Compare your results with those of your classmates.

1. If you put oil and water together, . . .
   - **a.** the oil floats at the top
   - **b.** they mix

2. If the temperature outside drops below 32 degrees Fahrenheit, . . .
   - **a.** water freezes
   - **b.** ice melts

3. If you stay in the sun a lot, . . .
   - **a.** your skin stays young and smooth
   - **b.** your skin wrinkles

4. If you raise the temperature of water to 100 degrees Celsius, . . .
   - **a.** it boils
   - **b.** it melts

5. If you combine two atoms of hydrogen with one atom of oxygen, . . .
   - **a.** you get hydrogen peroxide
   - **b.** you get water

6. If you don't refrigerate milk, . . .
   - **a.** it stays fresh
   - **b.** it spoils

7. If you fly west, . . .
   - **a.** you gain time
   - **b.** you lose time

8. If you fly east, . . .
   - **a.** you lose time
   - **b.** you gain time

9. If your body temperature is 103 degrees Fahrenheit, . . .
   - **a.** you are well
   - **b.** you are sick

# Focus 2

## MEANING

# Expressing Habitual Activity

MEANING

- Factual conditionals also express relationships based on habits. Habitual conditionals are common in everyday conversation.

  **(a)** If I cook, my husband washes the dishes.

  **(b)** If I lied, my mother punished me.

# Focus 3

## FORM

# Tenses in Factual Conditionals

FORM

- **Fact:** With factual conditionals based on physical law, use the simple present tense in both the *if clause* and the **main clause.** There is a comma after the *if* clause.

  **If Clause**              **Main Clause**

  If you mix black and white,  you get gray.

- **Habit:** Factual conditionals based on habit can express present or past relationships that are generally true. Use the same tense in both clauses: present in both clauses if the habitual relationship refers to present time; simple past in both clauses if the habitual relationship refers to past time.

  **(a)** If my husband **cooks,**                    I **wash** the dishes.

  **(b)** If my children **behaved** well,            I **rewarded** them.

- Note: In sentences with factual conditionals, it is possible to substitute *when* or *whenever* for *if,* and still express the same idea.

  **(c) When(ever)** you mix black and white, you get gray.

  **(d) When(ever)** I cook, my husband washes the dishes.

# Exercise 2

Use the cues to complete the *if* clauses below. Say your sentences aloud and compare your ideas with your classmates' ideas.

1. If you have elderly parents, / worry
2. When you live with a roommate, / share
3. If you buy things on credit, / pay
4. If you take a vacation every year, / feel
5. If you don't own a car, / use
6. Whenever someone sneezes, / say

## Exercise 3

In some cultures people say, "If you go out with wet hair, you get sick." Statements of this type are called "old wives' tales" because they aren't based on fact, but on what people say. Read the following "old wives' tales" and decide in your group if they are true or not.

1. If you go out with wet hair, you catch a cold.
2. If your ears are ringing, someone is talking about you.
3. If you eat chicken soup, your cold goes away.
4. If you hold your breath, your hiccups go away.
5. If you eat spinach, you get big and strong.

   Now add a few old wives' tales from your own country.

## Exercise 4

How long will you live? Read the following questionnaire and figure out how long you will live. Start with the number 74.

74

1. If you work out every day, add three years.
   If you don't get much exercise, subtract three years. _____

2. If you always try to stay calm, add 3 years.
   If you are aggressive, or nervous (have sleepless nights or bite your nails), subtract 3 years. _____

3. If you are under 30 and have traffic tickets, or have had an accident, subtract four years.
   If you always wear a seat belt, add one year. _____

4. If you know your blood pressure, add one. _____

5. If you are 65 or older and still working, add 3. _____

6. If any grandparent is 85, add 2.
   If all grandparents are 80, add 6.
   If a parent died before age 50, subtract 4. _____

7. If you smoke more than 2 packs of cigarettes a day, subtract 9; one or two packs a day, subtract 6; less than a pack a day, subtract 3. _____

8. If you drink more than two drinks daily, subtract 2. _____

9. If you are a female, add 3.
   If you are a male, subtract 3. _____

10. If you are overweight by 50 pounds or more, subtract 8; by 30–40 pounds, subtract 4; by 10–29 pounds, subtract 2. _____

11. If your age is 30–39, add 2; 40–49, add 3; 50–69, add 4; 70 or over, add 5. _____

    **Your Final Score** _____

# Focus 4

## Order of Clauses in Factual Conditionals

USE

- In factual conditionals, the *if* clause is almost always in first position.
- But, when the *if* clause contains **new information** we want to focus on, the *if* clause can be in second position. When the *if* clause is in second position, there is no comma between the two clauses.

  **(a)** How do you get an A in this class?

  **(b)** You get an A **if you do all of the work.**

- Note: It is also possible to change the order of clauses with *when / whenever.*

  **(c)** You get gray **when(ever) you mix black and white.**

  **(d)** My husband washes the dishes **when(ever) I cook.**

## Exercise 5

Answer the questions below using an *if* clause or *when(ever)* in second position.

1. How does milk turn sour?
2. When do you miss home?
3. How do you catch a cold?
4. When do you have trouble sleeping?
5. When did your parents punish you?
6. When were your parents pleased with you?
7. When do you listen to music?
8. When do you get angry?
9. How do you learn English?
10. How often do you reread this grammar book?

# Activities

## Activity 1

Psychologists say there are 2 personality types: A and B.

"Type A" people worry, get nervous, and are under stress all the time. "Type B" people are calm and try to enjoy life.

Which personality type are you? Read the following conditions and complete each with a result. Discuss your results in your group. Decide who in the group are "Type A" personalities and who are "Type B."

1. Whenever there is a change in my life, I....
2. If I have a test, I....
3. When I get stuck in traffic, I...
4. When I meet someone of the opposite sex for the first time, I....
5. When another driver on the road makes a mistake, I...
6. If a friend hurts my feelings, I...
7. If I don't get letters from home, I...
8. When I have a lot of things to do in one day, I...
9. When I don't succeed at something, I...
10. When someone criticizes me, I...

## Activity 2

Do you have any special eating problems or unusual habits? Write down any habits you have. Share your statements with your group. Try to find the person with the most unusual eating habits.

> **EXAMPLES:** *If I eat chocolate, I get a headache.*
> *If I drink more than three cups of coffee a day, I can't sleep.*

## Activity 3

Think about your childhood. Make five sentences with *if* clauses about past habits.

> **EXAMPLES:** *If my sister teased me, I hated her.*
> *If my mother yelled at me, I was miserable.*

## Activity 4

Compare habitual activities in your different cultures. Read the conditions below and complete each statement with a result that is appropriate in a country you know.

> **EXAMPLE:** In the United States, when you have dinner in a restaurant, you leave a tip.

## CONDITIONS:

a couple announces their engagement

a man is ready to get married

someone pays you a compliment

someone says "thank you"

someone gives you a gift

a woman has a baby

someone sneezes

someone invites you to dinner

someone dies

**331**

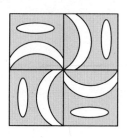

# Index